C0 CDA 274

Shakespeare for the wiser sort

CABRINI COLLEGE LIBRARY
610 KING OF PRUSSIA ROAD
RADNOR, PA 19087

MANCHESTER
1824

Manchester University Press

Shakespeare for the wiser sort

Solving Shakespeare's riddles in *The Comedy of Errors, Romeo and Juliet, King John, 1–2 Henry IV, The Merchant of Venice, Henry V, Julius Caesar, Othello, Macbeth* and *Cymberline*

Steve Sohmer

Manchester University Press
manchester and new york

distributed exclusively in the USA by Palgrave

PR
3072
.S58
2007

18747661

Copyright © Steve Sohmer 2007

The right of Steve Sohmer to be identified as the author of this work has been asserted
by him in accordance with the Copyright, Designs and Patents Act 1988.

Published by Manchester University Press
Oxford Road, Manchester M13 9NR, UK
and Room 400, 175 Fifth Avenue, New York, NY 10010, USA
www.manchesteruniversitypress.co.uk

Distributed exclusively in the USA by
Palgrave, 175 Fifth Avenue, New York,
NY 10010, USA

Distributed exclusively in Canada by
UBC Press, University of British Columbia, 2029 West Mall,
Vancouver, BC, Canada V6T 1Z2

British Library Cataloguing-in-Publication Data
A catalogue record for this book is available from the British Library

Library of Congress Cataloging-in-Publication Data applied for

ISBN   978 0 7190 7667 1 hardback

First published 2007

16 15 14 13 12 11 10 09 08 07   10 9 8 7 6 5 4 3 2 1

Typeset by IML Typographers, Birkenhead, Merseyside
Printed in Great Britain by Cromwell Press, Trowbridge, Wiltshire

For Lisa, David and Tully
with love adoring

Reade him, therefore, and againe, and againe:
And if then you doe not like him, surely you are
in some manifest danger not to understand him.
And so we leave you to other of his Friends,
whom if you need, can bee your guides ...

(John Hemminges and Henry Condell, *To the Great Variety of Readers*, First Folio of 1623)

Contents

Illustrations

Preface

For twenty years my principal interest in the study of Shakespeare has been twofold. First, to better understand Shakespeare the writer, what sort of man he was and how his mind worked. Second, to resolve and explain certain passages in his texts long believed by scholars inscrutable. It has always been my conviction that these interests were two sides of the same coin. Knowing Shakespeare better, we are better equipped to know his plays. Better knowing his plays brings us closer to knowing Shakespeare.

During my studies at Oxford I perceived among my colleagues rather less appreciation for the keenness of Shakespeare's intelligence than was, in my opinion, warranted. Even today, the eighteenth-century notion that Shakespeare was an ill-educated country rube who 'warbled his woodnotes wild' has its adherents. Indeed, this undervaluing of Shakespeare's intellect has animated any number of conspiracy theorists – some extremely well organized – who offer the Earl of Oxford or Christopher Marlowe or Francis Bacon or other pretenders – as the 'actual' author of Shakespeare's plays. But when Hemminges and Condell produced their Folio, William Shakespeare had been dead seven years; surely enough dust had settled for the author of *The Tempest* to reveal him- or herself. Yet no one stepped forward. And the dedicatory poems which precede the plays point to the man from Stratford. In the rantings of Shakespeare's nay-sayers – and the forces who would co-opt him now to serve their own philosophical or religious agendas – the playwright may still be paying the price for his natural modesty, reticence, and 'civill demeanor.'

As to Shakespeare's apparent lack of a college education, it is well to remember that English higher education then as now centered on a program of 'directed reading' rather than taught courses. From the thousands of disparate quotations and allusions which litter his plays we can deduce that Shakespeare was a prodigious reader. Though his course of reading was, perhaps, self-directed, it was colossal – witness his vocabulary: unique words in Shakespeare total more than 17,000 (many of his own invention) – four times the vocabulary of today's average college graduate and twice as large as John Milton's. It was not until the publication of Sister Miriam Joseph's *Shakespeare's Use of the Arts of Language* in 1947 that scholars recognized how vast was Shakespeare's grasp of formal rhetoric and how adroit his facility in using it. Only in the latter decades of the twentieth century have scholars grasped the depth of Shakespeare's readings in ancient history, law, medicine, and other disciplines – including, as the present book exhibits, time and chronometry.

Are we really arrogant enough to believe we are the first generation to recognize these elements in Shakespeare's plays? Surely there were among his first auditors (and readers) men and women whose breadth of knowledge and understanding rivaled Shakespeare's? And just as surely, the writer must have believed this. Otherwise, would he not have felt himself an Orpheus playing to an audience who had no ears?

This book suggests that Shakespeare wrote not only for the mass audience, but simultaneously for that stratum of *cognoscenti* whom Gabriel Harvey dubbed 'the wiser sort.' And that Shakespeare did so because he was vexed by questions of morality, custom, politics and faith which he determined to interrogate mimetically. In so doing, Shakespeare pursued the tradition of socially relevant, topical, morally challenging drama as old as Aeschylus and as contemporary as today. The creation of literature *demands* that the author write about those subjects which society or government or church commands one *not* to write about. As Stanley Kunitz observed, a writer of literature must condemn himself to lead a 'counter-life.'

Shakespeare did so. And by exercising his prodigious talents with Joycean 'silence and cunning' he thrived by writing for two audiences: one, the great mass of entertainment-seeking playgoers; the other, a wiser sort who were themselves wrestling with those problems of conscience which the age, the government, and the churches imposed upon all thinking persons.

After a thousand years of enslavement, the fifteenth century had seen the human mind begin to revivify. On the continent of Europe – in those benighted precincts where the Inquisition burnt Bruno and Tyndale and condemned Galileo – just as, in other districts, Lutheran iconoclasts defaced a cultural legacy of fifteen centuries – a heavy yoke still burdened human aspiration. But in England – where large-scale violence against this or that religious group was no longer in prospect when William Shakespeare came up from Stratford to London *circa* 1582 – where a unique and novel tolerance of *don't ask, don't tell* had taken hold – the environment was fertile for the flowering of dramatic art which vigorously interrogated ideas.

True, by modern standards England was no paradigm of tolerance. But by the standards of Reformation Europe, surely it was. In my view it is precisely because Elizabethan and Jacobean England tolerated both the Catholic and Protestant confessions – thereby compelling their adherents to live cheek-by-jowl and share a common language, customs, traditions – even patriotism – that Shakespeare found the freedom to write as he did. He was tolerated, and he was tolerant. He found the *via media,* and from that vantage point looked upon and considered all things human. Which is why his genius still speaks so eloquently – and challengingly – to us today.

This book – indeed, all my study of Shakespeare – would hardly have been possible without the friendship and encouragement of the late Dennis Kay, who taught and inspired so many who miss him today. I also wish to thank Manchester University Press for their enthusiastic, unflagging support. Finally, thanks to Mark Rylance and the company and staff of Shakespeare's Globe (London) for staging *The Tragedy of Julius Caesar* at 2 p.m. on the Summer Solstice, 22 June 1999, the precise moment of the four-hundredth anniversary of both the opening of the first Bankside Globe and the world première of Shakespeare's Roman tragedy. I think he would have been pleased; my David and Tully were.

ONE

'to please the wiser sort':
Shakespeare's other (smarter) audience

John Hemminges and Henry Condell could be confident their splendid folio of William Shakespeare's works would encounter a great variety of readers. The thirty-five plays they assembled and published in 1623 had entertained three generations of Englishmen and -women of every stripe: royal and common, rich and poor, learnèd and unlettered, sophisticated and countrified, naïve and cannily wise.[1] In consequence, Shakespeare's first editors anticipated a universe of readers comprising both the simple and clever; prudently, they cautioned in their preface, 'Reade him, therefore, and againe, and againe: And if then you doe not like him, surely you are in some manifest danger not to understand him. And so we leave you to other of his Friends, whom if you need, can bee your guides ...'[2]

This prominent caveat raises an intriguing question: why would Shakespeare's first editors exhibit such an admonition in the head pages of a collection of familiar, popular, stage-worn plays?

We moderns, when we were students entering upon the study of Shakespeare, certainly had difficulty understanding him. Though Shakespeare wrote in our language, his forms and syntax are archaic, his spelling and punctuation obsolete, and many words in his vast vocabulary disused and unfamiliar. But the buyers of the First Folio were the playwright's *immediate* contemporaries; Shakespeare's English, though poetic, was as familiar to them as breathing. Why, then, would Hemminges and Condell caution buyers that Shakespeare's plays *require* reading and rereading – and that a reader who doesn't embrace Shakespeare must not understand him? And why, rather than offer elucidation, would they encourage the reader to seek Shakespeare's meanings in discourse with the playwright's 'Friends'?

Surely we require no further evidence that there is more to Shakespeare's texts than appears on the page?

Unfortunately, polemicists from Frances Yates to Clare Asquith have inferred from this caveat that Shakespeare wrote in some sort of philosophical, religious or political 'code.'[3] With tireless ingenuity they have argued Shakespeare laced his plays with recondite 'messages' – whispers of the playwright's secret predilection for Rosicrucianism, Catholicism, the Kabala, or some other equally dangerous *-ism*. This book is not an entry into those debates – though, admittedly, it is difficult amid the present sound and fury not to take note of issues raised. In the following chapters I will, occasionally, have something to say about William Shakespeare's religious leanings, what we reliably know about them, and what we can reasonably infer from his plays. But I doubt my views will succor any of the legions of militant scholars battling to appropriate Shakespeare for their own religious agendas.[4] At least, I hope not.

Over the past four hundred years an enormous community of scholars have heeded assiduously Hemminges' and Condell's advice; they have read and reread (and reread) Shakespeare, edited his language, modernized his punctuation, parsed usages, debated intentions, and analyzed his words with tests syntactical, historical, linguistical, and digital. Yet even today Shakespeare's texts remain riddled with passages, whole scenes, and plot twists which baffle and confound his cleverest commentators. Why, for example, didn't Hamlet succeed to the throne of Denmark at the instant of his father's death? (It's not because the Danish throne was elective.) Why does Chorus promise his audience 'two houres trafficke of our stage' when anyone can see *Romeo and Juliet* runs almost three hours? Why does *Othello* seem to unfold in double-time? What did Cicero say as he watched Caesar swoon? and why won't Casca dare repeat it? Why do the Capulets have a servant named Sampson, and Lady Faulconbridge a man named James Gournie? Why is the half-dead Michael Cassio suddenly appointed governor of Cyprus? How is it that Old Hamlet sent his son to school in (Protestant) Wittenberg but his Ghost was sent to (Catholic) Purgatory? and is there cause-and-effect here? Why would Shakespeare rewrite a creaky old play about King John in 1596? and how could he resist a glance at *Magna Carta*? (He didn't.) Who is the historical figure behind the shadowy Frenchman Lamord? How can Lancelot Gobbo be correct (and he is) when he claims Black Monday (the day after Easter) and Ash Wednesday (the forty-first day *before* Easter) once fell on the same day? And what, in heaven's name, is a 'dram of eale'? This book solves these riddles and many others.

In these chapters I will investigate many of the nagging cruces in Shakespeare's plays which scholars have never been able to unravel. I will demonstrate that, while Shakespeare was the most popular playwright of his age (and ours), he did not at all times and in every instance write for the popular audience. I will identify many passages in the plays which Shakespeare fashioned to communicate with a handful of auditors only – coteries, cliques, and affinity groups who shared some special interest or knowledge. I will show that parsing these passages not only resolves famous cruces but casts new light on Shakespeare's mind and method, and illuminates anew even the most familiar of his plays.

These chapters will also paint the portrait of a Shakespeare we have not encountered elsewhere in the critical literature. He is, of course, profoundly gifted, learned, witty – some would say inspired – and he knew how to make the groundlings roar and weep. But we have the word of the aesthete Gabriel Harvey (1550?–1631) – an admirer, though no great friend – that Shakespeare also wrote for a rarefied stratum of society, certain *cognoscenti* whom Harvey labeled 'the wiser sort.' I will show that Harvey's wiser sort recognized a Shakespeare who was unflinching, judgmental, and caustic by turn, teasing, loyal, deeply skeptical, politically enlightened, independently minded, rather courageous, goodhearted – irrepressibly, incorrigibly playful – and remarkably tolerant for his era (and ours). Shakespeare wrote for a mass audience – yes – but not always. Scholars who deny this – who deny that Shakespeare's auditors were as heterogeneous as London itself[5] – who refuse to accept that some passages in his texts were opaque to the mass but pregnant with meaning for a chosen few – those scholars risk falling into shallow-mindedness and self-delusion. I will demonstrate that Shakespeare often wrote for coteries – sometimes very small coteries – as few in number as the immediate families of his patrons. I will show that he wrote for cliques who shared specialist knowledge of, for example: Continental or English common law; Roman, French, and English history; heraldry and the martyrology; astrology and astronomy; the calendar and time-keeping.

These select few auditors comprised Harvey's wiser sort – and perhaps after encountering Shakespeare they were wiser still.

There's a convenient example of Shakespeare writing for a tiny clique in *Julius Caesar,* the tragedy he purpose-wrote to christen the new Bankside Globe in 1599. Shakespeare composed his Roman tragedy for the delectation of a mass audience who shared a common appetite to see a tyrant ridiculed and slain. But Shakespeare also wrote into this play more than one passage intelligible *only* to that handful of the wiser sort who had read Plutarch and knew their Suetonius. In *Julius Caesar* 1.2, Caska describes for Cassius and Brutus how Caesar thrice refused Antony's offer of a crown — and then fainted as the multitude gasped and senators looked on. Cassius asks:

Cassius Did *Cicero* say any thing?
Caska   I, he spoke Greeke.
Cassius To what effect?
Caska   Nay, and I tell you that, Ile ne're looke you i'th'face againe. But those that understood him, smil'd at one another, and shooke their heads: but for mine owne part, it was Greeke to me.

(382–8)[6]

Only an astute few who knew that Caska spoke Greek could have inferred what Cicero said – words so dangerous Casca dared not report them in 1.2 – words as dangerous in Shakespeare's London as in Cicero's Rome.[7] (The curious will find the solution to this crux in the Appendix.)

Into *Macbeth* Shakespeare injected a detail accessible only to the few intrepid souls brave or reckless enough to have cast the horoscope of King James I – it was treason to do so – but probably including the king himself, who was profoundly superstitious and took a keen interest in the calendar. Scene 2.1 opens with a stage direction: '*Enter Banquo, and Fleance, with a Torch before him.*'[8] It is a portentous night; before cock-crow King Duncan will be dead and the line will be drawn which will lead James VI of Scotland to the English throne in 1603. Ominously, a dialogue between father and son begins

> Banquo   How goes the Night, Boy?
> Fleance   *The Moone* is downe: I have not heard the Clock.
> Banquo   And she goes downe at Twelve.

(2.1.1–3)

Editors of *Macbeth* have noted that the entrance of a torch signaled night to an audience in a daylit playhouse, and receive Banquo's remark on the time of moonset merely as a colorful aside. But careful reckoning reveals that Shakespeare crafted into this fleeting exchange far more than a sense of darkness – as a *very* select few among his auditors would have recognized.

Modern historians attribute the murder of Duncan to the night of 13/14 August 1040. On that night, moonset at Dunsinane occurred not at Midnight but at 8:00 p.m. As the chart below illustrates, an observer looking west from Dunsinane Castle (56°31″N, 3°13″W) on the night of 13/14 August 1040 would have seen the trailing limb of the moon dip below the horizon at 8:00 p.m. local time.[9] Consequently, Banquo's observation that the moon set at midnight cannot be correct (see figure). Banquo's gaff has not discomforted Shakespeareans; we were taught our playwright was careless about matters of time and the hour. But we were taught wrong. Though accessible only to a handful of Shakespeare's first auditors (and none of his scholar-commentators) Banquo's allusion to moonset illustrates *how precise* Shakespeare could be about time.

We know Shakespeare's principal source for *Macbeth* was Raphael Holinshed's *Chronicle*. Holinshed gives the correct day but the wrong year – 14 August 1046 rather than the correct 14 August 1040 – for Macbeth's coronation as king of Scotland. Holinshed wrote, 'The bodie of Duncane was first conveied unto Elgine, & there buried in kingly wise; but afterwards it was removed and conveied to Colmekill, and there laid in a sepulture amongst his predecessors, in the yeare after the birth of our Saviour, 1046.'[10] In Shakespeare's accelerated account of events on the morning after the king's

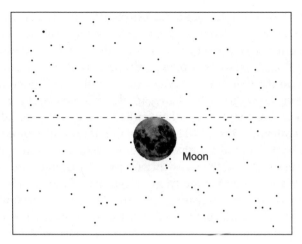

Moonset at Dunsinane 13/14 August 1040, 8:00 p.m.
The horizon appears as a horizontal broken line.

murder (2.4), Duncan's body is said to have been carried to Colmekill while Macbeth has been named king and gone to Scone to be crowned (31–2) – a mere two-hours' ride from Dunsinane. If Shakespeare accepted Holinshed's wrong date – that is, 14 August 1046 – for Macbeth's investiture, he must have inferred the murder of Duncan took place on the night of 13/14 August 1046. As Jacobean astrologers could easily divine, on that night the moon did set at Midnight (see chart).[11]

An observer looking west from Dunsinane at Midnight on 13/14 August 1046 would have seen the trailing arm of the moon dip below the horizon at

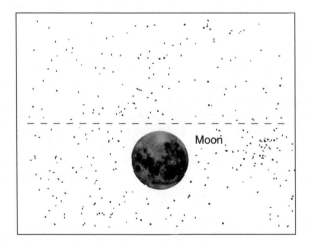

Moonset at Dunsinane, 13/14 August 1046, 12:01 a.m.

12:01 a.m. So Banquo's reference to the time of moonset is accurate *within one minute*. Shakespeare – having accepted the wrong date for the night of Duncan's murder – got the time of moonset exactly right. And we are not the first to grasp that. Shakespeare would hardly have troubled to recover the hour of moonset on the night of Duncan's murder unless he was confident that *someone* among his auditors – perhaps a royal someone – would recognize it.

In the following chapters I will examine some dozen plays Shakespeare wrote in the interval 1592–1610 – along with relevant historical materials. I will offer a fresh array of insights into an unrecognized level of discourse between Shakespeare and the wiser sort among his first auditors – a decades-long dialogue about honor, honesty, royal legitimacy (and illegitimacy), time, faith, Scripture as literal history, and freedom of expression. Though Shakespeare may have whispered these sentiments in a voice inaudible to the great majority of his audience, some surely heard it. Now, we will too.

Notes

1 The only certainties were that readers of the First Folio would be literate and monied; bound in calf the book cost some eighteen shillings, a serious sum in 1623.
2 Charlton Hinman (ed.), *The First Folio of Shakespeare* (New York: Norton, 1968), p. 7.
3 For example: L.W. Rogers, *Occultism in the Shakespeare Plays* (1909, rpt. Kila, Montana: Kessinger, 1996); Frances Yates, *The Occult Philosophy in the Elizabethan Age* (London: Routledge, 1979); Clare Asquith, *Shadowplay: The Hidden Beliefs and Coded Politics of William Shakespeare* (New York: Public Affairs, 2005); Gerald M. Pinciss, *Forbidden Matter: Religion in the Drama of Shakespeare and his Contemporaries* (Newark: University of Deleware Press, 2000), and one less familiar and little but dandy psychological/conspiracy theory: Graeme Bryson, *Shakespeare in Lancaster* (Liverpool: Sunwards, 1997).
4 For example: E.A.J. Honigmann, *Shakespeare: the Lost Years* (Manchester: Manchester University Press, 1998); Richard Wilson, *Secret Shakespeare: Studies in Theater, Religion, and Resistence* (Manchester: Manchester University Press, 2004); and Stephen Greenblatt, *Will in the World: How Shakespeare Became Shakespeare* (New York: Norton, 2004).
5 The subject has an exhaustive literature including Alfred Harbage, *Shakespeare's Audience* (New York: Columbia University Press, 1964); Ann Jennalie Cook, *The Privileged Playgoers of Shakespeare's London* (Princeton: Princeton University Press, 1981); Janet Hill, *Stages and Playgoers: From Guild Plays to Shakespeare* (Montreal: McGill-Queen's University Press, 2002), and of course Andrew Gurr, *Playgoing in Shakespeare's London* (Cambridge: Cambridge University Press, 2004).
6 Text and lineation from Hinman, *First Folio*.
7 S. Sohmer, 'What Cicero Said,' *Notes and Queries* (vol. 44, no. 1, March 1997), 56–8.

8 Text of *Macbeth* from Hinman.
9 Prepared by the author using *Redshift2* software, © Maris Media 1998.
10 Raphael Holinshed, *The Chronicles of England, Scotland and Ireland* (London: Henry Denham, 1587), 2.171 with marginal note, 'Duncane's burial. 1046. H.B.'
11 *Redshift 2.*

TWO

'Doubt thou the starres are fire':
The new philosophy in *Hamlet*

In the second act of *Hamlet* Polonius reports a poem composed for Ophelia by the prince. With these verses Hamlet invites his love to

> *Doubt ... the starres are fire,*
> *Doubt ... the Sunne doth move,*
> *Doubt truth to be a lyer,*
> *But never doubt I love [thee].*

(Q2 2.2.116–19, original italic)

Though Hamlet's lines are simple-seeming, behind them rages one of the great battles for men's minds and souls of the Counter-Reformation, a veritable Sixteenth-century *Star Wars*. Hamlet is bandying matters of cosmology which were burning issues (literally) throughout William Shakespeare's lifetime.[1]

In the eyes and canons of the Catholic Church the creation myth of Genesis – the so-called 'Mosaic cosmogony' – was received as *literal* history. Believers were required to accept that God, at a stroke, had created the universe from nothingness – *productio totius substantia ex nihilo sui et subjecti*; or, as the Old Testament book of the Maccabees put it, 'Look upon heaven and earth, and all that is in them: and consider that God made them out of nothing' (II Mac. 7:28). The Lateran Council (1215) formulated this *condidit ex nihilo* to include the creation of time itself – *ab initio temporis* – as well as evil and free will. A mature summa of the dogma can be found in the *Summa* of Albertus Magnus, which epitomizes the view of the Schoolmen of Shakespeare's era — and the cosmology taught at the Sorbonne in Paris when his Laertes matriculated.[2]

Furthermore, so say the Schoolmen and their intellectual heirs and assigns, the advent of Earth and our species was a unique event unreplicated elsewhere in the universe; *QED*, we humans are the focus and apotheosis of all Creation. As if biblical authority and Scholastic logic weren't sufficient proof of the preeminent position of mankind in God's design, empirical evidence was also visible to any observer; one had only to look to the heavens to see that His Sun, stars, and planets – indeed, the entirety of His cosmos – rotate around mankind's fixed, unmoving Earth. Clearly, the species to whom God gave dominion over the fauna and flora of Earth (so ran the dogmatic wisdom) must be the linchpin and fulfillment of His creation.

This (supremely arrogant) geocentric cosmology was not, however, original with Jews and Christians; like so many of the rites and rubrics adopted by the remarkably eclectic early Christians, their geocentric *gestalt* was borrowed. The centrality of Earth in the universe had been evident to pagans long before the birth of Christ; the Schoolmen took comfort that no less an authority than Aristotle (384–322 BC) held that the Earth stood at the center of the universe. Likewise, the relative latecomer Claudius Ptolemaeus (fl. AD 150), in his *Mathematicke Syntaxis* (*aka* the *Almagest*), argued that every thing in the universe either moves toward the center of the Earth or orbits around it. (The Church chose to ignore the view of Aristotle's near-contemporary, Aristarchus of Samos, who conceived the Earth revolving around the Sun.) As a consequence, Aristotle's inference and Ptolemy's cosmology – backed by the power and glory of the Holy See – held sway well into the fifteenth century.

But in the mid-sixteenth century, a new cosmology – a so-called 'Copernican model' – burst upon the Western consciousness. Remarkably, though Copernicus himself was devoutly Catholic, it fell to Lutherans to turn his theories into a revolution.

Nicolaus Copernicus (1473–1543) was no religious reformer. In addition to studying astronomy and medicine, Copernicus had earned a doctorate in canon law at Ferrara in 1503; thereafter, he lived many years in the palace of his bishop-uncle and remained a professing Catholic throughout his life.[3] Good Catholic Copernicus was reluctant to publish his theories; he recognized his radical map of the solar system (and, by entailment, the insignificance of Earth in the scheme of things cosmic) would puncture the Church dogma which held that Earth and mankind were the centerpiece of Creation. Although in the 1530s two popes, Clement VII and Paul III, had given at least tacit approval to Copernicus' theoretical work, it was the Lutherans who embraced and delivered it to the world.

In the 1530s rumors of Copernicus' breakthroughs had begun making the rounds of intellectual circles in Europe. In 1539, George Joachim Rheticus (1514–74), a professor of mathematics at Luther's (and Hamlet's) university of Wittenberg was given leave to study with Copernicus at Frauenberg in Poland. Rheticus wrote and published an epitome of Copernicus' vision, the *Narratio Prima* (1540), which excited much discussion and enthusiasm. Rheticus would himself have seen Copernicus' masterwork, *De Revolutionibus,* through the press had he not been called to a chair of mathematics in Leipzig. Rheticus entrusted the publication to a Lutheran minister and theologian, Andreas Osiander (1498–1552), who identified a Lutheran Nuremberg printer and produced the first edition of *De Revolutionibus* in 1543.[4] Its contents were (literally) earthshaking.[5]

Copernicus concluded that Earth, not the cosmos, rotates on its axis every twenty-four hours; that the axis of the Earth wobbles as the planet rotates, which accounts for the precession of the equinoxes; and, most significantly, Earth and the other planets orbit the Sun (as Aristarchus had guessed). We moderns know this cosmology as well as our own names. But we have forgotten that Copernicus also propounded the view that the Sun, like the stars, *does not move* and is fixed in space. So a sixteenth-century Copernican would *Doubt ... that the Sunne doth move.* In Copernicus' plan of the solar system, a fixed Sun sits at the focus about which six planets orbit. Beyond the orbit of Saturn lies a ring of fixed stars.

Furthermore, Copernicus was convinced that at least some of the stars *were not fire* – including *The Wanderers* (planets) and the Sun. Galileo's observations confirmed with ocular proof that the planets were not fire. Therefore, a convert to the new Copernican philosophy could *Doubt ... that the starres are fire.*

Assessing the impact of the Copernicus' cosmology on the wiser sort, in his *An Anatomy of the World* written a decade after *Hamlet* (1611), John Donne wrote (with echoes of the Danish poet-prince)

> new philosophy calls all in doubt,
> The element of fire is quite put out,
> The sun is lost, and th'earth, and no man's wit
> Can well direct him where to look for it.
> And freely men confess that this world's spent,
> When in the planets and the firmament
> They seek so many new; they see that this
> Is crumbled out again to his atomies.
> 'Tis all in pieces, all coherence gone,
> All just supply, and all relation;
> Prince, subject, father, son, are things forgot ...
>
> (205–15)

... perhaps like a certain hobby-horse.

That the Sun does not move – that some stars are not fire – these are new ideas of a new philosophy, and a new view of mankind's place in the cosmos – a Copernican, Lutheran cosmos. (See Appendix, p. 170, Dr Peter Usher on *Copernicus, Stars, and Fire.*)

The Copernican model of the solar system, sensible and familiar to us, was immediately branded heretical by the Catholic Church. Proponents of Copernican cosmology such as the gadfly Giordano Bruno (1548–1600) – who, in a leap to the ultramodern, imagined a universe dotted with thousands of solar systems containing thousands of Earths each with its own Creation and Garden of Eden – paid for their openness of mind at the stake.[6] For supporting Copernicus' views, Galileo – born nine weeks before Shakespeare – suffered two bitter bouts with the Inquisition, was compelled to recant and spent the last ten years of his life in misery under house arrest. One cannot pass from a discussion of Catholic rage against heliocentrism without noting that Galileo, the father of experimental science, was partially rehabilitated in 1992 (!) by Pope John Paul II.[7] However, the pope did not repudiate Galileo's conviction for heresy. The persistence of such a preposterous judgment is incontrovertible proof of the resilience of human stupidity.

To Americans living in the first decade of the twenty-first century, conflicts like the battle over heliocentrism during Shakespeare's lifetime – which pit empirical science against religious ideology – have become sadly familiar. One has only to listen to the dogmatic rhetoric of the opponents of stem-cell research or the Kyoto Protocols on global warming – or to the misguided zealots who would replace Darwin with the fantasy of evolution by 'intelligent design' – to appreciate how religious fanaticism frustrated the advancement of knowledge and the betterment of the human condition in Shakespeare's age as it would do in ours.

This is not to say that all members of Reformed churches enthusiastically embraced heliocentrism. Though Luther himself, a resolute empiricist, took an interest in the new science,[8] Tycho Brahe (1546–1601) – perhaps the greatest observational astronomer of all time, and both a Lutheran and Hamlet's countryman – rejected Copernicanism and clung to the notion of a geocentric universe until his dying day.[9]

In Shakespeare's England the Copernican revolution was a Continental event dimly perceived (if at all) by the everyday English. But it was of cosmic consequence to the wiser sort. In 1576 mathematician Thomas Digges (1546–95), whose son contributed a ghastly doggerel to the forepages of the First Folio, first published in English Copernicus' plan of a heliocentric solar system.[10] Digges was the first scientist to conceive a universe that was infinite (a risky notion bruited by Catholic theologian-philosopher Nicolaus of Cusa in the fifteenth century). In a later chapter I will show that Shakespeare had read Digges carefully and quotes another of his books, *Stratioticos* (1595), as a previously unrecognized source of *Othello*.[11]

While Digges' infinite universe and Copernicus' solar system were freely discussed in London, Wittenberg, and other reformed regions, in Catholic states the evil powers of the Inquisition were doing their worst to suppress the new *gestalt*. Bruno went to the stake in 1600. Copernicus' *De Revolutionibus* was placed on the Index of forbidden books in 1616 (it was removed only in 1835). For defending Copernicus' theorems Galileo was sentenced to house arrest from 1633 until his death in 1642.

Which brings us back to *Hamlet*. In Shakespeare's Danish tragedy written *ca* 1600 – in the very thick of this titanic collision between hoary dogma and vibrant new ideas which would forever alter the place of man in the universe – a prince returns home from school in Lutheran Wittenberg where Copernican cosmology is taught. There he encounters the Ghost of his father – an 'honest ghost,' mind you – who delivers a detailed description of his place of suffering which is, indisputably, the Catholics' Purgatory. (To leave no doubt about it, Hamlet swears to the Ghost's truth 'by Saint *Patrick*,' the traditional gatekeeper of Purgatory.)

Now, how can this be? How can the Copernican universe *and* Catholic Purgatory concurrently coexist?

The solution to this paradox – surely one of the most vexatious in the Shakespeare canon – will give cold comfort to scholars who have sought to appropriate the playwright for their own religious agendas. The peaceful coexistence of the Copernican universe and Purgatory is an artifact of the environment of tolerance in England which followed the accession of Queen Elizabeth I (1558) and her 'Religious Settlement' of 1559. In Shakespeare's England it *was* possible for a Copernican universe and a Catholic Purgatory to coexist, just as Elizabeth had shown it was possible for her Protestant and Catholic subjects to coexist without treason, without bloodshed, and most important, without surrendering their consciences.[12]

The passage through parliament of the statutes which constituted Elizabeth's Religious Settlement was one of the Queen's most extraordinary feats of statecraft. Contrived with her Lord Privy Seal Nicholas Bacon and the divine Matthew Parker (whom she named Archbishop of Canterbury in December of that year) her Settlement is both politically pragmatic *and* an enlightened social masterstroke. It would bestow upon England decades of (relative) religious tolerance.

After thirty years of religious strife, Elizabeth's first step toward an armistice, The Act of Supremacy, abolished the civil power of the papacy in England and established the monarch as 'Supreme Governor' rather than 'Supreme Head' of the Anglican Church of England – a critical concession accepted by the largely Catholic House of Lords. Later that year the Act of Uniformity restored the Protestant prayer book of 1552. But Elizabeth wisely permitted a number of Catholic practices to persist, e.g. candles on the altar, episcopacy, the appareling of priests. Outwardly, Elizabeth's Church *looked* Catholic. The Queen also made provision for the individual conscience; her newly drafted description of the Eucharist *could* be interpreted to accommodate the Real Presence of the body and blood of Christ, a dogma precious to her Catholic subjects.

Elizabeth's intention was to separate political issues – most specifically, the dictates of patriotism and loyalty to the crown – from matters of personal faith. To a large extent she succeeded. As long as her Catholic subjects remained loyal – and observed their holy days and rituals discreetly – Elizabeth and her ministers were content to look the other way. Her Settlement was the original *don't ask, don't tell* arrangement. Considering that a succession of popes had declared the Queen a bastard, vacated her claim to the throne, and placed a price on her head, Elizabeth's Religious Settlement was an exemplar of magnanimity. No, it did not satisfy everyone on either side. Calvinists and Puritans railed against the episcopacy and the paraphernalia. And Jesuits who preached insurrection were still hunted down. But Elizabeth's overarching objective was to end the religious conflict which had wracked England and threatened to destabilize the throne between 1525 and 1558. By and large, she made it work.

William Shakespeare, born in 1564, was a child of this Religious Settlement. While there can be no doubt that there were numerous Catholics in his (and every other) extended family in Tudor England, that fact does not entail that William was himself recusant. His father, John (d. 1601), may well have signed the Catholic 'Last Will of the Soul' discovered in 1757 in the rafters of the house where William was born. Edward Arden, a cousin of Shakespeare's mother, certainly kept a priest disguised as a gardener; Sir Thomas Lucy arrested the two – and Arden's son-in-law, John Sommerville – for plotting to assassinate Elizabeth. In 1583 Arden was hanged at Tyburn and his head set up on London Bridge. E.A.J. Honigmann and Richard Wilson hypothesize that at about this time Shakespeare was serving as schoolmaster to the recusant de Hoghton family of Lancaster where he may have met the Jesuit martyr Edmund Campion (d. 1581).[13] We also know that Shakespeare's daughter, Susanna, was cited for recusancy in 1606.

But all the above being noted, the documentary evidence of Shakespeare's baptism, marriage, and death suggest he was born, lived, and died in conformity with Elizabeth's Anglican Church.[14] Not incidentally, his first editors, John Hemminges and Henry Condell, were both practicing Anglicans – which seems to belie any inference that their caveat to buyers of the Folio can be taken as proof that Shakespeare's plays contain recondite recusant Catholic messages.[15]

My own view is that William Shakespeare's religious opinions reflected the complexities – and relative tolerance – of Elizabeth's Religious Settlement. There are any number of Catholics (good and bad) in Shakespeare's plays – along with scores of good and bad Protestants, pagans, and a scattering of Jews – just as there were such persons in his family, his England, and in Europe. Shakespeare's texts are dotted with likable friars and monks, and allusions to suppressed Catholic holy days – some as illustrious as the Feast of Saint James the Greater (*Romeo and Juliet*), others obscure as the Feast of Saint Leonardus (*Twelfth Night*).[16] Shakespeare regularly alludes to rituals of the old Church –

baptism in *Comedy of Errors*, shriving and confession in *Hamlet*, creeping to the cross in *Julius Caesar*, pilgrimage in *All's Well*, and Holy Saturday rituals in *Othello*. In *Hamlet* Shakespeare even treats Purgatory with respect. None of this proves beyond doubt that Shakespeare was Catholic. But it does prove he was tolerant.[17]

Shakespeare's Old Hamlet *was* Catholic. And if his Ghost walks – well then, despite Lutheran arguments against the existence of ghosts – Shakespeare and his Hamlet are tolerant enough to let him walk. The Protestant prince – though schooled at Wittenberg – accepts that. Indeed, Hamlet rebukes his Melanchthonesque Wittenberg school chum: 'There are more things in heaven and earth *Horatio* / Then are dream't of in your philosophie' (1.5.166–7).

It's worth noting that in Elsinore tolerance cuts both ways. According to tradition, ghosts were expected to beg of living mortals three things: prayer, pilgrimage, and donations to the Church – activities believed efficacious in reducing the ghost's painful stay in Purgatory. But Old Hamlet's Ghost asks none of these – knowing they would not be forthcoming from his *Protestant* Wittenberger son. He demands only revenge.

Old Hamlet sincerely believed that the rite of Extreme Unction (a sacrament to Catholics but not to Protestants) could have spared him from the fires. Movingly, he laments that he died

> Unhuzled, disappointed, unanueld,
> No reckning made, but sent to my account
> Withall my imperfections on my head
> O horrible, o horrible, most horrible.

(Q2 1.5.77–80)

But *all* those who die in *Hamlet* die unshriven. Hamlet's Catholic father *believed* in Purgatory so thoroughly that his Ghost went there. Young Hamlet's Protestant ghost, on the other hand, wings directly to heaven – if the reliable Horatio is to be believed when he says 'flights of Angels sing thee to thy rest' (5.2.371). For Hamlet and Horatio Purgatory does not exist; for Old Hamlet's Ghost it does. And Shakespeare presents both views sympathetically. This is the apogee of religious tolerance. No author who was a convinced Catholic or confirmed Protestant could have written *Hamlet* so even-handedly. There is no axe-grinding here.

Prince Hamlet – lately returned from Wittenberg – has, perhaps, persuaded Ophelia of the new cosmology – and that he loves her. But in his poem he explains he is willing that she doubt the Copernican model. She might even suspect the (Copernican) Truth about these cosmic entities may be false – which sounds to us an oxymoron but certainly wasn't in 1603. In Hamlet's poem all the contentious cosmic fiddlefaddle which pitted reformers against inquisitors is quite beside the point. What's important is that Ophelia *never* doubt Hamlet loves her. That's what matters. And it matters more to him than either of the rival cosmologies. So says Hamlet's poem, a minor paean to tolerance.

As I will demonstrate in a later chapter, from a very early stage in his authorial career William Shakespeare stood something apart from the principal organized religions of his era, their dogmas, doctrine, and peculiar passions.[18] He was remarkably tolerant for his time. Then again, given Europe's bloody history of intolerance, so was the Religious Settlement contrived by Elizabeth, Bacon, and Parker. Shakespeare was possessed of a universal sympathy, a quality alien to absolutists and polemicists. One hopes to see an end in our time to the excesses of the Counter-Reformation.

Notes

1 On the *Star Wars* of the Counter-Reformation see for example: Thomas S. Kuhn, *The Copernican Revolution* (Cambridge: Harvard University Press, 1957). For an apologia, see Olaf Pedersen, *Galileo and the Council of Trent* (Città del Vaticano: Specola vaticana, 1991).

2 R. Bosquet (ed.), *Albertus Magnus, Summa,* I, tr. xiii; Q. liv, vol. 31, p. 551 (Paris: 1895).

3 For accounts of Copernicus and the progress of his ideas see, for example: William C. Dampier, *A History of Science and its Relation with Philosophy and Religion* (Cambridge: Cambridge University Press, 1961) or Fred Hoyle, *Nicolaus Copernicus: an Essay on his Life and Work* (London: Heinemann, 1973).

4 The impenetrable book is available in translation: Charles Glenn Wallis (tr.), *On the Revolutions of the Heavenly Spheres* (New York: Prometheus, 1995).

5 Osiander inserted an unauthorized, unsigned and deprecating preface into the work, and added the words *Orbium Coelestium* to Corpernicus' title.

6 These and other of Bruno's musing are translated in Dorothea Waley Singer, *Giordano Bruno: His Life and Thought, etc.* (New York: Henry Schuman, *ca* 1950). An epitome of Bruno's scientific thought can be found in Hilary Gatti, *Giordano Bruno and Renaissance Science* (Ithaca: Cornell University Press, 1999).

7 One may read the whole grisly tale in Maurice A. Finocchiaro, *Retrying Galileo, 1633–1992* (Berkeley: University of California Press, 2005) or, more succinctly, in Peter Machamer (ed.), *The Cambridge Companion to Galileo* (Cambridge: Cambridge University Press, 1998). For a counter-perspective: James Brodrick, *Galileo and the Roman Inquisition* (London: Catholic Truth Society, 1963).

8 Luther's supposed and often-misquoted remark about Copernicus was made four years before the publication of *De Revolutionibus.*

9 Victor E. Thoren, *The Lord of Uraniborg* (Cambridge: Cambridge University Press, 1990).

10 Most of the material for this book had been compiled and drafted by Thomas Digges' father, Leonard, who died in 1571 but, notwithstanding, appears as the author: Leonard Digges [*sic*], *A prognostication everlastinge, etc.* (London: Thomas Marsh, 1576).

11 Again, father Leonard appears as the author: Leonard Digges, *An arithmeticall militare treatise, named Stratioticos, etc.* (London: Henrie Brynneman, 1579).

12 Still an invaluable resource is John Strype, *The Life and Acts of Matthew Parker* (London: John Wyat, 1711). For Bacon's role see Robert Tittler, *Nicholas Bacon: the Making of a Tudor statesman* (Athens: Ohio University Press, *ca* 1976). A fascinating glimpse behind-the-scenes is accessible in Henry Norbert Birt, *The Elizabethan Religious Settlement: A Study of Contemporary Documents* (London: G. Bell, 1906). The settlement did not go down well everywhere; see Roger B. Manning, *Religion and Society in Elizabethan Sussex* (Leicester: Leicester University Press, 1969). For the Catholic *summa* of the checkered history of religion in England see the comprehensive but hardly impartial Philip Hughes, *The Reformation in England* (London: Hollis and Carter, 1952).

13 Wilson, *Secret Shakespeare.*

14 Judging solely by *Othello,* one could go so far as to declare Shakespeare an enthusiastic Protestant; see my later chapter in this book and Martha Tuck Rozett, *The Doctrine of Election and the Emergence of Elizabethan Tragedy* (Princeton: Princeton University Press, 1984).

15 For another perspective see James C. Bryant, *Tudor Drama and Religious Controversy* (Macon: Mercer, 1984).

16 S. Sohmer, *Shakespeare's Mystery Play and the Opening of the Globe 1599* (Manchester: Manchester University Press, 1999), p. 210.

17 But see Jonathan Dollimore, *Radical tragedy: Religion, Ideology, and Power in the Drama of Shakespeare and his Contemporaries* (Durham: Duke University Press, 1993).

18 Alternatively see Jeffrey Knapp, *Preachers and Players in Shakespeare's England* (Berkeley: Center for Hermeneutical Studies, 1995).

THREE

'The time is out of joint':
Queen Elizabeth's calendar muddle

Shakespeare and his contemporaries grew up in a world caught between two irreconcilable, adversarial views of existence. One of the principal artifacts of the collision between the Catholic and Protestant cosmologies – indeed, its most pervasive aspect, inescapable as time itself – was the existence of two rival calendars. During Shakespeare's lifetime Julius Caesar's old Julian calendar (45 BC) prevailed in England and in other Protestant enclaves and Greek Orthodox regions. Its rival, the scientifically correct (Catholic) Gregorian reformed calendar of 1582, dominated most of Europe. Not only were these two calendars asynchronous by ten days – 1 January in London was 11 January in Rome – but their companion-piece martyrologies were incongruent as well. Catholics and Protestants could not even agree on the date of Easter, which they often celebrated five weeks apart.

Unlike the clever *via media* of the Elizabethan Religious Settlement, the conflict between the rival calendars admitted no middle way. Either today was 25 July and the Feast of Saint James the Greater, or today was 15 July and Saint Swithun's day – and, of course, today couldn't be both (although I will show that it is in *Romeo and Juliet*). Shakespeare and his contemporaries struggled to come to terms with this paradox in ingenious, intriguing ways. As a consequence – and in an ongoing appeal to reason – Shakespeare suffused his plays with references to calendrical anomalies. Some of these are heart-wrenching, as when Othello, who lives by a Gregorian-style calendar[1] reenacts on the *Julian* Holy Saturday the Catholic ritual of *Tenebrae* (extinguishing of candles) as he murders Desdemona (3.2.7–12). Some of these passages are funny – as when Lancelot Gobbo recalls a Black Monday that fell on Ash Wednesday (*MV* 2.5.22–7). Gobbo's lines are *screamingly* funny – and sharply satirical – to auditors (and readers) who recognized that Lancelot is conflating the two calendars.

How there came to be two rival calendars in Europe … why the Julian calendar was in error and how the Gregorian came to be correct … and why the English and a scattering of other Protestant (and Greek/Russian Orthodox) regions stubbornly rejected the Gregorian reform in the face of overwhelming evidence of its correctness … is a curious and remarkable tale, and a monument to human foolishness. Here, briefly, is what lettered Elizabethans (including William Shakespeare) would have understood about this monumental boondoggle.

From his extensive reading of Caesar, Plutarch, Ovid, and Cicero, Shakespeare knew a good deal about the Roman calendar and the Julian reform.[2] On 1 January 45 BC Julius Caesar had imposed on the Roman world a new solar-based calendar; Caesar's objective was to correct the prevailing lunar-based Roman republican calendar (*ca* 153 BC) which was only 355 days long. When a calendar is shorter or longer than the solar tropical year, the dates of the equinoxes and solstices drift (as do the seasons) and holy feasts are gradually displaced from their proper observance. Plutarch described the confusion which confronted Caesar in 46 BC: 'For the Romanes using then the auncient computacion of the yeare, had not only such incertainty and alteracion of the moneth and times, that the sacrifices and yearly feasts came by litle and litle to seasons contrary for the purpose they were ordained: but also in the revolution of the sunne (which is called *Annus Solaris*) no other nation agreed with them' (791).

To reform the republican calendar Caesar's Alexandrian arithmetician, Sosigenes (on loan from Cleopatra), estimated the length of the solar tropical year at 365.25 days. To account for the 0.25 day, Caesar decreed that an additional day should be intercalated every four years. A so-called 'bissextile' day was to be intercalated following 23 February in every fourth year.

Having determined the form of his new calendar, Caesar moved to set it afoot. To correct the prevailing displacement of the seasons, he added a total of ninety days to 46 BC, making it the 'long year' of 445 days. Caesar also moved New Year's day from 1 March to 1 January. Apparently, his intention was to create a correspondence between the four principal solar events and certain well-established Roman festivals; the vernal equinox, for example, was linked with the Roman *Hilaria* – which fell in late March – and from which our April Fools' Day tradition may have descended. This was also the feast of Cybele, mother of Jove; perhaps that's why early Christians set the anniversary of the Annunciation on 25 March.[3]

Early Christianity was a wonderfully eclectic religion, and first-century Christians adopted all four of Caesar's dates for the principal solar events to commemorate the (lost) dates of the conception and nativity of the founders of their religion. In addition to adopting Caesar's date for vernal equinox (24/25 March) as the Annunciation, Caesar's summer solstice (23/24 June) supplied the date of the (lost) birthday of John Baptist, and Caesar's autumnal equinox (23/24 September) was adopted as the date of John's conception. Christians eventually co-opted Caesar's winter solstice (24/25 December), too – as the anniversary of the birth of Jesus Christ.[4]

But the Church would soon discover that Caesar's calendar was imperfect. Sosigenes' estimate of the length of the solar tropical year – 365.25 days – was too long by eleven minutes fourteen seconds. Though this tiny error was undetectable in a Roman's lifetime, it accumulated to a full day every 128 years. By the time the Council of Nicaea met in AD 325, Sosigenes' error had accumulated to three days and the vernal equinox had regressed from 24 to 21 March. This confounded the dating of Easter, which depends on identifying the Paschal moon. When the Council's arithmeticians failed to resolve the difficulty, the Nicaean fathers formulated a new Easter rule. They fixed 21 March as the 'official' date of the vernal equinox and decreed that Easter would be observed on the Sunday after the first full moon following. Though based on a palpable absurdity, this became the Easter rule of the Catholic Church.

Although the Nicaean decree conformed the observance of Easter throughout the Church, it did nothing to correct the slippage inherent in the Julian calendar. By the time the Venerable Bede correctly estimated Sosigenes' error (AD 730) the date of the vernal equinox had advanced even further – to 18 March. This unrelenting precession led to the bizarre medieval practice of designating the true Easter Sunday *Pascha verum* and the observed Easter Sunday *Pascha usitatum*.

In an effort to resolve this embarrassing confusion, in 1472 Pope Sixtus IV engaged the German arithmetician Johann Müller to reform the calendar. But the issue was factious and explosive. Müller died – perhaps by poison – and plans for reform were abandoned. Almost a hundred years later, Pius V summoned mathematicians to Rome to study the problem; he died before they submitted their recommendation. It fell to Pius' successor, Gregory XIII (1502–85), to complete the work and promulgate a new calendar two months before Shakespeare's eighteenth birthday.

The Papal Bull which Gregory signed on 24 February 1582 – Caesar's old bissextile day, perhaps a nod from one *Pontinfex Maximus* to another – clashed with a number of English traditions. Gregory confirmed 1 January as the start of the civil year – which contradicted the English practice of dating the new year from 25 March. By excising the ten days 5–14 October 1582 from the calendar, Gregory restored the date of the equinoxes to the radix of the Council of Nicaea – which left the English Julian calendar ten days behind. Gregory further decreed that only those centennial years divisible by 400 henceforth would be leap years – which would drop England another day behind in 1700.

Gregory's bull cast Queen Elizabeth on the horns of a dilemma. Johannes Kepler and other leading Protestant mathematicians – including Englishmen

Thomas Digges, Henry Savile, and John Dee – endorsed the Gregorian reform. Trouble was, the three consecrated documents of Elizabeth's Church were the Bible, the Book of Common Prayer *and* the Julian calendar. Elizabethan Bibles and prayer books routinely included a calendar in their forepages.[5] Like the words of Christ, these were printed in red – because the calendar was thought to be revelatory; its orderly succession of holy days 'revealed a profound logic of resonances and connections. The meaning of these may escape the modern mind but their ancient significance was perfectly familiar' to Elizabethans.[6] 'In the liturgy and in the celebrations which were its central movements people found the key to the meaning and purpose of their lives'.[7] We moderns live by many calendars – fiscal, academic and simply chronological – all of them secular. But the Elizabethan calendar *was* the Church calendar. And it was holy.

Still, Elizabeth was not one to be left ten days behind the whole world; she determined to impose an English calendar reform. After consulted John Dee (among others), the Queen urged Archbishop Edmund Grindal (*ca* 1519–83) – who had succeed Matthew Parker in 1576 – to approve an English calendar reform without delay. To Elizabeth's consternation Grindal refused, stubbornly arguing that calendar reform would entail a revision of the Book of Common Prayer – which could be moved only by parliament, and certainly not by the Antichrist Bishop of Rome. Further, argued Grindal, since the end of the world (and time) was believed to be near, why tinker with the calendar *now*?

In fact, the wily Grindal had a price for accepting Elizabeth's calendar reform: an ecumenical review of the matter by his Anglican Church '*in concert with our brethren overseas*'.[8] This was a price Elizabeth could not and would not pay. Allowing Grindal to refer an English calendar reform to an international convocation would effectively repeal the Act of Appeals *and* debunk the Queen's claim to supreme governorship of her national Church.[9] Checked, Elizabeth chose the lesser of two evils (for her); she determined England would continue to live and pray according to Caesar's scientifically discredited Julian calendar. This (tyrannous) decision turned England into a national anachronism – which it remained until Lord Chesterfield's calendar reform took effect in 1752.

But even Elizabeth's authoritarian rule could not quash the issue of English calendar reform. Any Englishperson with eyes could see that the solstices and equinoxes were falling on the wrong dates. And every confessing English Christian knew that the Anglican Church was celebrating Easter, Pentecost, and Christmas on the wrong days.

The inexorable precession of the equinoxes made Elizabeth's calendar controversy grist for the pulp publishers of England. To stir the pot for an English reform writers of almanacs regaled their readers with a detailed history of Caesar's calendar while cheekily printing the rival Julian and Gregorian calendars side-by-side – as an aid to travelers, so they claimed.[10] These ubiquitous paperbacks gave literate Englishpersons a detailed lesson in Elizabeth's Julian calendar (and its glaring flaws). To cite one example, in his almanac for 1584 John Harvey explained how the ancient Romans 'a long tyme to have labored, and paynefully travayled in searchyng out the direct course and true space of the yeere' (Harvey Bii^r) – how Numa Pompilius (666 BC) revised the primitive calendar of Romulus – how Caesar recruited Sosigenes, and how the 'most puissaunt Captayne, and learned Astronomicall Emperour' imposed his Julian calendar (Harvey Bii^r). Harvey explained Sosigenes' error and closed his scholarly treatise by inviting readers to 'have recourse to Suetonius ... to the fyrst booke of Macrobius Saturnalia, or to an Epistle of S. Iherome directed ad Eustochium ... which are all copious in this argument' (Harvey Biii^v). This bibliographical reference suggests a popular appetite for information about the roots of the calendar controversy.

Other almanac-makers were more aggressive in pressing for reform. Farmer's almanac for 1586 included a table of the true and observed Easters over a period of thirty-two years. During this interval the English celebration of Easter had been wrong by one week in eight years, wrong by four weeks during five years, and wrong by five weeks during four years. Discreetly, Farmer declined to pursue this evidence to its logical conclusion: 'Thus have I after rude and simple maner made manifest the chiefe causes of this late [Gregorian] Alteration,' he wrote, 'but whether there be any necessitie that we should do lyke or not [in England], I referre that to the judgement of the reverent Divines, and learned Astronomers, who are sufficiently able to determine that cause: The one, in respect of conscience, the other in respect of the communitie of Computation' (c2^r). In the face of Elizabeth's rejection of Gregory's calendar, reform was not a subject upon which *any* writer dared appear outspoken. Given that the Julian calendar was a consecrated state document, attacking it – particularly after the Supreme Governor of the Church had confirmed it – would have been heresy or treason, or both.

Then in 1598 a phenomenon occurred which brought the calendar controversy to a head. That year saw the most extreme variation (five weeks) between the Catholic and English Easters. In 1599, a pamphlet published in Scotland and distributed in England captured the widespread confusion and frustration:

In the yeare of our Lord 1598 lately by past, according to the decree of the Nicene Councell, and late Kalendar, set out by [Italian arithmetician] Lilius, Easter day fell upon the twelft daie of March in the olde Kalendare and Almancks whereby we yet reckon in England and Scotland: And Whit Sunday upon the last daye of Aprill: And Fastings even upon the twenty foure of Ianuary: Whereas after the vulgare maner and count, Easter daie was celebrate that yeare, the sixteenth daie of Aprill; Whit Sunday, the fourth of Iune: And Fastings eve, the last of February. Yee see the distance betweene the one calculation and the other is more then the space of a Moneth: what errour it may growe to by the proces of time it is easie by this example to perceive.[11]

As this pamphlet was passing through the printer's press William Shakespeare was writing *Julius Caesar*. His tragedy written to christen the Bankside Globe depicts the assassination of the tyrant who imposed the Julian calendar. *Julius Caesar* would open the Globe on England's official *and wrong* date of the Summer Solstice.

The Scottish pamphlet and Shakespeare's play pinpoint a historic moment in the English calendar controversy – a moment when 'the most basic category by which men order their experience [time] seemed subject to arbitrary political manipulation.'[12] Being compelled to celebrate Easter on the wrong day – when everyone knew it was the wrong day – had turned the English Easter services of 1598 into a theater of the absurd. Imagine yourself a devout Christian in an English Church on 16 April 1598 – reciting the anthem 'Christ is risen,' hearing the Gospel's tale of Jesus' haunting whisper to Mary Magdalene – all the while knowing that the true Easter had passed, ignored, on 12 March.

Gregory's newfangled calendar may have been Catholic, but it was correct. To an English Christian, being compelled to worship by Caesar's calendar – a calendar repudiated by the whole world – wasn't merely absurd; it was degrading, humiliating, scandalous, mortifying. It was tyranny. Those who wonder why Shakespeare chose 1599 to write his play about the murder of the tyrant who authored the Julian calendar perhaps need seek no further.

I have now rehearsed as much of the root and cause of the Elizabeth's calendar controversy as her average lettered subject might have known. Even so, it is difficult for twenty-first-century minds to grasp the oppressive day-to-day experience of living and worshipping under a scientifically discredited Julian calendar. Every winter the English holy year dissolved into a series of jangling discordances. On 21 December Elizabethan Protestants observed the Feast of Saint Thomas. But they knew that the rest of Europe (and their Catholic recusant neighbors) had already celebrated Christmas, St Stephen's Day, and Holy Innocents, and were preparing to see in the New Year that very night. By the time the English Protestants' 1 January rolled around, the Twelve Days of Christmas were long-gone for their Catholic neighbors, who were already dating their correspondence with a new year. As Elizabethans prepared billets-doux on the Eve of St Valentine 1598, Catholic Europe was celebrating Shrove Tuesday 1599. And while Elizabethans were exchanging Valentine greetings, the rest of the world was gravely observing Ash Wednesday and the onset of Lent. Even Julius Caesar's anniversaries were muddled: on the English Ides of March (15 March) the Catholic world was observing the Annunciation to the Blessed Virgin Mary. Worse, the Elizabethans' date of the Annunciation fell on the Catholic Palm Sunday. Worst of all, the true Easter, 11 April 1599

Gregorian, fell on the date the English observed April Fools' Day. These are a few of the bizarre clashes of dates the English suffered under their antiquated Julian calendar. And everyone had to go along with Elizabeth's madness. It wasn't that the empress had no new clothes – but she certainly couldn't tell time.

Throughout his career William Shakespeare wrote for an audience whose way of thinking about time (and the cosmos) was radically different from our own. To understand Shakespeare – to share his first auditors' perception of his plays – we must school ourselves to think as they did. This is not easy. Our habits of mind, and theirs, severely diverge.

Our twenty-first-century year is governed by a scientifically exact, secular civil calendar. Elizabeth's calendar was fatally flawed in ways that any of her subjects could understand … but which the entire population of England was powerless to correct. The English also followed a state-sponsored, pervasive liturgical calendar which was held to be God-given and sacrosanct; Shakespeare and his contemporaries remembered (though we have largely forgotten) that Jesus began His mission by proclaiming He had come to 'preach the acceptable year of the Lord' (Lk 4:19).

Whereas the minutes of our day are metered by the rate of decay of atoms of Cesium, in Shakespeare's age timekeeping relied on the transit of the sun, notoriously faulty mechanical clocks, the gradual phasing of the moon and the ponderous slow wheel of the Zodiac. Our foreground calendar is the minutely calibrated Gregorian with its superstructure of secular and religious holidays. Shakespeare's contemporaries followed the liturgical calendar of the Reformed church – with scores of suppressed but unforgotten Catholic holy days ghosting in its cellar. We do not date births, marriages, contracts, leases, wills, and deaths by reference to holy days. Elizabethans did. Simply by working their fingers in the *computus manualis* while mumbling a doggerel *Cisio Ianus* – even an illiterate Elizabethan could quickly calculate (for example) that Shakespeare's Juliet, born on Lammas Eve at night, was conceived on All Hallows' Eve. We don't entertain such leaps of mind; at least some Elizabethans did.

We are Newtonians; we can measure gravity even if we cannot explain it, and we have some grasp of celestial mechanics. The vast majority of Shakespeare's first auditors were pre-Copernicans who inhabited a geocentric universe where the constant guiding hand of God was required to steer the planets and stars. In a very real sense, they lived in a perpetual miracle. We hardly believe in miracles at all.

We consider astrology an amusement. Shakespeare's contemporaries accepted astronomy and astrology as the descriptive and predictive aspects of a single discipline. They regarded the movements of celestial bodies – and every other event in the universe – as elemental to God's grand plan and, therefore, potentially revelatory. Centuries of observation by countless skywatchers had created remarkably accurate ephemeredes – charts of the nightly positions of the stars and planets. Elizabethans regarded the casting of horoscopes as a respected skill; most mathematicians and astronomers engaged in the practice. I will show that Shakespeare's arithmetician and counter-caster Cassio does so – just as a Jacobean audience would have expected him to do. No Englishperson of means would embark on an undertaking of any significance without first consulting an astrologer; the Earl of Leicester even asked the polymath John Dee to chose a propitious date for Queen Elizabeth's coronation.

We moderns are pragmatic rationalists; Shakespeare's countrymen were superstitious and, broadly speaking, more religious than we are. They were compelled by law to attend church regularly, something most of us decline to do. We do not read the Bible daily nor hear it declaimed each Sunday as Elizabethans and Jacobeans did. Nor do the majority of us accept the Old Testament or the Gospels as literal, infallible history. To varying degrees Shakespeare's contemporaries believed in magic, witchcraft, numerology, and Christianity.[13] By contrast, our modern outlook is scientific and stubbornly secular.[14]

We don't know the martyrology. Shakespeare's contemporaries did. A comprehensive and minutely detailed calendar of the liturgical year was printed in the forepages of their Bibles and Books of Common Prayer. Though stripped of hundreds of saints' days by Henry VIII's reforms, the liturgical calendar under Elizabeth and James was still peppered with holy days which imposed obligatory observances, oblations and rituals, including some rather bizarre. For example, the English had to be mindful that 25 March was Lady Day; it was both the solemn anniversary of the Annunciation and the first day of their New Year. Observant Christians had to track the varying date of Easter and its moveable feasts so as to clear their larders no later than Shrove Tuesday night in obedience to the rubrics of Lent. Shakespeare's contemporaries knew 23 April was the gala feast of England's patron, Saint George (so do we). But they also remembered that 25 July was the feast of Saint James *and* the eve of Saint Anne – even though Henry VIII had struck both occasions from his books and declared idolatrous the swarms of pilgrims who made their way to James' shrine in Campostela, Spain; in a later chapter I will show these disused holy days underlie Old Capulet's reference to his 'old accutom'd feast' and Nurse's oath by 'my halidom.'

We don't read through the psalms each month. Many of Shakespeare's contemporaries did. Their Book of Common Prayer provided a rigid scheme for reciting all 150 psalms during the course of every month. Every day, specific clutches of psalms were prescribed for the morning and evening prayers. For example, Shakespeare's auditors recited the 23rd Psalm on the fourth day of every month and the 115th Psalm ('*Non nobis,*' as in *Henry V*) on the 23rd day of the month. Through this repetition, in the minds of many (including Shakespeare), certain psalms became linked to specific dates. I will show that Iago's drinking song, 'O, man's life's but a span' is a paraphrase of the 39th Psalm, which Elizabethans recited on the eighth day of every month.

The rigid schedule of readings in the Book of Common Prayer led Shakespeare's contemporaries through the New Testament twice each year (the Book of Revelation excepted) and through the Old Testament once each year (Solomon's racy bits excepted). Thanks to this lifelong repetition, in the memories of Shakespeare and his auditors many best-loved passages of the Old and New Testaments became indelibly linked with specific dates in the calendar. As a consequence, Shakespeare could convey to his audience the date of an onstage action merely by quoting or paraphrasing a snatch of Scripture. For example, when the Cynicke Poet storms the tent of Brutus in *Julius Caesar* 4.3 shouting 'Love, and be Friends, as two such men should bee' the pious among Shakespeare's audience could hardly fail to recognize a parody of Jesus' commandment to love one another, John 15:12–17. Those who followed the calendar of readings in the Book of Common Prayer had read this passage *that very morning*. John 15 was the Gospel reading for St Barnabas Day, 11 June. Because the English lived by Caesar's outmoded Julian calendar, 11 June was the Summer Solstice in London in 1599. As I demonstrated in *Shakespeare's Mystery Play*, this was the date on which the first Globe theater opened, and the date on which Shakespeare's *Julius Caesar* was first performed.

There is another crucial point of difference between Shakespeare's contemporaries' perception of time and our own. They were sunwatchers. We're not. Nowadays clocks and watches are commonplace. But in Shakespeare's England clocks of any kind were a rarity and portable watches nonexistent. Instead, sundials and almanacs which tabled the times of sunrise and sunset for each day of the year were ubiquitous, as were ephemeredes which plotted with remarkable accuracy the positions of the stars and planets. After the Bible, these ephemeral pamphlets and one-sheets were the most widely circulated printed documents in England. Everyone who was anyone had one. Church sextons used these tables at sunrise and sunset to reset the notoriously unreliable tower clocks of the age. Shakespeare glances at this practice in *King John* – 'Old Time the clock-setter, that bald sexton Time' (3.1.250) – and brings one of these 'absolute' sextons to life in the graveyard in *Hamlet*.

Shakespeare's contemporaries had many reasons to be deeply and continuously concerned about time – reasons no longer relevant to our modern lives. It's unlikely the present reader will be aware of either the phase of the moon tonight, or the time of sunrise and sunset, or of moonrise and moonset. But this was important information in Shakespeare's age. There were no streetlamps and a new, unrisen, or early setting moon entailed a night of utter darkness. Walking abroad on a moonless night could be dangerous. When Banquo tells son Fleance that the moon set that night at midnight he is teaching his boy prudence – and the need to stay *au courant* with the ephemeredes – a family tradition which the superstitious and calendrically minded King James I maintained.

The early modern English attached to the phasing of the moon a variety of powerful superstitions which we have forgotten. New Moon was considered the propitious time for planting or moving house. Full Moon was apposite to these activities. Jacobean auditors may well have grasped that Shakespeare's Lear plans to move between his daughters' houses at each New Moon. His division of a kingdom – his 'darker purpose' – takes place on such a moonless night – which is why Kent can fight Oswald by the light of a full moon two weeks later – details which commentators have never recognized.

Whereas our theatrical companies perform a single play (or a few in repertory) eight times a week and hope each run will continue indefinitely, by contrast Shakespeare's companies had a broad repertoire and often consulted an almanac and/or the liturgical calendar when selecting a play for a performance date. Thomas Platter's report of a performance of *Julius Caesar* at the Bankside Globe on 21 September 1599 indicates a choice of material informed by an ephemeredes.[15] September 21 was the 'official' date of the autumnal equinox. But the English Julian calendar was ten days in error and the equinox had been observed in London on 13 September. By playing Julius Caesar on 21 September Old Style – the Julian *and incorrect* date of the equinox – Shakespeare and company delivered a cheeky comment on Elizabeth's Julian calendar. An English audience compelled to live and worship by the antiquated Julian calendar could hardly have overlooked this irony. There is also compelling evidence that, several months prior to opening their new Bankside playhouse, the Globe sharers consulted an almanac for June 1599. Working from Wenceslas Hollar's *Long View of London* (1647), John Orrell deduced that the axis of the Globe was aimed at a point on the horizon 48.7° north of East.[16] This point on the horizon approximates the rising of the sun on the Summer Solstice. Since the Globe construction commenced during winter, the sharers and their builder must have consulted an almanac or ephemeredes to determine this azimuth of sunrise when they laid the groundplan for their new playhouse. In *A Midsummer Night's Dream* Shakespeare spoofs this practice; as Peter Quince and the Mechanicals set about their rehearsal, this dialogue ensues:

> Snout   Doth the moon shine that night we play our play?
> Bottom   A calendar, a calendar – look in the almanac, find out moonshine, find
>   out moonshine.
> Quince   Yes, it doth shine that night.
>
> (3.1.48–51)

Robin Starvling is delegated Moon, and the play revised to accommodate the moon's and Robin's presence (*MND* 5.1.239, 252–4.).

Shakespeare's company also consulted the liturgical calendar when scheduling plays for playing dates. We know the company played *Henry VIII* – a play depicting that monarch's historic break with the Church of Rome – on the feast of the pope, St Peter's Day, 29 June 1613. This ironic match of play-to-date suggests that spoofing old holy days may have been acceptable within limitation. The Chamberlain's Men also performed *Twelfth Night* at the Middle Temple on 2 February 1602.[17] In this play Olivia – whom Feste addresses as 'Madonna' – attempts to seduce a cross-dressed virgin, Viola-Cesario. There's a palpable irony here: 2 February is Candlemas, the Feast of the Purification (not the seduction) of the original Madonna.

In sum, for us time has little to do with politics – but in Shakespeare's era time was the object of intense political and religious controversy. Throughout the playwright's career Elizabeth's three consecrated state documents – the Protestant Bible, the Book of Common Prayer, and the antiquated Julian calendar – were under siege by the concerted forces of Roman Catholicism. In 1582 Pope Gregory not only had published the new and scientifically correct Gregorian calendar, he also unveiled a revised martyrology *and* the first Catholic New Testament in English *and* a revised book of canon law. These coordinated publications constituted a major offensive in the war for Christian hearts and minds. Within a year at most, every lettered Englishperson had to face the fact that their Julian calendar was outmoded, scientifically discredited, and corrupt. As we school ourselves to think about time and the cosmos as Shakespeare's contemporaries did, I will demonstrate that the rivalry between the Catholic and Protestant calendars runs through his plays like a glowing silver thread.

Why and how William Shakespeare developed his interest in time and the calendar is another intriguing question. There is suggestive evidence that Shakespeare's parents shared the conventional superstitions of the age; Samuel Schoenbaum speculated that Shakespeare was born on 23 April but not christened until 26 April – three days after his birth rather than the usual two – because 'superstition intervened – people considered St Mark's Day [25 April] unlucky. 'Black Crosses' it was called; the crosses and altars were almost to Shakespeare's day hung with black, and (some reported) the spectral company of those destined to die that year stalked the churchyard.'[18] If Schoenbaum's inference is correct, the boy Shakespeare may have grown up in a household which regarded the calendar and martyrology as a kind of gazetteer to the universal mysteries. Then again, Shakespeare's interest in the calendar might have been nourished by mere dramatic necessity. Francois Laroque noticed that 'Given that one of the greatest problems of the theatre and dramatic representation … is to find visual and gestural equivalents to the abstract categories of thought and speech, it is easy to see how Shakespeare seized upon … the medium of the calendar linked with the various traditions and games of the major festivals [to] endow his plays with the extra semantic dimension of temporal symbolism.'[19] Whether or not Shakespeare imbibed the fear of St Mark's Day with his mother's milk, the playwright could have high confidence that members of his audiences would recognize the 'temporal symbolism' of holy days … which requires of us a brief backward glance at *Macbeth* and the night that King Duncan's murder set the Stuart line on course for the throne of England.

The Macbeth saga is for us the stuff of legend. But for Jacobean playgoers in 1606 it was literal – and highly topical – political history. There had been a real Macbeth, a real Duncan, a real August night, a real murder-under-trust. And as a direct consequence a flesh-and-blood descendant of Banquo possessed the English throne.[20] Banquo's uncannily accurate reference to the time of moonset at Dunsinane on the night of 13/14 August 1046 – a detail which could have been recovered by Shakespeare himself or by one of scores of London's practicing astrologers – is certainly no coincidence. On the contrary, it typifies one mode of calendar-play which recurs repeatedly in Shakespeare's work. When writing about an historical event which occurred on a known date, the playwright often made reference to salient astronomical details. I will demonstrate that Shakespeare employs this tactic to lament *Magna Carta* in *King John*.

Shakespeare also applied this rubric when writing (or revising) a play for performance on a date certain. Scholars accept that Shakespeare's play 'Comedy of Errors (like to *Plautus* his *Menechmus)* was played by the Players' at Gray's Inn on 'Innocents-Day at Night,' 28 December 1594 (Foakes, 116–17). Some believe, as I do, that the play was purpose-written (or substantially revised) for this performance date – and the proof is in the text.

The action opens with old Egeon condemned to die at sunset: 'Yet this my comfort: when your words are done, / My woes end likewise with the evening sun' (1.1.26–7). As the execution party approaches in Act Five, a remarkably observant bystander reckons

> By this [procession], I think, the dial point's at five.
> Anon, I'm sure, the Duke himself in person
> Comes this way to the melancholy vale,
> The place of death and sorry execution …

> (5.1.119–22)

The Duke – *Solinus* – is named for the sun whose light casts the gnomon's shadow, 'the [sun]dial's point.' But Egeon's fatal rendezvous is only one of several meetings set for 5 p.m. on this fateful day. At 1.2.26–7, a Merchant agrees to meet Antipholous of Syracuse, 'Soon at five o'clock … I'll meet with you upon the mart.' The goldsmith Angelo tells a creditor that Antipholus of Ephesus 'had of me a chain. At five o'clock / I shall receive the money for the same' (4.1.10–11). These three markers entail a sunset *ca* 5:00 p.m. But on 28 December 1598 Julian there was no sunset at London at 5:00 p.m. (see figure).

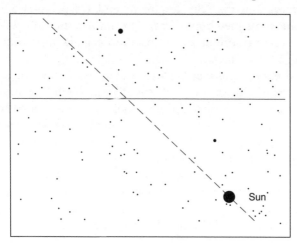

Sunset at London, 28 December 1594 (Julian), 5:00 p.m. The sun is well below the horizon line.

At London (51°15'N, 0°10'W) on 28 December 1594 Julian, the winter sunset had ended at 4:09 p.m. By 5:00 p.m. the disk of the sun was well below the horizon (chart above). In fact, a sunset at London *ca* 5:00 p.m. could have been expected in mid-October.

But, remarkably, *at Ephesus* (37°55'N, 27°19'E) on 28 December 1594 Julian, sunset began at 4:58 p.m. (see figure).

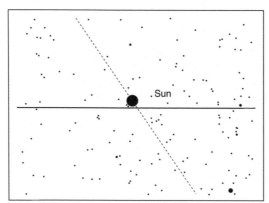

Sunset at Ephesus, 28 December 1594 (Julian), 4:58 p.m.

At Ephesus on the night *Comedy of Errors* was performed sunset occupied the interval 4:58 to 5:08 p.m. Is it possible that Shakespeare could have determined that 5 p.m. was the time of sunset at Ephesus on the Julian Innocents' Day 1594, the evening his company performed *Comedy of Errors*? Yes, in point of fact. The longitude and latitude of Ephesus – and many other sites referenced in the Old Testament and Gospels – were available to Elizabethans in printed books. From this information it would be a simple matter for one of London's astrologers to calculate the time of sunset at Ephesus on 28 December.

Extraordinary as this may be, there was an even more suggestive celestial event occurring in the sky over Ephesus at 5 p.m. on the evening Shakespeare's company performed *Comedy of Errors*. Looking east-northeast at Ephesus that evening with the setting sun at one's back, an observer would see the rising of the celestial twins, Castor and Pollux, the Zodiacal sign of Gemini (see figure). Can it *really* be coincidence that this celestial tableau – a setting sun *and* the rising of Gemini – serves as the backdrop for the reunion of two sets of twins at 5 p.m. on 28 December, the performance date of *Comedy of Errors*? The complexity of this calendrical trope is even more remarkable since it appears in a play written very early in William Shakespeare's career.

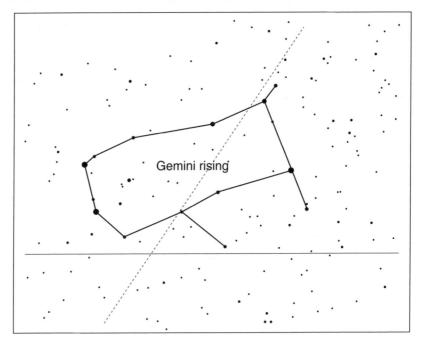

Looking east–northeast at Ephesus: Gemini rising on 28 December 1594 (Julian) at 4:58 p.m.

But our playwright was inclined to calendar-mischief *even earlier* in his development. To my knowledge *The Fasti* of Ovid has not been recognized as the source of the opening soliloquy of *Richard III*. But I suggest the connection is unmistakable. Ovid introduced the month of March:

> *Bellice, depositis clipeo paulisper et hasta,*
> *Mars, ades et nitidas casside solve comas.*
> *forsitan ipse roges, quid sit cum Marte poetae:*
> *a te, qui canitur, nomina mensis habet.*
> *ipse vides manibus peragi fera bella Minervae;*
> *num minus ingenuis artibus illa vacat?*
> *Palladis exemplo ponendae tempora sume*
> *cuspidis: invenies et quod inermis agas.*
> *tum quoque inermis eras, cum te Romana*
> *sacerdos cepit, ut huic urbi semina magna dures.*
>
> (*Fasti* 3.1–10)

Sir James Frazer's translation runs:

> Come, warlike Mars; lay down thy shield and spear for a brief space, and from thy helmet loose thy glistering locks. Haply thou mayest ask, What has a poet to do with Mars? From thee the month which now I sing doth takes its name. Thyself dost see that fierce wars are waged by Minerva's hands. Is she for that the less at leisure for the liberal arts? After the pattern of Pallas take a time to put aside the lance. Thou shalt find something to do unarmed. Then, too, wast thou unarmed when the roman priestess captivated thee, that thou mightest bestow upon this city a great seed. (Frazer, 121)[21]

Hasn't Ovid's thought and diction informed Shakespeare's famous invocation of Mars:

> Now is the winter of our discontent,
> Made glorious summer by this sonne of Yorke:
> And all the cloudes that lowrd upon our house,
> In the deepe bosome of the Ocean buried.
> Now are our browes bound with victorious wreathes,
> Our bruised armes hung up for monuments,
> Our sterne alarmes changd to merry meetings,
> Our dreadfull marches to delightfull measures.
> Grim-visaged warre hath smoothed his wrinkled front,
> And now in steed of mounting barbed steeds,
> To fright the soules of fearfull adversaries,
> He capers nimbly in a Ladies chamber,
> To the lascivious pleasing of a loue.
>
> (1.1.1–13)[22]

It may be that Shakespeare co-opted Ovid's diction because his source (again, Holinshed) recorded that King Edward IV was crowned at Westminster on 4

March 1461.[23] But I prefer to believe the playwright's cue was that 'this son of York' was Earl of March.

There is another type of Shakespeare's calendar-play which I will examine in this book. And its wit relies on so detailed a knowledge of the rival calendars of the Renaissance as to have remained resiliently opaque to scholars for hundreds of years. A case in point is Shakespeare's only overt jibe at the confusion created by the Gregorian calendar reform of 1582. In Act Two of *The Merchant of Venice*, Lancelot Gobbo recalls his nosebleed on 'Black Monday last at six o'clock i' th' morning, falling out that year on Ash Wednesday was four year in th' afternoon' (2.5.22–7). Commentators have dismissed Gobbo's reckoning as nonsense. After all, Black Monday is the Monday after Easter. Easter Sunday must fall in the period 22 March to 25 April, an interval of only 35 days. Since Ash Wednesday and Easter Monday are separated by 48 days it follows that they cannot fall on the same date in different years. In a later chapter I will demonstrate that in Shakespeare's age this could happen, and that Shakespeare's joke – an irony lost for centuries – is that Gobbo has his dates and holy days right, but he is conflating the two rival two calendars.

I have offered these instances of Shakespeare's invention at the outset of this book as examples of the range and precision of Shakespeare's sophistication (and delight) in writing for the wiser sort. Some of the chapters which follow will offer evidence that the overwhelming majority of temporal references in Shakespeare's plays are exacting and precise, and that many are pregnant with levels of meaning commentators have never suspected. Recovering these unrecognized nuances will profoundly enrich our understanding of the most important literary documents in English, as well as illuminating anew the mind of their creator.

These chapters will show that Shakespeare possessed a remarkably detailed knowledge of the rival calendars of the Renaissance – not only the Julian and Gregorian but also the Venetians' singular variant, the *More Veneto*. Shakespeare was also conversant with the calendars of other states – including Venice and Cyprus – and other ages, including the Etruscan and Roman. He committed to memory long passages of the Bible (taking special pleasure in the Psalms and Epistles of Saint Paul). In Shakespeare's mind – as in the minds of his first auditors – many of these passages of Scripture are linked to specific days of the month – or dates in the year – via the repetitious recitals prescribed by the liturgical calendar of the Book of Common Prayer.

Though students of Shakespeare have long been taught their author was indifferent to details of time and date, the chapters in this book will demonstrate the contrary is true; Shakespeare dotted his plays with scenes set on specific days of the week, on solar and lunar holy days, even on the solstice. Shakespeare set some of his plays in specific years; I will show that the *annus praesens* of *Romeo and Juliet* is 1582 and of *Othello* 1603. Relying on the chronology in the second edition of Wells' and Taylor's *Oxford Shakespeare*, I will trace the development of Shakespeare's writing for the wiser sort. Whereas the playwright seems indifferent to the calendar when he writes *Two Gentlemen of Verona* and *The Taming of the Shrew* (1589–91), by the time he has battled through a number of historical dramas (*1–2–3 Henry VI, Richard III, Titus Andronicus, The Rape of Lucrece*) he emerges with an intense interest in the calendar, time, and time-keeping – along with a rather dry skepticism toward received religion – in *The Comedy of Errors* (1594). He explores the Gregorian reform and confusion ensuing in *Romeo and Juliet* (1595) and, in the same year, writes an occasional, date-specific play, *A Midsummer Night's Dream*. By the time Shakespeare writes *King John* (1596) his skill is sufficiently sophisticated for him to allude to a Solstice in order to make a recondite political statement on *Magna Carta*.

Then in 1598/9 a remarkable innovation in Shakespeare's technique occurs. Into *Henry V* (set *ca* AD 1412), his last play written for performance at The Curtain, Shakespeare injects an unmistakable allusion to the Earl of Essex's contemporary adventure in Ireland (March 1599) – a passage which could not help but jar his audience out of the early fifteenth century and into their present-day London. Into his next play, *Julius Caesar* – which everyone knows takes place in 44–42 BC – Shakespeare injects an anachronistic striking clock which tolled his audience from ancient Rome to contemporary England. Anachronism was a long-established, well-recognized tactic for linking onstage events to contemporary events in England.

As he set to work in the new Bankside Globe, Shakespeare adopted another new and exciting tactic: he began to shuffle planes of times like a dealer riffling cards. In *As You Like It* (1599–1600) the seasons become pied because there are no clocks in the forest. In *Twelfth Night* (1601) a Christmas carol conveys that the English Julian 12th of December was the actual solar date of Christmas. In *Othello* (1603–4), a group of Gregorian-calendared Venetians occupy an island which lives by the Greek (and English) Julian calendar – and all manner of time-confusion ensues. These plays are exemplars of a master at work. They interrogate the rival calendars and the bitter religio-political conflict, of which – for Shakespeare and the wiser sort – these calendars are the most pervasive, ineluctable evidence.

A later chapter in this book takes special notice of Shakespeare's Q2 rewrite of *Hamlet* (1602–3) to illustrate the mature playwright's absolute mastery over dramatic time. The Prince Amleth of Saxo Grammaticus, if he lived at all, would have flourished *ca* AD 900. And, indeed, there are hints of the early medieval era in *Hamlet*; for example, England is a Danish fief. But there are anachronisms in *Hamlet*, too: cannon, for one, another striking clock, and the prince's post-Copernican verses to Ophelia. Hamlet's university, Wittenberg, was founded only in 1502; this city in the Protestant district of Germany followed the Julian calendar. Which is why Hamlet, who has only just returned from Julian Germany to Gregorian Denmark, cannot remember how long it is since his father died – 'But two months dead, nay not so much, not two … within a month … A little month … within a month.' The wiser sort would have understood Hamlet's calendar confusion; it was common to international travelers after the Gregorian reform of 1582 (I will show that Desdemona has a bout of it on Julian-calendared Cyprus). Shakespeare's time-setting for *Hamlet* – which seems in relentless flux between the medieval and Tudor eras – has vexed commentators time out of mind. But I believe the instability of the time-setting is as intrinsic to Shakespeare's dramatic design in *Hamlet* as it is in *Othello*. The time *is* out of joint at Elsinore, just as it was in Elizabeth's and James's England. Against this unstable backdrop Shakespeare incises a rigid calendar into *Hamlet* which is neither solar nor lunar but biological. Hamlet is thirty. He was born on the day Old Hamlet overcame Old Fortinbras, the very day on which the absolute Clown became sexton – the clock-setter – of the church. This dating is of paramount importance to the drama, as it was to the Danish (and English) succession; I will show that Hamlet was conceived before the marriage of his parents (as was Queen Elizabeth) and, therefore, is illegitimate and incapable of the Danish throne. It is the calendar of Hamlet's nativity which shapes the drama of Shakespeare's Danish tragedy; that is the calendar he wished his wiser sort to contemplate.

The American poet, Stanley Kunitz, taught his many students that in order to succeed as a writer of literature it was necessary to lead 'a counter-life.' By this Kunitz meant that a writer of literature must swim against the stream, and move socially, intellectually, and spiritually *against* the currents of one's own age. William Shakespeare perhaps gave the world more literature than any other writer living or dead. He could not have done so without leading a counter-life. Whether he was a conforming Anglican or a Catholic raised or converted, Shakespeare could not have written as freely and widely and profoundly had he embraced either idiom wholeheartedly. Writers of literature *must* keep their distance. They can thrive only by living in what James Joyce called 'silence, exile, and cunning.'

Notes

1 Actually, by the Gregorian-based but unique Venetian *More Veneto*, of which more in a later chapter.
2 For example: Sir Thomas North, *Plutarch's Lives* (London: 1579), pp. 791–5.
3 The rites engrossed the period 15–25 March. The 24 March was the 'Day of Blood,' and centered on animal sacrifice. The rites concluded on 25 March with the ritual bathing of a statue of Cybele. Simon Hornblower and Anthony Spawforth (eds), *The Oxford Classical Dictionary* (Oxford: Oxford University Press, 1999), p. 416.

4 The winter solstice had long been recognized in Parthia and Rome as the birthday of an earlier man-god, Mithras. In his reading of Plutarch's *Pompeius,* Shakespeare would have encountered a reference to Pompey's legionnaires performing 'many straunge sacrifices & certen ceremonies of religion amongest themselves, in the mount Olympus, & among other, the mistery of *Mithres,* which is the sunne' (North, p. 689). Also see E.A.J. Honigmann, 'Shakespeare's Plutarch,' *Shakespeare Quarterly* 10 (1959), 29.

5 R. Chris Hassel, Jr., *Renaissance Drama and the English Church Year* (Lincoln: University of Nebraska Press, 1979), pp. 7–8.

6 Francois Laroque, *Shakespeare's Festive World* (Cambridge: Cambridge University Press, 1993), p. 202.

7 Eamon Duffy, *The Stripping of the Altars* (New Haven: Yale University Press, 1992), p. 11.

8 British Library, MS. Add 32092, fols. 26–33.

9 Patrick Collison, *Archbishop Grindal and The Struggle for a Reformed Church* (London: Jonathan Cape, 1979), pp. 270–1.

10 For example, J. Harvey, *Leape Yeares. A compendious Prognostication, etc.* (London: Watkins and Roberetes) 1582, Biiiv ff, and William Farmer, *The common Almanacke or Kalender, etc.* (London: 1586), fol. 2r.

11 Robert Pont, *A New Treatise of the Right Reckoning Yeares, etc.* (Edinburgh: Robert Walde-grave, 1599), p. 61.

12 Sigurd Burckhardt, *Shakespeare's Meanings,* (Princeton: Princeton University Press, 1968), p. 6.

13 For a useful perspective see Clifford Davidson, *History, Religion, and Violence: Culture Contexts for Medieval and Renaissance English Drama* (Adlershot: Ashgate, 2002).

14 Despite the recent political successes of evangelicals and fundamentalists.

15 Ernest Schanzer, 'Thomas Platter's Observations on the Elizabethan Stage,' *Notes and Queries* (November 1956), 466–7.

16 John Orrell, *The Quest for Shakespeare's Globe* (Cambridge: Cambridge University Press, 1983), pp. 152ff.

17 Elizabeth S. Donno (ed.), *Twelfth Night* (Cambridge: Cambridge University Press 1992), p. 1.

18 Samuel Schoenbaum, *Shakespeare: a Compact Documentary Life,* (Oxford: Oxford University Press, 1977), p. 25.

19 Laroque, *Festive World.*

20 If the play was performed before James and Christian IV on the night of 13/14 August 1606 Gregorian (Sunday 3/4 August 1606 Julian), this would mark the 560th anniversary of Duncan's murder; it was also a night of New Moon, i.e. moonless. (See Appendix on whether two monarchs were among the first audience of *Macbeth.*)

21 Sir James Frazer (tr.), *Ovid: the Fasti* (Cambridge: Harvard University Press, 1959).

22 Text and lineation from W.W. Greg (ed.), *Richard the Third: Shakespeare Quarto Facsimiles no. 12* (Oxford: Clarendon Press, 1959), fol. A2.

23 Holinshed, 3.663.

FOUR

Shakespeare's time-riddles in *Romeo and Juliet* solved

In *Romeo and Juliet* William Shakespeare marks the passage of time 'with great precision'; why, then, can't commentators 'agree such a seemingly elementary chronological point as the number of days the plot covers'?[1] P.A. Daniel reckoned the action concluded on the sixth day;[2] John Munro argued for fewer than six;[3] Caroline Spurgeon[4] and G.B. Harrison[5] counted five; Harley Granville-Barker reckoned four[6] as did Raymond Chapman, who indicted Shakespeare for mixing short- and long-time references to endue his play with 'double-time' *à la Othello*.[7] Even contemporary editors don't agree; Arden and Cambridge content themselves with five days[8] while Jill L. Levenson ponders a sixth in her new Oxford.[9] And the numbering of days isn't the sum of discord. Scholars have yet to agree the date of Nurse's earthquake (1.3.22)[10] or explain why the Capulets were then away in Mantua. No one has identified the occasion for Capulet's 'old accustomd feast' (1.2.20) or why Romeo and Juliet speak as pilgrims when they encounter at his gaudy (1.5.96–114). If Old Capulet is so precise about One being *not* a number in Act One (1.2.32–3) why can't he remember what day it is in Act Three (3.4.18)? Nurse is just as dizzy; sent to meet Romeo at nine (2.5.1), she turns up at Noon (2.4.97–99) – what kept her? Which 'holy day' shutters the Mantuan apothecary shop in Act Five (5.1.58)? What was Friar Lawrence thinking when he promised Juliet 'two and fortie houres' sleep (4.1.106)? Why did Shakespeare birth his Juliet on 'Lammas Eve at night' (1.3.21) when all the sources set her birthday in September? And, finally, why does Chorus promise his auditors 'two houres trafficque of our Stage' (Prologue 12) when they are sure to discover the play runs almost three hours?[11]

By relating Shakespeare's texts, the Renaissance calendars and the liturgy – admittedly an idiosyncratic confluence of interests – I will produce a lexicon uniquely apt for parsing the time-riddles in *Romeo and Juliet* – because *all* this play's time-cruces – even its hugger-mugger pace of meet-love-marry-die – are artifacts of the playwright's previously unrecognized *mise-en-scène*. Shakespeare set his story in 1582, the shortest year in Europe in 2000 years, and calendrically the most confused since 46 BC. For confirmation, the wiser sort had to seek no further than Nurse's 'infancy narrative' of Juliet.

Modern scholars have roundly (and ill-advisedly) declared Nurse an unreliable chronographer.[12] Even the great E.K. Chambers cautioned us against using Nurse's reminiscence of Juliet's traumatic weaning to establish a coherent time-scheme for the play (1.3.18–38); that, he smiled, would be 'pressing Nurse's interest in chronology – and Shakespeare's – rather hard.'[13] But hard pressing is precisely what I intend. First, I'll suggest Nurse's chronicle is true and correct (and offer a pair of neglected sources as part-proof). Then I'll demonstrate that Shakespeare crafted Nurse's monologue – including her elusive earthquake and missing teeth – as a passkey to all his time-riddles in *Romeo and Juliet* for the wiser sort among his auditors.[14] Finally, I'll show that solving the time-cruces in this play provides a fresh insight into Shakespeare's mind, his interest in chronometry, and his remarkable knowledge of the rival calendars of the Renaissance.

My argument and Wife Capulet's conversation with Nurse begins,

Wife Thou knowest my daughters of a prettie age.

Nurse Faith I can tell her age vnto an houre.

Wife Shee's not fourteene.

Nurse Ile lay fourteene of my teeth, and yet to my teene be it spoken, I haue but foure, shees not fourteene. How long is it now to Lammas *tide*?

Wife A fortnight and odde dayes.

Nurse Euen or odde, of all daies in the yeare come Lammas *Eue* at night shal she be fourteene. Susan *and she, God rest all Christian soules, were of an age. Well* Susan *is with God, she was too good for me: But as I said, on* Lammas *Eue at night shall she be fourteene, that shall shee, marrie, I remember it well. Tis since the Earth-quake now eleuen yeares, and she was weand I neuer shall forget it, of all the daies of the yeare vpon that day: for I had then laide worme-wood to my dug, sitting in the sun vnder the Doue-house wall. My Lord and you were then at* Mantua *– nay I doo beare a braine. But as I said, when it did taste the worme-wood on the nipple of my dug, and felt it bitter, pretie foole, to see it teachie and fall out with the Dugge. Shake quoth the Dove-house, twas no need I trow to bid me trudge: and since that time it is a leven yeares, for then she could stand hylone, nay byth roode, she could have run and wadled all about: for even the day before she broke her brow, and then my husband, God be with his soule, a was a merrie man, tooke up the child, yea quoth he, doest thou fall upon they face? thou wilt fall backward when thou hast more wit, wilt thou not* Iule? *And by my holydam, the pretie wretch left crying, and said I: to see now how a ieast shall come about: I warrant, and I should live a thousand yeares, I never should forget it: wilt thou not* Iule *quoth he? and pretie foole it stinted, and said I.*

(Q2 1.3.10–38, italic in original)

Scholars have long wondered why Shakespeare introduced an earthquake into Nurse's chronicle. In his *Observations and Conjectures upon some Passages of Shakespeare* (1766), Thomas Tyrwhitt mused, 'How comes the Nurse to talk of an earthquake? There is no such circumstance mentioned in any of the novels from which Sh. drew his story ...' Nor have commentators agreed the date of Nurse's earthquake. Here is Levenson's useful *summa* of received opinion:

> In the eighteenth century Thomas Tyrwhitt first proposed ... a specific earthquake in England, on 6 April 1580, and [relying on Nurse's eleven-year interval] calculated the play's date as 1591[15] ... As recently as 1982 [E.A.J.] Honigmann discounted arguments against that calculation. Earlier, Sidney Thomas had cited a reference in William Covell's *Polimanteia* (1595) to a terrible earthquake on the Continent, on 1 March 1584, which makes it possible to date the play to 1595; Sarah Dodson added two references to landslips in Dorsetshire cited by chroniclers – Blackmoor, Dorsetshire, 13 January 1583 and Motingham, Kent, 4 August 1585 – that would allow other dates ... John W. Draper, who fixes the plot by year and day according to astrological references to days of the week and month and phases of the moon – thinks it [the play] was written or extensively revised in 1596.[16]

A general problem with all these calculations is that they seek to establish from an earthquake (or astrology) the play's *year of composition* rather than the *year of the action*. Certainly, there are Shakespeare plays in which the year of composition and the *annus praesens* of the action are one, *Merchant of Venice* (1596) and *The Moor of Venice* (1603) being two.[17] But this is not the case with *Romeo and Juliet*.[18]

In fact, the seismic event to which Nurse refers was not a single earthquake but a barrage of earthquakes and echo-tremors we call 'aftershocks' – more than 100 of them – which occurred in and around Ferrara, Italy, during the interval 11–21 November 1570. Inexplicably, scholars have given short shrift to Joseph Hunter, who in 1845 identified this cataclysm with Nurse's narrative. Hunter wrote, 'It will not be denied that Shakespeare might make an Italian character in an Italian story allude to [an earthquake] which occurred at London; but it is obvious that whole argument is of the most shadowy kind, and it seems to be entirely destroyed when the fact is introduced that in 1570 there did occur a most remarkable earthquake in the neighbourhood of Verona [*sic*], so severe that it destroyed Ferrara, etc.'[19]

This catastrophic event is vividly described in an anonymous letter published at London by Thomas Purfoote *ca* 1571; Howard Staunton (1857) quotes from the unique copy preserved in the British Library.[20] In a gripping description of upheavals which decimated Ferrara, the letter-writer plays insistently on 'the ruine and overthrow of an infinite number of ... howses' and of aftershocks 'wherewith many howses were overthrowen' including 'the Bishops howse' which suffered 'ruinous overthrowes' (fol. A.ii^v–A.iii^v). The palace of the Secretary to the Duke 'was also overthrowen' (A.iii^v). The disaster culminated in a final shock which felled 'many houses that had stoode not overthrowne' (A.iii^v).[21]

Now, we have been schooled to read *Romeo and Juliet* as a tragedy of two young lovers, but that is *not* how Shakespeare put his story to us. His Chorus focuses our attention on two *houses* – 'Two households both alike in dignitie' (Prologue 1). His tragedy turns on Mercutio's repeated cries – 'a plague a both your *houses* … a plague a both your *houses* … a plague a both your *houses* … [and as he swoons] your *houses*' (3.1.87–104, [my emphasis]). And the play climaxes with the heirs of Capulet and Montague (and Lady Montague) dead – entailing the extinction of both their houses – and County Paris dead without issue.[22] Shakespeare's Chorus promised the lovers 'pitteous overthrowes' (Prologue 7). And the playwright underscores the seismic aspect of his Veronese tragedy when Paris declares Juliet 'quite overthrown' by death (4.5.60). There is further evidence Shakespeare knew the letter Purfoote published. No one has explained why Shakespeare located Old Capulet and his wife in Mantua during the earthquake. But our letter-writer recorded that – as the 1570 earthquakes shook Ferrara – the Duke and Duchess slipped away … to Mantua (A.iii^v–iv^r).

I believe this letter and its earthquakes are a once-recognized but long-neglected source of Shakespeare's Nurse's reminiscence. For Elizabethans familiar with the letter and/or the catastrophe it describes, Nurse's reference to an earthquake would pin the date of Juliet's weaning to November 1570. If the action of *Romeo and Juliet* is taking place '*since the Earth-quake now eleuen yeares*' the wiser sort could instantly calculate that Nurse's conversation with Wife Capulet must be taking place between November 1581 and November 1582. Since we are told the scene transpires 'a fort'night and odde dayes' before Lammastide – the harvest festival which began with Vespers on 31 July – their conversation must take place in mid-July 1582. Shakespeare and Nurse are at pains to tell us twice that Juliet's fourteenth birthday will fall not on the *evening* but on the *night* of 31 July 1582 (1.3.18–19 and 21); therefore, Juliet must have been born after Compline – that is, between 9 p.m. and Midnight – on 31 July 1568. Recovering the date of Juliet's birth untangles one of the much-debated cruces of the play: Juliet's supposed late weaning. There has been considerable comment on Juliet weaning and waddling at age three.[23] But once we recognize that Juliet, born 31 July 1568, was weaned in mid-November 1570 – that is, at the age of two years and three months – we can accept Nurse's boast that her charge '*could stand hylone, nay byth roode she could haue run and wadled all about.*' We would expect this of a two year-old.[24]

So Shakespeare's Juliet was two years old – not three – when she was weaned, and she will marry at thirteen. These ages are important; they fix the holy day (and eve) on which the Nurse–Wife conversation transpires.[25]

Here I wish to introduce a second unrecognized source of Nurse's chronicle of Juliet's weaning: Jacopo de Voragine's best-seller, *The Golden Legend*, which ran through scores of English editions after Caxton first translated and printed it *ca* 1483.[26] Shakespeare borrowed Juliet's ages at weaning and at marriage, and her waddling and the sexual connotation of her fall, from de Voragine's fabulous life of Saint Anne. The hagiographer reports that Joachim and Anne brought their daughter, Blessed Virgin Mary, to live in the temple at Jerusalem on or about her third birthday. Naturally enough, the child had already been weaned: 'And when she had accomplished the time of three years, and had left sucking, they brought her to the temple with offerings.'[27] A decade later, Mary was ordered to marry: 'And in the fourteenth year of her age [i.e. at the age of thirteen], the bishop commanded in common that the virgins ... [who] had accomplished the time of age, should return to their houses and should after the law be married.'[28] But Mary refused, protesting that her father and mother had committed her to the service of the Lord. She accepted Joseph only after a miraculous episode in which *a dove* finds a curious perch: Joseph 'brought forth his rod, and anon it flowered, and a dove descended from heaven thereupon.'[29] Like Mary, Juliet was weaned before the age of three and marries before fourteen. Not incidentally, the *Legend* also describes three-year-old Mary adroitly climbing the temple's imposing steps:

> And there was about the temple ... fifteen steps or grees to ascend up to the temple, because the temple was high set ... And then our Lady was set on the lowest step and mounted up without any help as she had been of perfect age ...[30]

Of course, the agile Mary was blessèd; Shakespeare's Juliet is an ordinary mortal toddler. Though weaned in the shadow of a talking dove-perch and destined to marry at the same age as Mary, Juliet falls and earns a Cockerel's testicle instead of a halo (1.3.32, 42) – signifying that she will enjoy a normal sex life or, as Nurse's husband prophetically puts it, 'fall backward when [she] commest to age' (1.3.43–4).[31]

Though their destinies differ, Juliet shares Mary's chronology because Shakespeare infused Nurse's infancy narrative with clues to the holy day that began at Vespers on the evening when Nurse and Wife converse: the Feast of Saint Anne. Shakespeare drops another hint to this connection in Nurses' oath, '*by my holydam.*' The archaic word 'halidom' means 'holiness' or 'sanctity' (*OED*) of which Nurse has laughably little.[32] But its homonym, 'by my Holy Dame,' solicits a saint, and the patron saint of mothers is Anne.[33] Saint Anne's day is 26 July; it began with Vespers on 25 July.[34] We know the Nurse–Wife conversation is taking place during the evening by the abrupt entrance of the Servant to report a hubbub in the house: 'the guests are come, supper seru'd vp, you cald, my young Lady askt for, the Nurse curst in the Pantrie, and everie thing in extremitie ...' (1.3.87–9).

But how can Nurse's conversation with Wife Capulet be taking place on the evening of 25 July when Wife tells us they are conversing 'a fort'night and odde dayes' before Lammas Eve – that is, in mid-July? Dr Philippa Berry has inferred this could be a glance at Saint Swithun's day, 15 July, the popular English feast regarded by the superstitious as predictive of weather for the ensuing forty days.[35] I believe Berry infers correctly that some of Shakespeare's auditors might have detected this connection. But if her inference is correct and the date is 15 July, how can I support my suggestion that Old Capulet is about to feast Saint James and the date is 25 July?

The resolution of this ten-day discrepancy – and the key to Shakespeare's unrecognized time-play in *Romeo and Juliet* – lies in the ten-day discrepancy between the English Julian and Catholic Gregorian calendars. When it was the 15 July in Protestant London (Saint Swithun's Day) it was 25 July in Catholic Verona, the Feast of Saint James and the eve of Saint Anne.

Commentators have long found the breathless pace of Shakespeare's *Romeo and Juliet* remarkable – particularly given the sources' leisurely versions of the lovers' tale. The recognition that Shakespeare compressed the action cannot be a modern insight only; there were numerous editions of the lovers' story in circulation in Elizabethan England.[36] In each version the tragedy transpires over a period of months. A reader of any of these books could have recognized that Shakespeare had collapsed the prolonged action into a mere handful of days. The wiser sort who identified Nurse's earthquake with the disaster that shook northern Italy in 1570 and recognized 1582 as the *annus praesens* of the play, could have perceived Shakespeare's tactic as an expression of the unique compression of time in that singular and remarkable year. Thanks to the ubiquitous English almanacs, Shakespeare and lettered Elizabethans knew that 1582 had been the shortest year in European history since Numa Pompilius corrected the Etruscan calendar in 666 BC.[37] The defunct pre-Roman lunar calendar had been 355 days long; so was 1582 after Pope Gregory extracted the ten days between 4 and 15 October. Lettered Englishpersons knew that, beginning in 1582, every day had two dates – one Julian, one Gregorian – and that those dates were ten days apart. Though bizarre to us, Elizabethans who routinely dated their correspondence from 1 January to 24 March with a stroke between two years – as, for example, 1583/4 – could adapt to the fact that a single day had two alternative dates. Elizabethans (particularly the recusants) knew that while they were dodging raindrops on Swithun's Day 15 July, Catholic Europe was busily laying the feast of Saint James on 25 July.

This raises a second question: if Old Capulet is laying the Feast of Saint James, why does he refer to it as 'an old accustomd'? To parse Shakespeare's phrase one must briefly recall how this important Catholic feast day disappeared from the English calendar. On 18 March 1532 Henry VIII's 'Reformation Parliament' presented the king with a Petition of the Commons enumerating several clerical abuses including this one: 'The number of holy days is excessive, *especially in harvest,* and are the occasion of idle and wanton sports' [my emphasis]. The resulting 'Act made for the abrogation of certain holy days' (1536–7) banned 'all those feasts or holy days which shall happen to occur ... in the harvest time, which is to be counted from the first day of July unto the xxix day of September ...' Thus was the Feast of Saint James suppressed. Its Catholic identity is remembered in Old Capulet's word 'accustomd,' which meant not only 'habitually practiced' but also 'by or according to custom'; the English reformers had divided religious practices into those necessary for salvation and those which were indifferent. The latter – a vast array of Catholic 'abuses' including pilgrimages – were characterized as 'customs' of the Church which lacked a legitimate basis in Scripture and were, therefore, neither rituals nor rites but mere customs. They were banned. From Shakespeare's reference to the coming on of Lammas any lettered (or recusant) Elizabethan auditor could recognize that Capulet's 'old accustomd feast' was the suppressed Feast of Saint James.

But the fact that Swithun's Day in London was James' Day in Verona does not entirely explain why Old Capulet is celebrating a feast of 25 July while Wife Capulet believes the date is 15 July. Gregory condensed 1582 by extracting ten days from the month of *October.* Wife and Nurse are nattering on in *mid-July,* two-and-one-half months' earlier. If Old Capulet has already begun reckoning by the Gregorian calendar, he must be jumping the gun.

Indeed, anticipating the Gregorian reform was one aspect of the confusion which accompanied the imposition of the new calendar; landlords and businessmen had no choice but to pre-order their affairs to anticipate Gregory's alteration. A Vatican study published in 1982 suggests that all Catholic Europe meekly adopted Gregory's reform.[38] This is not correct. Medieval and early modern astronomers, scholars, and clergymen had long recognized the necessity of extracting not ten days but *thirteen* days from the Julian calendar in order to return the equinoxes, solstices, *and Christmas* to their proper dates at the time of the birth of Jesus Christ.[39] As a consequence, rival plans for calendar reform had been intensely debated in Catholic universities for a decade before Gregory's bull appeared. As I've noted elsewhere, the pope's bull threw Europeans and their calendars into pandemonium.[40] In France, the day after Sunday 9 December 1582 was declared Monday 20 December. In the Catholic areas of Switzerland, Germany, and the Netherlands the day after Friday 21 December was Saturday 1 January 1583 (they did without Christmas). The Protestant Netherlands thought they could turn 15 December into Christmas by fiat; then cooler heads prevailed and 1 January was chosen as the day of transition. Depending on which country one were in, 12 December could have been New Year's Day or the first day of Winter or the Feast of Saint Thomas. There were countries where the 12

December didn't exist. And countries where 12 December was Christmas – among them, Shakespeare's England. According to no lesser authority than the Sun, the English 12 December was Christmas – which is what *Twelfth Night* is about and why Sir Toby parodies the carol, *The Twelve Days of Christmas*, when he sings, 'O, the twelfth day of December' (2.3.79). Here is the commonsense (though simplistic) math:

Years between 1 BC and AD 1601 (inclusive) = 1602
Years for the Julian calendar to slip one day = 128
Therefore: $1602 \div 128 = 12.52$ days

Adding 12.52 days to 12 of December brings us to Christmas, 25 December.

When Gregory's reform was announced in February 1582, men of affairs like Old Capulet – to whom time was money – had no choice but to begin anticipating the coming loss of ten days for the excellent reason that a loan, contract, or lease for a term of one year signed on, say, 15 July 1582 would not mature on 15 July 1583, but on 25 July 1583. The Old Capulet who hustles his mourning daughter to marry on three days' notice – and then trumps himself by advancing her nuptial from Thursday to Wednesday – is a Gregorian anticipator. According to Wife Capulet's old-fashioned Julian reckoning the date is 15 July. But to Gregorian-minded Old Capulet it is already 25 July. That is why Shakespeare devised his young lovers' 'pilgrim dialogue':

Romeo   My lips two blushing Pylgrims did readie stand, To smoothe that rough
        touch with a tender kis.
Juliet Good Pilgrim you do wrong your hand too much ... For saints have hands,
        that Pilgrims hands do tuch, And palme to palme is holy Palmers kis.
                                                                    (1.5.98–103)

This I take to be proof positive that Shakespeare's young lovers are meeting on the Feast of Saint James, whose relics at Santiago de Campostela, Spain, were the principal destination of all European pilgrims.

Shakespeare provides another clue to his Gregorian mischief when Nurse offers to wager fourteen of her teeth that Juliet will turn fourteen years old on Lammas Eve. Then, abruptly, Nurse remembers: she has but four teeth. By this tactic Shakespeare calls our attention to ten missing teeth and, by inference, ten missing days. Wasn't it 'Devouring time' that extracted 'keen teeth from the fierce tiger's jaws' in Sonnet 19?

Below, I'll demonstrate that recognizing 1582 as the *annus praesens* of *Romeo and Juliet* allows us to recover a number of Shakespeare's other clues to his sixteenth-century time-warp – such as the significance of the play's first word, 'Gregorie.'[41] The servant Sampson swears, 'Gregorie, on my word weele not carrie Coles' (1.1.1).[42] The name is Shakespeare's wink at the pope who decreed the calendar reform, the root of all confusion. But first, I wish to offer two more proofs that Shakespeare meticulously searched the calendars and ephemeredes when he prepared the time scheme of *Romeo and Juliet*.

Moments after dancing with Juliet, Romeo realizes to his horror she's a Capulet (1.5.123–4). At that instant Benvolio counsels Romeo to depart, 'Away begon, the sport is at the best' (125). Overhearing them, Old Capulet interjects, 'Nay gentlemen prepare not to be gone, / We have a trifling foolish banquet towards' (127–8).[43] Then, abruptly, the old man continues

> Is it ene so? why then I thanke you all.
> I thanke you honest gentlemen, good night:
> More torches here, come on, then lets to bed.
> As sirrah, by my saie it waxes late,
> I'll to my rest.
>
> (1.5.129–33)

Capulet's startled 'Is it ene so?' suggests one of the young men has spoken something to him which was inaudible to the audience. Helpfully, Q1 interpolates a stage direction, '*They whisper in his eare*.' No commentator has attempted to supply the unheard line but, on hearing it, Old Capulet abruptly forsakes his 'foolish banquet' and calls for light to show his way to bed. I suggest the unheard whisper refers to the arrival of the hour of Midnight. Minutes later Romeo identifies Juliet with the Sun – famously (and prophetically) –

> But soft, what light through yonder window breaks?
> It is the East, and *Iuliet* is the Sun.
> Arise faire Sun and kill the envious Moone,
> Who is alreadie sicke and pale with greefe …
>
> (2.2.2–5).

It must be after Midnight when Romeo speaks; at Verona on the night of 15 July 1582 the Moon did not rise until shortly after Midnight (12:15 a.m.). And the Moon was in its last quarter – which accounts for Romeo's 'sicke and pale' – and low to the horizon, which may account for how it 'tips with silver all these frute tree tops' (2.2.109). Having pointedly identified Juliet with the Sun, Shakespeare now causes the changeable Romeo to swear by (and identify himself with) the changeable Moon, 'Lady, by yonder blessed Moone I vow, etc.' (2.2.109).[44] In the catastrophe of the play the consequence of the lovers' union is mutual extinction; a liaison in which the Moon covers the Sun (which extinguishes both) is a solar eclipse. Indeed, an annular eclipse of the Sun was visible at Verona (and London) on the morning of 31 July 1590 Gregorian. The eclipse began shortly after sunrise *ca* 6:40 a.m. local time, achieved its maximum magnitude (0.76) at 7:53 a.m., and ended *ca* 9:15 a.m.[45] Whether Shakespeare was aware of the eclipse of 1590 is a nice question; I believe he was. According Old Capulet's Gregorian reckoning Romeo and Juliet are found dead in the tomb on the night of 30 July – and it is the morning of 31 July when Escalus provides an apt description of an early morning eclipse: 'A glooming peace this morning with it brings: / The sun for sorrow will not show his head' (5.3.313–14).

What's been lurking in the cellarage of *Romeo and Juliet* for the past four hundred years is AD 1582. Shakespeare is writing of times that are *literally* changing. And while some of Shakespeare's characters have accepted (and even anticipated) the Gregorian reform, others including Wife and Nurse still reckon the old-fashioned Roman way. This explains why Nurse, whom Juliet dispatches to meet Romeo at 9 a.m., arrives when the 'the bawdie hand of the dyal … is upon the prick of noone' (2.4.98–9). Like Friar Lawrence, Nurse reckons in old Roman hours – and 'Noon' derives from 'None,' the ninth hour.[46] We know Noon is the ninth hour of the day on which Nurse meets Romeo from Capulet's cry, 'Come, stir, stir, stir, the second cock hath crowed. / The Curphew bell hath roong, tis three a clock' (4.4.3–4). Sunrise in mid-July in Verona was *ca* 5 a.m..[47] But the curfew bell, the second cock, *and* the Angelus sounded at first light – daybreak – *ca* 3 a.m. in Verona in mid-July, making the ninth hour of this day Noon. In case we missed the Angelus connection, Shakespeare underscores it in Capulet's next line: 'Looke to the bakte meates, good *Angelica*' (4.4.5).[48] Moments earlier, Shakespeare's Juliet drinks the sleeping potion – *ca* 3 a.m. – as she does in the source plays. In Act Five, the Watchman – like Hamlet's Gravedigger-Clown typical of Shakespeare's precise minor-character reporters – remembers Juliet 'heere hath laine this two daies buried' (5.3.184), meaning she was interred on Wednesday and the present hour is prior to Midnight Thursday. Friar Lawrence promised Juliet she would sleep 'two and fortie houres' (4.1.106); forty-two hours after 3 a.m. Wednesday is 9 p.m. Thursday. This is the hour when Juliet awakens. Lawrence hurries to the tomb, saying, 'Within this three houres will faire *Iuliet* wake' (that is, prior to Midnight; 5.2.25). Later, Lawrence confesses to his Prince that he arrived precisely on time, only 'some minute ere the time / Of her awakening' (5.3.265–6). Since Romeo has been in the tomb 'Full halfe an houre' (5.3.136) when Lawrence arrives, this fixes Romeo's arrival *ca* 8:30 p.m.

We could readily accept Lawrence's chronology were it not equally apparent that it is after Midnight when Duke Escalus arrives. Although the stage direction '*Enter the Prince*' immediately follows the Chief of the Watch's order 'stay the Frier too' (5.3.195), we know it is no longer late at night but early morning by the Duke's first words, 'What misadventure is so early up / That calls our person from our morning rest?' (5.3.196–7), and from his biting irony, 'Come *Montague*, for thou art early up / To see thy sonne and heire, now earling downe' (5.3.216–7).

Scholars have struggled mightily to reconcile Lawrence's 'two and fortie houres' with the Duke's apparent reference to an abortive sunrise. Evans summarized the commentators' frustration,

Although Shakespeare carefully reinforces (with frequent temporal signposts) the time-scheme … he appears to trip himself when the Friar tells Juliet that the potion will take forty-two hours (4.1.105) to run its course. Since she drinks the potion shortly before 3 o'clock on Wednesday morning [*sic*] (4.4.4) and awakens shortly before dawn on Thursday (5.3), the time elapsed is around twenty-seven hours, not forty-two. If, on the other hand, Shakespeare inadvertently thought of the play as ending on the early morning of the sixth day (Friday), the forty-two hours period is not long enough.[49]

From Escalus' comments we know the play ends on Friday morning. But Shakespeare hasn't tripped himself. Under dark of night in the graveyard of Verona time has collapsed – exactly as Pope Gregory condensed time at the stroke of Midnight on 4/5 October 1582 when he extracted ten days – not two-and-forty hours, but two-hundred-forty hours – from the calendar.

In Act Five of *Romeo and Juliet* Shakespeare is exhibiting in miniature the master-tactic which informs his rewrite of the sources' leisurely story: the compression of time. Romeo enters the tomb *ca* 8:30 p.m.. Forty lines later, half an hour has elapsed and Romeo is dead. Juliet wakes at 9 p.m. (5.3.156). Forty lines later it is after Midnight when Escalus arrives. One hundred-twenty lines later it is early morning Friday as the play concludes – on the sixth day of action which began on Sunday – confirming Levenson's numbering of days. Unraveling the collapse of time in the graveyard finally explains Corus' erroneous promise to the auditors of 'two hours traffic of our stage.' Shakespeare will compress time in his Verona – and drive his impetuous lovers at a hypersonic pace to meet, love, marry and die.

Readers may feel I have dismissed too lightly the 'two and fortie houres' crux. Saying merely that we must accept a Juliet who awakens forty-two hours after 3 a.m. Wednesday (that is, at 9 p.m. Thursday) – and that Escalus's striking references to morning are an artifact of Shakespeare's compression of time – may seem an oversimplification. But the real riddle here is *not* the hour at which Juliet awakens. It's why Shakespeare settled on 'two and fortie houres.' He didn't find that number in his immediate source, Arthur Brooke's *Romeus and Juliet*; Brooke's Lawrence doesn't specify the duration of the potion's effect. The other possible sources give either forty-eight hours or forty hours more or less.[50] Then again, if Shakespeare merely intended Juliet to awaken and die before Thursday Midnight he could have specified three-and-forty hours, or even four-and-forty, to the same effect. So why did he fix his Lawrence upon 'two and fortie houres'?

Here it is important to recall that when Lawrence gave Juliet the potion *they both believed that she would marry on Thursday* (4.1.1, 43). Had Juliet drunk the potion at 3 a.m. on Thursday morning and slept 'two and fortie houres' she would have awakened at the hour of Compline on Friday night – the night of 30 July. Romeo would have spirited her away from Verona as the dawn rose on

31 July – Juliet's fourteenth birthday and the day she reached the age of consent to marriage under prevailing English law.[51]

Above, I suggested that recognizing the interval 25–30 July as the span of the action in *Romeo and Juliet* would allow us to recover other unrecognized instances of Shakespeare's intensive time-play. Elizabethan auditors who knew their martyrology – or remembered their *Cisio Ianus*[52] – would have detected in *Romeo and Juliet* overtones of *every one* of the holy days in the interval 25–30 July:

Sunday 25 July is Saint James' day, the inspiration for Romeo's and Juliet's pilgrim poesy at the feast – and the eve of Saint Anne, whose legend inspired the weaning, toddling Juliet of Nurse's memory.

Monday 26 July, the day upon which Capulet and Paris agree to Juliet's marriage, was the holy day of Saint Anne, another parent who married-off a thirteen-year-old daughter.

Tuesday 27 July. Friar Lawrence gives the sleeping potion to Juliet on the Feast of the Seven Sleepers of Ephesus.[53] These martyrs immured themselves in a cave to escape persecution. God put them to sleep. Eventually, they awoke – and immediately died (as does Juliet).

Wednesday 28 July is the feast of Saint Sampson, whose name Shakespeare settled on the servant who refuses to carry coals (1.1.SD). Saintly Sampson was a Welshman.[54] Aren't the Welsh renowned for carrying coal? This is Shakespeare at his deftest, slyest, wiser-sort-teasing best.

Thursday 29 July. On this night, Romeo discovers Juliet apparently dead in the tomb. But it's the feast of Saint Martha to whom Jesus said, 'I am the resurrection and the life: he that believeth in me though dead yet shall he live: And whosoever lives and believes in me shall never die. Believest thou this?' Martha answered, 'Yes, Lord' (Jn. 11:25–7).[55] And because of her faith, Jesus called to her brother Lazarus in the tomb and raised him from the dead. Isn't this Shakespeare's inspiration for Romeo's dream – 'I dreamt my Lady came and found me dead … / And Breathd such life with kisses in my lips, / That I revivde' (5.1.6–9)?

Recovering Shakespeare's exploitation of these holy days explains why the playwright relocated Juliet's birthday from 10 (or 16) September as the sources have it. It also allows us to resolve a minor but much-debated crux in the text. When Lady Capulet asks her daughter 'How stands your dispositions to be married?' in both Q2 and F Juliet replies 'It is an houre that I dreame not of' and Nurse echoes, 'An houre, were not I thine onely Nurse, I would say thou / hadst suckt wisedome from thy teate' (1.3.53–5). Some scholars would substitute Q1's 'honour' for 'houre.'[56] Given Shakespeare's intensive time-play in *Romeo and Juliet*, surely we should follow Dr Johnson and accept 'houre.'

I promised to conclude with evidence that William Shakespeare had expert knowledge of chronometry and the rival calendars of the Renaissance. This requires a close encounter with Old Capulet, a role the playwright perhaps played. Paris tells us Capulet is of 'honourable reckoning' (1.2.4) – which commentators have taken to mean 'esteem, estimation, reputation.'[57] But 'reckoning' could also mean 'counting, computing, calculating.'[58] On Paris' cue Capulet promptly flaunts his precision with numbers;[59] inviting the County to his feast Capulet reckons 'One more, most welcome, makes my number more' (1.2.23). Then, a few lines later, Capulet says that Juliet 'being one, / May stand in number, though in reckning none' (1.2.32–3). This sounds arcane or pointless. But Shakespeare's auditors who had learned their numbers in an Elizabethan schoolroom knew Pythagoras held that One was not a number and that Aristotle agreed: 'One is regarded as not being itself a number because a measure is not those things measured, but the measure of the One is the beginning (or Principle) of number.'[60]

But if Capulet is punctiliously precise about numbers in Act One, why can't he remember the day of the week in Act Three? At 3.4.18 he asks Paris, 'But soft, what day is this?' Paris replies, 'Monday my Lord,' and Capulet laughs 'Monday, ha ha …' What strikes Capulet as funny is that his feast honoring Saint James on 25 July was yesternight; consequently, today's date must be 26 July – which was a Thursday to a Gregorian anticipator in 1582. But Paris, who reckons the old-fashioned Julian way is ten days behind; he believes the date is 16 July, which was Monday in 1582. This day-of-the-week confusion was common under the rival calendars; Shakespeare plays the same joke on Lancelot Gobbo and Desdemona.[61] In *Romeo and Juliet* Shakespeare caps his joke with Capulet's 'A thursday let it be, a thursday tell her … / what say you to Thursday'? Paris gasps, 'I would that thursday were to morrow' – to which Capulet replies in a dazzling *double-entendre*, 'a Thursday be it then' (3.1.18–31). The letter 'a' could mean 'on' – or it could be the indefinite article.

This day-of-the-week confusion also explains why the Mantuan apothecary shop is closed. Romeo grumbles, 'Being holy day, the beggers shop is shut' (5.1.58). Some editors render this 'Being holiday,'[62] though they can't identify the holiday. But Shakespeare isn't referring to a 'holiday'; his Romeo is telling us the shop is shut because it's the *holy day* of the week – Sunday. Romeo left Verona on Tuesday 17 July Julian. Juliet drank the potion at 3 a.m. Wednesday 18 July. Balthazar arrives with his report of Juliet's death and burial *not* on Wednesday, but on Thursday 19 July. If the Mantuans were anticipating the Gregorian reform, the date in Mantua would be 29 July, a Sunday.

Now for my overdue proof of Capulet's (and Shakespeare's) expert knowledge of the Renaissance calendars. As the masquers dance at his feast, Capulet says to Cousin,

> How long ist now since last your selfe and I
> Were in a maske?

2 Capulet	Berlady thirtie yeares.
1 Capulet	What man tis not so much, tis not so much,
	Tis since the nuptiall of Lucentio:
	Come Pentycost as quickly as it will,
	Some fiue and twentie yeares, and then we maskt.
2 Capulet	Tis more, tis more, his sonne is elder sir:
	His sonne is thirtie.
1 Capulet	Will you tell me that?
	His sonne was but a ward 2. yeares ago.

(1.5.30–40)

No crux in *Romeo and Juliet* has been given a wider berth by commentators; even *The Variorum* is silent. But Shakespeare clearly intends us to perceive Old Capulet is right. Because if Lucentio married thirty years ago *and* his son is thirty, that would have the double-effect of dating his son's conception *prior* to his parents' marriage, which would render the boy illegitimate and an unattractive prospect for wardship; Elizabethan auditors knew illegitimates could not inherit.[63]

To anyone who knew the calendar, Capulet's assertion that next year's Pentecost will fall on the same date as Pentecost twenty-five years ago would sound completely preposterous. Pentecost is a moveable feast, the fiftieth day after Easter, and everyone who has studied the calendar knows the repeat cycle of Easter (and, by entailment, Pentecost) *isn't* 25 years. To cite one example: in 1582 Easter fell on 15 April. Beginning with the year AD 507, the repeat cycle of Easters falling on 15 April was 11 years, 11 years, 62 years, 11 years, 11 years, 11 years, 62 years, 11 years, 11 years, 73 years … and so on.

In fact, since the birth of Christ the repeat cycle of Easter has been twenty-five years only during one anomalous period. This was the unique tranche of time that began with the Gregorian reform of 1582 and ended in 1699. During this interval only, the *Julian* date of Pentecost in Year X was identical with the *Gregorian* date of Pentecost in Year X-plus-25.[64] Punctilious Capulet, speaking in July 1582 and referring to the date of Pentecost 1583, is absolutely correct. And he *must* be referencing the dual calendars. Because only during the era of dual calendars did the date of Pentecost repeat every twenty-five years – and 1583 was the first year in which this unprecedented phenomenon occurred. Pentecost in Gregorian 1583 was Sunday 29 May – the same date on which Pentecost fell when Lucentio married in Julian 1558. Old Capulet is right. Shakespeare knew it. Some of the wiser sort in his audience knew it. And now, so do we.[65]

Romeo and Juliet is a play about the overthrow of noble houses. It warns us that humans may advance the calendar – but that won't make them older or riper or wiser. For Shakespeare's first auditors – who knew they were living under a scientifically discredited Julian calendar and ten days out of step with the rest of the world – *Romeo and Juliet* was about people living on the cusp of precariously changing times – people like themselves. But for modern scholars *Romeo and Juliet* now provides an insight into William Shakespeare's mind which his editors – even the editors of his Sonnets – have never grasped. Shakespeare was not captivated by time in a poetical way merely; he had a profound interest in chronometry and possessed a most exacting knowledge of the rival calendars of the Renaissance. We know now that Shakespeare stuffed his *Romeo and Juliet* with allusions to disused saints' days and examples of the confusion ensuing in the aftermath of Gregory's calendar reform. And next time we hear Chorus promise to get his play off the stage in two hours, we'll be in on Shakespeare's joke.

Notes

1 G. Thomas Tanselle, 'Time in *Romeo and Juliet*,' *Shakespeare Quarterly* 15 (1964), 349.

2 P.A. Daniel, 'Time Analysis of the Plots of Shakespeare, etc.,' *The New Shakspere Society's Transactions 1877–9* Series 1, Vols. 5–7 (London: 1879), 6.191–4. Delivered *viva voce* at the 47th meeting of the society, 13 December, 1878.

3 John Munro (ed.), *The London Shakespeare* (London: Eyre and Spottiswoode, 1958), 5.120.

4 Caroline Spurgeon, *Shakespeare's Imagery and What it Tells Us* (Cambridge: Cambridge University Press, 1935), p. 312.

5 G.B. Harrison (ed.), *Shakespeare: Works* (New York: 1952), p. 471.

6 Harley Granville-Barker, *Prefaces to Shakespeare* (Princeton: Princeton University Press, 1947), 2.302.

7 Raymond Chapman, 'Double Time in *Romeo and Juliet*,' *MLR* 46 (1949), 372. In fact, Shakespeare employs some short-time, long-time sleight-of-hand when Balthazar claims he 'presently took poste' (5.1.21) to bring the news of Juliet's death to Romeo. The word 'poste' suggests the servant traveled by the fastest means available, perhaps by a relay of post-horses which could be hired at stations placed at intervals of about ten miles on main roads between cities. Editors have assumed that 'presently' entails that Balthazar left Verona 'immediately' after Juliet's funeral, for example Jill L. Levenson (ed.), *Romeo and Juliet*, (Oxford, 2000), p. 331n. But 'immediately' is *not* the only possible interpretation; 'presently' could also mean 'soon,' 'shortly,' or at the earliest possible occasion (*OED*). In the sources Romeo's servant arrives on the day *after* Juliet's burial. Mantua is a mere twenty miles from Verona, but one wonders if Shakespeare knew this. Apparently he believed Mantua far enough from Verona to be a remote place of exile for Romeo – and distant enough for the Capulets to escape the effects of the cataclysmic earthquake, as did the Duke and Duchess of Ferrara.

8 G.B. Evans (Cambridge: Cambridge University Press, 1984), p. 10; Brian Gibbons, *Romeo and Juliet* (London: Routledge, 1980), p. 54.

9 Levenson, p. 307n.105.

10 In this chapter, text and lineation of *Romeo and Juliet* rely on Quarto 2 (1599) in P.A. Daniel (ed.), *Parallel Texts* (London: Trubner, 1874).

11 An earlier version of this chapter appeared in *English Literary Renaissance* (September 2005).

12 To cite just two: E.K. Chambers, *William Shakespeare: a Study of Facts and Problems* (Oxford: Oxford University Press, 1930), 1.345, and Barbara Everett, 'The Nurse's Story,' *Critical Quarterly* 14 (1972), 132–3.

13 Chambers, *Study*, i.345.

14 Which might explain why Nurse's speeches to Lady Capulet in 1.3 of Q1 and Q2 are the only speeches set in italic type (other than four lines by the Clown in Q1 (1.3.100–3). Any inference about this use of italic cannot but be speculative. For example, W.W. Greg, *The Editorial Problem in Shakespeare* (Oxford: Oxford University Press, 1942) p. 62: 'The most obvious evidence of the dependence of Q2 on Q1 is the common use of italic type for the earlier speeches of the Nurse. [But] the reason for it in Q1 is problematical. The most obvious explanation is than an actor's part, written in Italian script, had been cut up and pasted into the copy.' Not conclusive, but good enough for Jay L. Halio: 'The usual explanation for this anomaly is that the alleged reporter somehow obtained the actor's part (or 'side'), which was written in an Italian script rather than English secretary hand like the rest of the play … Possibly a shortage of type in [the printer] Danter's shop was responsible for the peculiarity in Q1, which Q2 follows.' *Shakespeare's Romeo and Juliet: texts, contexts, and interpretation* (London: Associated University Press, 1995), p. 150n.6. A more likely explanation is Evans's (p. 71n), which cites the rare spelling 'aleven' here and in *Saint Thomas More* to suggest this passage may have been set from Shakespeare's autograph copy.

15 Tyrwhitt surmised, 'it therefore seems probably that he had in view the earthquake which had really been felt in many parts of England in his own time, viz., on the 6th of April 1580 … If so, one may be permitted to conjecture that this play, or this part of it, at least, was written in 1591, after the 6th of April, when the *eleven years since the earthquake* were completed, and not later than the middle of July, *a fortnight and odd days* before *Lammas-tide*.' Tyrwhitt's fallacious logic infiltrated the editions of George Steevens (1778), Malone (1780), and Isaac Reed (1785), and has bedeviled editors ever-after.

16 Levenson, 99–100. Cf. Sarah Dodson, 'Notes on the Earthquake,' *Modern Language Notes* (February 1950), 144.

17 Both these plays incorporated the unique Venetian calendar, the *More Veneto (MV)*; Professor Lisa Hopkins has suggested that this may account for their alliterative titles, *Merchant of Venice* and *Moor of Venice*. See S. Sohmer, 'Another Time: The Venetian Calendar in Shakespeare's Plays' in Holger Klein and Michele Marrapodi (eds), *Shakespeare in Italy* (Lewiston NY, 1999), pp. 141–61.

18 Assigned to 1595 by Wells and Taylor, *Textual Companion*, p. 118.

19 Joseph Hunter, *New Illustrations*, (London: 1845), pp. 120–1. Gibbons notices Hunter and suggests 1581 as the date of action (p. 26).

20 Anonymous, *A coppie of the letter sent from Ferrara the xxii of November 1570* (London 1571?, STC 10830). Howard Staunton's précis is cited in Horace Howard Furness, *The Variorum Romeo and Juliet* (Philadelphia: Lippincott) 1874, p. 45.

21 'Any stonye harte,' so writes our correspondent, 'would have been moved to pitie & compassion … [by] the pitifull lamentacion of the noble gentlewomen' (A.iiv).

22 The 'Old' Capulets have buried their children and have passed childbearing age. The Montagues are younger. So Shakespeare abruptly kills off Mrs. Montague – 'Alas my liege, my wife is dead to night' (5.3.218) – to put the period to their line.

23 Evans, p. 199.

24 Levenson cites Maynard Mack, 'Rescuing Shakespeare,' *International Shakespeare Association Occasional Paper* (no. 1, 1979), 10–11. Gail Kern Paster thought it 'particularly significant for Nurse's narrative that Juliet's parents were absent at, also perhaps oblivious to, her weaning – a biological event widely and correctly regarded as physically critical and marked here by its timing on her third birthday [*sic*].' *The Body Embarrassed* (Ithaca: Cornell University Press, 1993), p. 222.

25 Shakespeare's Juliet is three years younger than Brooke's, four years younger than Boiastuau's Julietta, three years younger than Bandello's Guilietta, and four years younger than da Porto's lass.

26 He lived 1230–98 and was sometime Archbishop of Genoa.

27 F.S. Ellis (ed.), *The Golden Legend … as Englished by William Caxton*, (London: 1900, rpt. 1931), 5.101.

28 Ellis, 5.102.

29 Ellis, 5.103.

30 Ellis, 5.101–2.

31 '*Shake quoth the dove-house*' is Nurse's recollection. A dove is also associated with a disembodied voice after the baptism of Jesus in Matt. 3:16, Mark 1:10, and Luke 3:22.

32 But it could also be an oath by the Blessed Virgin Mary. According to *OED*, 'The substitution of -*dam*, -*dame*, in the suffix was apparently due to popular etymology, the word being taken to denote 'Our Lady'.'

33 And if Nurse is the mysterious 'Angelica' to whom Old Capulet refers at 4.4.5, Anne may be Nurse's name-saint. For Nurse's talking Dove-house there is a famous precedent and an intriguing explanation: in three of the Gospels John's baptism of Jesus includes the descent of a dove accompanied by a disembodied voice (Matt. 3:16, Mark 1:10, and Luke 3:22). Shakespeare could have known that the cathedral of Ferrara was dedicated to Saint John Baptist; among the great buildings overthrown, the Purfoote letter-writer noticed 'S. John Baptist the chiefe Churche all fallen' (fol. A.ivr).

34 Saint Anne's feast was assigned to 26 July in 1462.

35 Philippa Berry, 'Double Dying and Other Tragic Inversions' in *Shakespeare's Feminine Endings* (London 1999), pp. 23–43.

36 Among them Luigi da Porto's *Istoria novellamente ritrovata di due Nobili Amanti* (*ca* 1530), Matteo Bandello's *Novelle* (Lucca 1554), the *Histoires Tragiques* of Pierre Boiastuau (Paris 1559), *The Tragicall Historye of Romeus and Juliet* of Arthur Brooke (1562), and William Painter's *Palace of Pleasure* (1567).

37 Another account was readily available in North, pp. 78–9.

38 S.T. Coyne, M.A. Hoskin, and O. Pedersen (eds), *The Gregorian Reform of the Calender, etc.* (Vatican, *Speculo Vaticana*, 1983).

39 That is, to conform to Julius Caesar's original calendar which was imposed on 1 January 45 BC and prevailed at the birth of Christ.

40 Sohmer, *Mystery Play*, pp. 200–1.

41 I'm indebted to Dr Berry for calling this to my attention.

42 My emphasis.

43 Capulet's allusion to his banquet as 'foolish' points to the Gospel for the Feast of Saint James, Paul to the Corinthians 1.4.9–15, which plays on the Apostle's familiar theme, 'We are fools for Christ's sake, etc.'

44 Romeo, desperately in love with the elusive Rosalind as the action begins, falls in love with Juliet at first sight (1.5). Friar Lawrence chides Romeo for his changeable (moonlike) fickleness (2.4.66–81).

45 Prepared by the writer using *Redshift 4.0* software, Maris Multimedia, 2001.

46 There's a vestige of this system which divided the day into eight canonical hours in Lawrence's 'Within this three houres will faire *Iuliet* awake' (5.3.25), three clock hours being the equivalent of one canonical hour.

47 *Redshift 4.0.* Sunrise is the moment when the sun fully clears the horizon.

48 My emphasis. The received idea that the Angelus was said at 6 a.m., Noon and 6 p.m. is not correct. Medieval believers recited the Angelus at Compline, i.e. not at sunset or twilight, but at first dark. It was also said at first light, accompanied by the ringing of the curfew bell and opening of the city's gates. In the eleventh century it was customary to recite three *Ave Marias* during the evening bell. In 1269 St Bonaventure urged the custom of the Franciscans, who recited *Aves* as the evening bell was rung. Reciting the Angelus in the morning grew out of the monastic custom of saying *Aves* while a bell rang at Prime.

49 Evans, 10n.5.

50 The relevant passage in Brooke is lines 2125–65.

51 Sir Thomas Littleton, *Littleton's Tenures in French and English* (London: 1813), p. 23: 'The age of discretion is said the age of xiiii. years.'

52 Nonsense rhymes comprising syllables from the names of saint's days which allowed even illiterates to memorize the martyrology. See C. Wordsworth, *The Ancient Kalendar of the University of Oxford, etc.* (Oxford: Oxford University Press, 1904). The *Cisio Ianus* appears on 166–8.

53 Ellis, 4.120–6

54 David Hugh Farmer (ed.), *The Oxford Dictionary of Saints* (Oxford: Oxford University Press, 1978, rpt. 1992), p. 426.

55 See Ellis, 4.135–40.

56 See for example Evans, 72n and 199: ' … though Q2 'houre' (retained by Johnson, Capell, and Hoppe) makes sense [in Juliet's line], it makes little or none in [Nurse's speech] and the two readings obviously must stand together.' The reversion to 'honour' is Pope's doing (1726). But isn't naïf Juliet referring to the matrimonial service and Nurse to the proverbially quick cooling of ardor after consummation?

57 Among many others, Evans and Gibbons.

58 *OED.*

59 Rather than say that Juliet is thirteen years old, Old Capulet tells Paris 'Shee hath not seene the chaunge of fourteen yeares' (1.2.9). Though his figure of speech may seem less precise, it is more accurate. On a child's first birthday she begins her

second year. Juliet was fully thirteen years old on the day of her thirteenth birthday, i.e. fifty weeks before Old Capulet's conversation with Paris takes place. In a very few days Juliet will reach her fourteenth birthday and begin her fifteenth year. To say Juliet is 'thirteen' would be to misstate her age by almost a full year.

60 In his *Metaphysics* A.986a. See Sir Thomas Heath, *A History of Greek Mathematics* (Oxford: Oxford University Press 1921), 1.69. For a hipper interpretation see Hippocrates G. Apostle [!] (tr.), *Aristotle's Metaphysics* (London: 1966), p. 258n.10. The Pythagoreans seem to have thought One is not a number 'because when added to a number the result is sometimes an odd and sometimes an even number, or because both even and odd numbers are composed of units, or because the *One* is composed of both the *Odd* and the *Even*. Logic among the Pythagoreans, of course, was not strong.'

61 See detailed discussion of the instances in later chapters in this book.

62 Among many others, Evans and Gibbons.

63 Under English common law illegitimates could not inherit. Under Continental civil law, they could – provided there were no ensuing legitimate issue. There's a lively discussion of this topic in John Fortescue's *De Laudibus Legem Angliae* (London: 1599), fols. 90–4, a book which I have cited as an unrecognized source of Hamlet's meditation on his own illegitimacy, i.e. the 'dram of eale' speech which expresses his incompetence to succeed to the Danish crown. See S. Sohmer, 'A note on Hamlet's illegitimacy identifying a source of the "dram of eale" speech' (Q2 1.4.17–38), *Early Modern Literary Studies* 6:3 (January 2001), 13.1–7.

64 Leap years excepted for the obvious reason that the addition of the bissextile day on 24 or 29 February falls prior to Easter and Pentecost.

65 This tactic – conflating two calendars – also accounts for Lancelot Gobbo's nosebleed on 'Black Monday last at six o'clock i' th' morning, falling out that year on Ash Wednesday was four year in th' afternoon' (*MV* 2.5.22–7).

FIVE

'two and fortie houres':
Did Shakespeare know Bandello?

The scholarly consensus holds 'there is no persuasive evidence Shakespeare knew the Italian or French versions [of *Romeo and Juliet*] at first hand.'[1] In this chapter I will disagree. By patient examination of the original Italian text of Matteo Bandello I will offer evidence that Shakespeare had read the story of doomed lovers in the *Novelle* (1554), and perhaps in Luigi da Porto's 1530 version, too. Furthermore, I will show that Shakespeare is *not* the first author to carefully link the events in this fictional story of star-crossed lovers to actual dates, holy days, and lunisolar events in a specific calendar year. I will show that Bandello reworked da Porto's story to conform the action to the solar and liturgical calendars of AD 1302. And I will suggest that Shakespeare's close reading of Bandello not only supplied his mysterious 'two and fortie houres,' but may have inspired Shakespeare to exploit the tale of Romeo and Juliet to interrogate the Gregorian reform of 1582 by linking events in his tragedy to actual dates and holy days in that topsy-turvy year.

Luckily for us, a soldier named Luigi da Porto (1485–1528) received a disabling wound in a skirmish on the river Natisone on 11 June 1511 and spent the next seventeen years in retirement. To beguile the hours at his villa in Montorso, da Porto penned several romances, among them *Giulietta e Romeo*. A generation after the story's posthumous publication, da Porto's tale was taken up as the principal source for a *novella* by Fr. Matteo Bandello, subsequently translated into French by Pierre Boaistuau and thence into English by Arthur Brooke, whose endless doggerel in poulters' measure is the universally acknowledged proximate source of Shakespeare's play.

In contrast to secular solider da Porto, Matteo Bandello (1485–1561 or 1565) was a cleric who rose from friardom to the bishopric of Agen, France. One would expect a man with his nose perpetually in a breviary to care deeply about time and the calendar. And, indeed, Bandello revised da Porto's tale to fit precisely the calendar of the year 1302, a fact never recognized by scholars. Bandello's time-scheme – which diverges radically from da Porto's – influenced each successive version of the story, including Shakespeare's. As da Porto did before him, Bandello reckons hours by the antique Roman method of counting twelve from sunrise and sunset, and twelve from sunset to sunrise.[2] In the preceding chapter I have shown that his device – which has tripped-up even knowledgeable modern scholars – found echoes in Shakespeare's text, though one can hardly infer that Bandello's use of Roman hours was Shakespeare's cue.

In the minds of clerics of the fifteenth century (and most laymen), the calendar of record was not the secular solar calendar but the Church calendar. Bandello revised the time-line of da Porto's tale to link its principal events to specific holy days. Pierre Boaistuau secularized and sentimentalized Bandello's text and, in large part, dismantled his predecessor's ecclesiastical time-scheme. So did English Protestant Arthur Brooke, about whom little is known other than he authored a source of Shakespeare's *Romeo and Juliet* and died young (some would reckon this an enviable biography).

Why did Bandello settle on the year 1302 as the setting for his story? In a certain sense, his literal mind had no choice. Like da Porto, Bandello set his tale '*Era alora signor di Verona Bartolomeo Scala*' (371) – that is, when Bartolomeo (della) Scala reigned in Verona. This *signore's* tenure was brief – an interval of only twenty-nine months commencing in October 1301 and concluding with della Scala's death on 7 March 1304.[3] While da Porto appears not to date his tale to a specific year, given that his story begins before Lent and concludes after Easter, it could not occur during della Scala's reign in the years 1301 or 1304; Scala did not hold the dukedom during Lent/Easter in 1301, and he died before Lent/Easter in 1304. Therefore, this story could take place only in 1302 or 1303. In Girolamo della Corte's *Historia di Verona* (1594–6) the tragedy of Romeo Montecchi and Giulietta Cappelletti is presented as a matter of historical fact and dated to 1303.[4] But as we will see, Bandello restructured the time-line of da Porto's story to make it conform – with remarkable precision – to the calendar (and ephemeredes) of the only other year in the reign of della Scala in which it could have taken place: 1302.

Bandello's first alteration to da Porto's time-scheme is to change the date of the masque at which the lovers meet. In da Porto this takes place during '*carnavale*' (21) – the Shrovetide celebrations which must fall in the interval 3 February to 9 March. Bandello reschedules the date and occasion of the lovers' meeting to the festivities between Christmas and Epiphany, observed 25 December through 6 January – '*dopo natale si cominciarono a far de le feste ove i mascherti concorrevano*' (371) – after Christmas, when folks began to hold parties and masques.[5] Below, I will identify Bandello's motive for shifting the Capelletti feast from Shrovetide to the Twelve Days of Christmas.

In every version of the story Romeo is in love with another woman when he arrives at the masque. Da Porto does not tell us how long Romeo has been carrying the torch for his (nameless) inamorata, but Bandello suggests 'circa dui anni' – about two years – long enough to seem hopeless. The Capelletti gala is a costume party, and da Porta's Romeo dresses as a 'ninfa' – a nymph or sprite – when he attends the feast in order to be near his unnamed, cruel inamorata – 'la sua donna seguendo, si condusse' (21). Intriguingly, this motive is absent from Bandello, Boaistuau, and Brooke, but reappears in Shakespeare's version. Only Shakespeare supplies Rosalind's name – presumably so Romeo may recognize her among Peter's list of invitees (1.2.68), thereby supplying the lad's incentive for attending Capulet's 'old accustomd feast.'[6]

In da Porto, Romeo's rival, Marcuccio, has hands which are always very cold 'il lugio come il gennajo' (22) – as cold in July as in January. As Giulietta dances with him her hand takes a chill. Consequently, when Romeo grasps Giulietta's hand and warms it, she welcomes his touch as a blessing: 'benedetta sia la vostra venuta qui presso me, messer Romeo' (22). In Bandello, Romeo responds, 'Madonna, e che benedizione è cotesta che mi date?' – Madonna, what is this blessing you give me? (375). Shakespeare, of course, moves Old Capulet's gala to the Feast of Saint James, the great object of pilgrimage – and laces the dialogue between Romeo and Juliet with pilgrim references.

Intriguingly, although Shakespeare's Romeo and Juliet meet in July, there is evidence the playwright associated their encounter with the Feast of Epiphany as Bandello did. Whereas in the sources Romeo goes alone to the masque, Shakespeare's Romeo arrives among a group of young men (1.4.1 SD) which includes two principal companions, Mercutio and Benvolio. But in Q1 there are not three but *four* in Romeo's party. The three gallants are attended by Romeo's Page whom Shakespeare christens 'Balthazar' (Q2 5.1.12) – the name of one of the three Magi whose pilgrimage to Bethlehem and adoration of the infant Jesus (Matt. 2) is celebrated at Epiphany, the holy day upon which the lovers meet *only* in Bandello. Shakespeare's echo of Epiphany – the feast only Bandello associates with the masque – is very nearly sufficient evidence to conclude that Shakespeare knew Bandello's version of the tale. But there's more evidence of this connection yet.

In da Porto, Romeo returns home after the party and 'considerata la crudeltà della prima sua donna' (23) – reflecting upon the cruelty of his first lady – determines to devote himself instead to the newfound Giulietta. Subsequently, over an extended period of months the two exchange glances 'dier principio quando in chiesa, quando a qualche finestra' (23) – at first in church or through some window. In Bandello, the pair eye each other through Guilietta's window on a succession of days and nights (377–8). Following Bandello, Boaistuau allows a period of several days to elapse – 'plusieurs jours' (74) – before Julliette spies Rhomeo in the alley beside her garden by the light of the full moon – 'par *la splendeur de la Lune'* (67). Brooke, too, describes Romeo watching Juliet's house over a 'week or two in vayne' (line 461).

Shakespeare compresses this interval of months into moments. But his notorious 'second prologue' – which falls between 1.5 and 2.1 – may be a vestige of the long interval between the lovers' first and second meeting in the sources. Professor Levenson quotes Dr Johnson, who wrote 'The use of this Chorus is not easily discovered,' and remarks that 'it fails to convey [appears to contradict] the speed and intensity of unfolding events.'[7] But I suggest Shakespeare was driving for and achieved the exactly contrary effect. A chorus was an Elizabethan stage convention for marking the passage of time; Shakespeare employs a Chorus to condense the timeframe in the *Henry IV – Henry V* plays. But in *Romeo and Juliet* only moments have elapsed when the action recommences; Shakespeare has intentionally stood the conventional intrusion of a chorus on its ear. Surely, this anomaly would tend to jar his first auditors who, hearing his Chorus, would expecting a length of time to have passed when the action restarts. Indeed, the disorientation would be felt particularly keenly by those readers familiar with the leisurely pace of action in the sources. Furthermore, Romeo's 'Can I go forward when my heart is here, / Turn back dull earth and find thy Center out' (2.1.1) plays on the dual meanings of 'earth,' i.e. Romeo's body and the planet Earth. Post-Copernicans knew that the rotation of the earth was the fundamental mechanism which metered the passing of the hours.

Of the lovers' subsequent meeting da Porto writes, '*Avvenne una notte ... la luna più del solito rilucendo, che mentre Romeo era per salire sopra il detto balcone*' (24) – there came a night when the moon shown more brightly than usual, while Romeo was in the midst of climbing over Juliet's balcony. For his part, Bandello sets this business on a night when the moon was full – '*la luna col suo splendo*' (378). Below I will indicate that this night of a full moon – and the following day – has a special significance in Bandello which has never been recognized.

Romeo returns many nights to court Giulietta. Then in da Porto on '*una sera, che molta neve cadea*' (24) – one evening, when much snow had fallen – the shivering Romeo pleads to enter Giulietta's bedroom. She refuses unless Romeo makes her his wife (25). Romeo quickly agrees. They discover Frate Lorenzo is their mutual confessor, and Romeo determines to ask him to witness their secret marriage. Da Porto created the model of frate Lorenzo da Reggio, '*dell' ordine minore di osservanza, filosofo grande e spirmentatore di molte cose, così naturali come magice*' (25) – a brother of the [Franciscan] order of Observant Friars Minor, a great philosopher and experimenter in many things, things natural as well as magic. This friar 'had already made Romeo his confidant, and had confessed to him his occult interests which were scarcely in harmony with his reputation for orthodoxy. He would not have dared therefore to refuse Romeo the favor of performing the wedding ceremony.'[8] Here and in other instances, Bandello – himself a cleric – revises da Porto's tale to protect the character of Lorenzo; Bandello's Lorenzo agrees to wed the pair only in the hope that their union might bring peace to the feuding houses of Montecchi and Cappelleti.

In Bandello, Lorenzo tells Romeo the wedding must wait until *'l'occasione del confessarsi'* (380) – the time of confession (that is, Lent), when both can come to the church at the same time. In Boaistuau (76) and Brooke (lines 611–2) the friar asks for a day's time to devise a means to perform the clandestine wedding; neither of these two (Protestant) translations mentions Lent. But the tradition of confession on Saturday is remembered in Boaistuau's *'le samedy suyvant elle demanderoit congé à sa mere d'aller à confesse'* (78), which Brooke translates: 'On Saterday, quod he, if Juliet come to shrift, / She shalbe shrived and maried' (lines 633–4). Then as now, the superstitious regard Saturday as a most unpropitious day for marriage.

Da Porto refers the wedding to no particular day of the week. But the season is certainly Lent – *'essendo la quadregesima'* – when his Giulietta feigns a desire to go to confession – *'la giovane un giorno fingendo di volersi confessare'* (26). In Bandello, too, *'Venne il tempo de la quadresigma'* (380)[9] – but his story is more convoluted. Bandello's Giulietta confesses her love for Romeo to her maid – *'l'una … che seco in camera dormiva'* – the woman who sleeps in her chamber. She, in turn, agrees to carry a letter to Romeo. As instructed, Romeo provides himself with a rope ladder and arrives before Giulietta's window at *'cinque ore de la notte'* (380) – about 11 p.m.[10] Giulietta tells Romeo she will go to confession next Friday at the hour of preaching – *'venerdí prossimo … ne l'ora de la predicazione.'* Indeed, on that day she and Madonna Giovanna *'andò a San Francesco … ed entrata in chiesa'* – go to church (381).[11]

Prior to the Council of Trent (1545–63), the *Friars Minor* were one of only two orders of licensed preaching friars.[12] While the hour of preaching could vary, it was most closely associated with Terce *ca* 9 a.m. Giulietta and Romeo enter the confessional where, in the presence of Lorenzo *'per parole di presente'* – by *de presenti* vows – *'Romeo la bella giovane sposò'* (26) – Romeo weds the lovely young woman. Here and elsewhere, Bandello conforms his story to satisfy canon law; only his couple wed by *verba de presenti*; only his time-scheme allows for reading of the Giulietta–Paris banns on three successive Sundays; only Bandello's Romeo makes a good act of contrition before dying. In all other versions – including Shakespeare – Romeo dies unshriven. In the treatment of the clandestine wedding by the Protestants Boaistuau (79) and Brooke (lines 763–9) it is the cleric who speaks the words which make the couple man-and-wife.[13] Their Romeo gives Giulietta a ring.

One wishes to recover the date of the Friday on which Romeo and Giulietta marry in Bandello's version. This is difficult because their *verba de presenti* marriage is seriously deficient. Lent (along with Advent) was a *tempus clausus* when marriage was forbidden to Catholics. However, a 'forbidden time' does not limit 'the personal capacity of the contracting parties … but only the solemn celebration of the marriage; although, in truth, used commonly as if [a *tempus clausus*] forbade marriage.'[14] Fr. Bandello must have been sensitive to this nuance. And he certainly knew that the clandestine setting was a diriment impediment which rendered the marriage null and void from its inception.[15] But Bandello retains both of these details which he inherited from da Porto. Nor is Boaistuau's translation particularly helpful; he reports merely that Rhomeo and Julliette have been married '*quelque moys or deux*' (82) by Eastertide; this could place their wedding on any Friday between the third Friday in Lent and the Friday before Sexagesima Sunday.

Notwithstanding these obstacles to identifying the day on which Bandello's Romeo and Giulietta marry, for several reasons Friday 13 April 1302 seems the most likely date. The traditional English practice of confessing at Shrovetide derived from Anglo-Saxon Abbot Ælfric's (*ca* AD 1000) dictum that 'In the week immediately before Lent everyone shall go to his confessor'. But many Catholics preferred to make confession as late as possible during Lent, thereby minimizing opportunities for sinning again prior to Easter Sunday. In 1302, Easter Sunday was 22 April. Two of the Fridays in Lent were inappropriate for a wedding: Ember Friday (16 March) and Good Friday (20 April). But one of the remaining Fridays – in fact, the last Friday in Lent appropriate for confession – was Friday 13 April 1302. On that night there was a full moon – which sorts well with Bandello's newlyweds consummating their union by moonlight on a bench in Giulietta's garden (382). Although the union takes place in Julliette's bedroom in Boaistuau, Bandello's open-air setting is remembered in the camp-bed – '*le lict de camp*' – prepared by Giulietta's maid (80), which becomes the 'fieeldbed' in Brooke (line 897) which is remembered in Mercutio's complaint that 'This field-bed is too cold for me to sleep' (2.2.40).[16]

The inference that Romeo and Juliet consummate their marriage on a night of a full moon is supported by another extraordinary calendrical detail in Bandello's text. Early in the courtship – many days after their first encounter but before the Quadragesima – Bandello describes Romeo and Giulietta speaking at her window by the light of a full moon (378). Bandello found his cue for this detail in da Porto's '*la luna più de solito rilucendo*' (24). In 1302 there was a full moon which occurred several days after Epiphany (377–8) but before Quadragisema (380). It appeared on the night of 13 February, Saint Valentine's Eve.[17] As I indicated, there were *two* years in the reign of Bartolomeo Scala which could have accommodated Bandello's calendrical structure for Romeo and Giulietta – 1302 and 1303. Among these, Bandello chose the former. Then he rejigged da Porto's story so that the lovers meet not at carnival time, but on Epiphany – the holy day of discovery and revelation –

and unwittingly pledge themselves to marry on Friday the thirteenth, since pre-Roman times a date universally regarded as unlucky.[18]

After the wedding and consummation, the bliss of da Porta's couple lasts '*più notti*' – a few nights (26) before Romeo slays Tebaldo Cappelletti in the the town's most public place, the *via del corso* (27).[19] Bandello does not remark on how long Romeo and Giulietta are married before the death of Tebaldo; but if the couple married on 13 April, the interval of some ten days is compatible with da Porto. Bandello sets the fight '*Erano le feste de la pasqua de la resurrezione*' (382) – about the time of Easter. Boaistuau, who fails to detect Bandello's link between the full moon of Friday 13 April 1302 and the wedding, writes that Rhomeo and Julliette enjoy '*contentement incroyable*' – for some month or two – '*quelque moys ou deux*' (82) – which provides Brooke's unconsidered 'month or twayne' (line 949).

In Boaistuau Rhomeo kills Thibault during '*Les festes de Pasques (comme les hommmes sanguinaries sont volontiers coustumiers, après les bonnes festes, comettre les mechantes oeuvres)*' (82). William Painter's Elizabethan translation of Boaistuau renders this 'in the Easter holy dayes, (as bloudy men commonly be most willingly disposed after a good time to commit some nefarious deede)' (228). But Brooke is more specific and writes, 'At holiest times, men say most heynous crimes are donne; / The morowe after Easter day the mischiefe new begonne' (lines 959–60). The Monday after Easter was ominously called 'Black Monday.' Shakespeare may remember the occasion when Romeo laments 'This day's *black* fate on moe days doth depend' (3.1.110) and Lady Capulet refers to the brawl as 'this *black* strife' (3.1.169 [my emphasis]). In the aftermath, the Cappelletti appeal for justice to the prince of the city, who decrees the banishment of Romeo in all the sources.[20]

Giulietta is inconsolable when she learns of Romeo's banishment. In da Porto, Madonna Giovanna suspects the cause of her daughter's protracted melancholy is a wish to be married, coupled with a reluctance to ask her parents for a husband (29). Bandello says this is understandable given '*tutte le sue compagne esser il carneval passato divenute spose e che di lei non si parli di darle marito*' (387) – all Giulietta's friends married during the previous Shrovetide, but she has no fiancé. In da Porto, Madonna Giovanni believes Giulietta should marry before her beauty begins to decline and the girl becomes a domestic problem. Da Porto's Giulietta is already eighteen years old – '*che ogni modo ella diciotto anni questa santa Eufemia fornì*' (29) – in any case this (last) Sainte Euphemia's day she achieved eighteen years. Da Porto makes it clear that Giovanna's determination to marry off her daughter has nothing to do with the girl reaching the age of discretion or consent, or her sexual maturity; in any case, Roman Catholic canon law fixed the marriageable age (puberty) 'at twelve years for girls and fourteen for boys.'[21] It's not Giulietta's age that motivates da Porto's Giovanna. Rather, she warns her husband

e le donne, come questi di molto trapassano, perdono più tosto che avanzino della loro bellezza. Oltra ch' elle non sono mercantanzia da tenere molto in casa; quantunque io las nostra in verun atto veramente non conoscessi mai altro che onestissima. (29)

That is, '… and young women as they pass beyond this age lose rather than gain of their beauty. Besides, they are inclined to remain away much from the house although ours in every act I have truly never known other than most honest.'[22] Giovanna is saying that Giulietta has reached 'the pretty age,' after which her beauty must decline and make her less attractive to a husband. One cannot help but wonder whether this inspired Shakespeare's Lady Capulet to say to Nurse, 'Thou knowest my daughters of a prettie age' (1.3.10–11).

By contrast, Bandello's Giulietta is a year younger; '*a questa santa Eufemia che viene compirá i suoi diciotto anni*' (387) – she will achieve the age of eighteen on (next) Saint Euphemia's day. But Bandello is not lowering Giulietta's age to create an impediment to marriage. Rather, he is shifting Giulietta's eighteenth birthday from past to future so that he will be able to stage her recovery from seeming death on the feast of Saint Euphemia, a virgin martyred under Diocletian who might have earned the nickname *The Unkillable*; miraculously, Euphemia survived one rape attempt and five attempted murders.[23] Could Bandello have set the birthday of Giulietta on a more appropriate saint's day?

In Protestant Boaistuau's version any reference to Saint Euphemia has vanished and his Julliette is not yet eighteen – '*n'avoit encores attainct l'aage de dix et huict ans*' (94). Brooke's Juliet is even younger – 'Scarce saw she yet full xvi. yeres … too yong to be a bryde' (line 1860). For his part, Shakespeare makes Juliet thirteen and supplies a new birthday – 'Lammas Eve at night' (1.3.16–7). Commentators have speculated that Shakespeare made his Juliet younger to emphasize her impulsive innocence. But a more likely explanation derives from prevailing English law which recognized fourteen as the age of discretion and eligibility for marriage. In Nurse's dialogue with Lady Capulet (1.3), Shakespeare is at pains to focus our attention on the night when Juliet will achieve marriageable age – the night of 31 July/1 August.[24] This was the vigil of Saint Peter *ad Vincula,* the feast which commemorates the saint's miraculous release from prison in Acts 12:4–11. The apostle, chained, is sleeping between two guards when an angel miraculously unbinds him and guides him out of jail. In a fury over Peter's escape, Herod puts his two guards to death (Acts 12:19). When Romeo places Paris' corpse within the Capulet tomb and commits suicide, Shakespeare contrives for Juliet to wake amid three dead men at the moment her ghostly father arrives (5.3.156).[25]

Because of Giulietta's age – or in spite of it – in each of the versions her father, Antonio, determines to match her.[26] In da Porto, a joyful Madonna Giovanna informs Giulietta that '*fra pochi giorni*' – in eight days, a Roman week – 'sarai ad un gran gentiluomo degnamente maritata' (29) – you will be married to a gentleman of great dignity. Of course, this sends her daughter – already married to Romeo – into a paroxysm of despair. On learning of his daughter's reluctance to wed, Antonio is 'molto turbato' and 'sopra la persona assai la minacciò' (30) – he threatens her with violence. But neither her mother's flattery nor her father's threats can move Giulietta to consent to the marriage (31). Rather, she determines to ask Lorenzo to help her find a way out. She asks her mother for permission to go again to confession (32). Once at the church, Giulietta confides to Lorenzo 'Io sento preparare le mie nozze ad un palagio di mio padre, i quale fuori di questa terra da due miglia verso Mantova' (32) – 'I understand they are preparing to marry me off at a palace of my father which is two miles from here [Verona] in the direction of Mantua.' She begs him for poison so that she and Romeo may escape the shame of her bigamy. Instead, Lorenzo gives her a powder which will put her into a deathlike sleep – which brings us to the threshold of the answer to the riddle: why does Shakespeare's Lawrence promise Juliet 'two and fortie houres' sleep?

In da Porto, the duration of the drug's effect will be 'quarantotto ore, ovver poco più o meno' (33) – forty-eight hours, more or less. After Giulietta is entombed, the friar promises to disinter and conceal her in his cell until it is opportune to take her to Mantua in the disguise of a monk (33). He instructs her 'togli questa polvere, e, quando ti parrà, nelle tre o nelle quattr' ore di notte insieme con acqua cruda senza tema la beverai' (34) – to take the powder and, when you are ready, at the third or fourth hour of the night, mix it with water and drink it. Giulietta agrees to the plan. But when Paris asks to see his bride-to-be and Giovanna arranges for Giulietta to go to the family's country house for this purpose, the young woman 'credendo che il padre così all'improvviso l'avesse fatta audare, per darla di subito in mano al secondo sposo' (35) – fears that her father is contriving to suddenly put her into the hands of a second husband. Therefore, 'la notte vicina alle quattro ore' – at about the fourth hour of the night, Giulietta asks her maid for cold water to prepare the potion. Da Porto describes the maid as 'che seco allevata s'era, e che quasi come sorella tenea' (35) – who had been raised with her, and whom Giulietta considered almost a sister. Only in da Porto is Giulietta's maid a young woman of her own age; in Bandello, Boaistuau, and Brooke Giulietta's maid is 'una vecchia' – an old woman. Shakespeare seems to recall the quasi-sister who serves Giulietta in da Porto in Nurse's otherwise inexplicable reverie about her own dead child: 'Susan and she [Juliet], God rest all Christian soules, were of an age. Well, Susan is with God, she was too good for me' (1.3.19–20).

Da Porto's maid observes Giulietta mix and drink the powder, but thinks nothing of it. Then Giulietta lowers her lamp and goes to bed. After her maid retires, Giulietta rises, dresses in her clothes, lies down on the bed, and crosses her hands on her breast. She does this in the belief that this presentation will convince those who find her that she's dead. In a little more than two hours the potion renders her seemingly dead (35). When her maid cannot wake her in the morning, the distraught servant despairs that the powder was poison and flings herself on Giulietta's body wailing, '*Io sola e voi e me, il vostro padre e la vostra madre ad un tratto averò morto*' (36) – I alone have killed you and your father and mother. The tableau persuades the mother and father that Giulietta is truly dead, and a doctor pronounces her already dead for six hours (36). Her body is returned to Verona '*con esequie grandi*' (37) and interred in the family tomb.

Bandello alters da Porto's version of these events in several important respects. His Giulietta is not yet eighteen years old and Antonio refers to her forthcoming birthday as a 'marriageable age' – '*Figiuola mia, veggendoti oggimai d'etá de marito*' (388). When Giulietta refuses the match with Paris, Bandello names the locale of Antonio's country house, accelerates the business of Giulietta's first meeting with Paris, and embellishes the threat of violence. Bandello's Antonio storms

> *fra tre o quattro giorni ella deliberasse andar con la madre ed altre parenti a Villafranca, perciò che quivi deveva venir il conte Paris con sua compagnia a vederla, e che a questo non facesse né replica né resistenza se non voleva che le rompesse il capo e la facesse la piú trisa figliuola che mai fosse nata.* (388)

That is, in three or four days she must determine to go with her mother and other elders to Villafranca where Paris will come with his friends to see her, and she must not reply [decline] or resist if she doesn't want her father to break her head and make her the saddest girl ever born. His colorful threat of violence – only obliquely suggested in Boaistuau (96) and Brooke (lines 1987–90) – may have suggested Shakespeare's Old Capulet's warning to his daughter, 'My fingers itch [to strike you].'[27]

Reluctantly, Bandello's Giulietta goes to Villafranca Paris observes her at mass, likes what he sees, and concludes the marriage agreement with Antonio. When Bandello's Giulietta returns to Verona she learns that '*le nozze s'apprestavano per mezzo settembre*' (389) – her wedding is set for the middle of September, a detail not present in da Porto. Since the mid-days of September are the 15th and 16th of the month, Bandello is drawing attention to Giulietta's birthday on 16 September without naming the date. Bandello must certainly have known that wedding dates in mid-September were limited by four exclusionary holy days: the Exultation of the Cross (14 September) and the three Ember Days which follow the Fifteenth Sunday after Pentecost. Bandello also tells us that Giulietta's nuptial was fixed on '*domenica, deveva publicamente esser sposata*' (394) – the Sunday when she was to be publicly married. There is only one year in the principate of Bartolommeo Scala in which Giulietta's birthday, 16 September, fell on Sunday – 1302. Bandello's choice of 16 September 1302 was no idle choice; in addition to being Saint Euphemia's day, in 1302 this was the Fifteenth Sunday after Pentecost.[28] Bandello would certainly have been aware this day was familiarly known as the 'Sunday of the Widow of Naim' after the Gospel reading for the day which records the raising of the widow's son from the dead:[29]

> And it came to pass the day after, that he went into a city called Nain; and many of his disciples went with him, and much people. Now when he came nigh to the gate of the city, behold, there was a dead man carried out, the only son of his mother, and she was a widow: and much people of the city was with her. And when the Lord saw her, he had compassion on her, and said unto her, Weep not. And he came and touched the bier: and they that bare him stood still. And he said, Young man, I say unto thee, Arise. And he that was dead sat up, and began to speak. (Lk 7:11–15)

Could there be a more appropriate day for Giulietta to fall into a deathlike sleep from which she – seeming dead – would awake, sit up, and speak? In the absence of evidence to the contrary – and given Bandello's long career as friar and bishop – his reference to the brief principate of Bartolommeo Scala, the full moon on the night of Friday the thirteenth when Romeo and Giulietta first pledge their love, the Full Moon on Friday 13 April when they marry and consummate – making two Fridays the Thirteenth – and the triple concordance of the day of her nuptials on 16 September with her birthday, Saint Euphemia's day, and the Sunday of the Widow of Nain – all these details argue that Bandello restructured da Porto's story with meticulous precision to link the principal events of the tragedy to dates in the ecclesiastical and lunar calendars which are rife with powerful overtones of meaning. But Bandello may also be glancing at the solar calendar; in 1302, 15 September was the date of the Autumnal Equinox – which occurred *ca* 8 p.m. (Coordinated Universal Time) – making 16 September a date on which there were an equal twelve hours of day and twelve of night, the significance of which I will discuss below. In Bandello's story time is not a passive medium in which the tragedy transpires. Time becomes an engine driving the disaster as their tale unfolds on a series of evil days.

In Boaistuau's reformed version of the drama's central crisis, after Tybaldo's death Rhomeo goes into hiding with Laurens while his banishment is pronounced. A few days later Rhomeo visits Julliette, says his farewells, and departs for Mantoue (92). In his rewrite of this encounter Brooke casually introduces another 'full moone' (line 1348) not found in Boaistuau (nor justified by the internal calendar of Brooke's version). In the days that follow, Boaistuau's Julliette persists in melancholy. Her mother comes to believe she is sad because most of her friends have married though she has not – '*La pluspart de ses compagnes mariées, et elle non*' (93). When Mere Montesche advances this notion to her husband, Antonio, he first expresses reluctance to see Julliette married since she is not yet eighteen years old – *'toutesfois, voyant qu'elle n'avoit encores attainct l'aage de dix et huict ans'* (94). Despite the deficiency of Julliette's age, Boaistuau's Antonio determines to match her with Paris, Comte de Lodronne. Boaistuau does not tell us how long she has been married to Rhomeo when Julliette refuses the match. As in his source, Pere Montesche waxes apoplectic:

> *J'atteste la puissance de ce luy qui m'a faict la grace de te produire sur terre que, si dedans mardy (pour tout le jour) tu faux á mon chasteau de Villefrance, oú se doit render le Comte Paris, et lá donner consentement à ce que ta mere et moy avons jà accordé, non seulment je te priveray de ce que j'ay des biens de ce monde, mais je te feray espouser une si estroicte et austere prison que tu maudiras mille fois le jour et l'heure de ta naissance.* (96)

That is, 'I swear by the power of He whose grace brought you to the world that if on Tuesday inside (for all the day) you fail to be at my chateau at Villefrance, or fail to present yourself to Comte Paris, and to him give consent to what your I and mother have already concluded, not only will I deprive you of my worldly goods, but I will marry you to one so strict and a jail so bare that you will curse a thousand times the day and hour of your birth.' Bandello's 'three or four days' has, arbitrarily, become next Tuesday. In Brooke, the date is – arbitrarily – 'Wensday next' (line 1973).

Under this terrible threat, Boaistuau's Julliette passes a sleepless night and on the following morning, *'feignant aller à mess avecques sa dame de chambre'* (97) – pretending to go to Mass with her nurse, she hurries to Laurens to plead for help. When Laurens asks when the formal steps toward matrimony are to begin, she replies

> *La premiere assignation, dist-elle, est á mercredi, qui est le jour ordonné pour receivoir mon consentement du marriage accordé par mon pere au Comte Paris; mais la solennité des nopces ne se doit celebrer que le dixiesme jour de Septembre.* (98)

That is, on Thursday Julliette must pledge her troth to Comte Paris, but the marriage ceremony will not be performed before the tenth of September. Brooke adopts this time-scheme (lines 2070–2). But Fr. Bandello knew that before a wedding could be performed the banns must be proclaimed in the respective parish churches of the bride and groom on three successive Sundays.[30] Therefore, his Giulietta must learn that her marriage is set for mid-September at least four weeks before the event. Indeed, shortly after learning of the date of her nuptials Giulietta asks permission of her mother to go to confession *'Era vicina la festa de la gloriosa assunzione de la sempre beatissima Virgine madre del nostro Redentore'* (389) – about the time of the glorious assumption of the blessed perpetual Virgin mother of our Redeemer. When they meet, Giulietta tells Lorenzo that her wedding is set for *'mese di settembre'*

(390). The date of the Feast of the Assumption is 15 August, four Sundays prior to 16 September. Although it may appear at first glance that Boaistuau (and Brooke) are following Bandello by assigning the wedding date to 10 September, I will indicate below that they are not doing so. Shakespeare accelerates the marriage sequence by combining both the troth-plight and nuptials into a single, looming event.

In response to Julliette's desperation Laurens provides a sleeping powder which will work in a quarter-hour (99); in Brooke this becomes 'halfe an howre' (line 2131). Laurens instructs Julliette to mix the powder with water and drink it *'le soir dont le jour suyvant seront tes espousailles, ou le matin avant jour'* – on the night before her espousal, or on the morning before sunrise (100).[31] Brooke translates this, 'on thy marriage day before the sunne doe cleare the skye' (line 2150). Laurens tells Julliette that the sleeping potion will bring on a deathlike sleep which will last *'quarante heures'* – forty hours (100). Brooke mentions no specific duration. There can be no argument but that Shakespeare found his cue for Juliet to marry on Wednesday in Brooke. But where did Shakespeare find his 'two and forty hours'?

Had Shakespeare turned to Boaistuau he would have found *'quarante heures pour le moins'* (100) – forty hours at the very least; if he turned to Painter, 'xl. houres at the least' (237). In da Porto, the interval was *'quarantotto ore, ovver poco più o meno'* (33) – forty-eight hours, or a little more or less. Bandello seems somewhat indefinite about the duration of the action of the potion – *'circa quaranta ore almeno e talora più'* (391) – about forty hours at least or a little longer. But later in his story Bandello is quite precise about the duration of the operation of the potion. He advances by six hours the time at which Giulietta was to drink it from da Porto's *'la notte vicina alle quattro ore'* (35) – about ten o'clock at night – to *'ne l'apparir de l'alba'* – the appearance of the dawn, which was *ca* 4 a.m. at this time of year.[32] Advancing the time at which Giulietta drinks the potion by six hours has the effect of reducing the duration of its effect from da Porto's forty-eight hours to forty-two hours ($48 - 6 = 42$).

Since the duration of the action of the sleeping potion – whether forty-eight, forty-odd, or two-and-forty hours – shapes the story's catastrophe, it will be useful to follow the development of the climactic action through the sources. In Boaistuau, Laurens promises Julliette that after he sees her sleeping body laid in the Capellets' tomb he will summon Rhomeo by letter, asking him to come the following night – *'la nuictée suyvante'* – when together the men will carry her, still asleep, to his cell to await the time when *'l'operation de la poudre parachevée'* – the operation of the power is completed (100). The timetable is the same in Brooke: 'he and I will take thee forth that night. And when out of thy slepe thou shalt awake again, etc.' (lines 2164–5). In da Porto, Lorenzo will remove Giulietta from the tomb when the time of her waking arrives (33). Only Bandello, with his characteristic attention to time, constructs a taut schedule. Whereas da Porta's Lorenzo told Giulietta that the powder would act through forty-eight hours and to drink it at nine or ten o'clock at night, Bandello's friar instructs Giulietta to drink the potion at first light. This time-shift of six hours reduces da Porta's forty-eight hours to forty-two, the source of Shakespeare's 'two and fortie houres.'

Bandello's Lorenzo tells Giulietta that '*poco dopoi ti addormenterai*' – a short time afterward [the potion] will put her to sleep – '*e a l'ora del levare veggend i tuoi che tu dormi*' – and at the time of rising she will be found asleep (393). Meanwhile, Lorenzo will advise Romeo of the scheme by letter and summon him back to Verona, and on the following night – '*La notte poi seguente*' – the two men will recover Giulietta from the tomb. When the night before Giulietta's wedding Sunday arrives – '*Venuta la notte che il di seguente, che era domenica, deveva publicamente esser sposata*' (394) – she is frightened by a vision of Tebaldo's ghost '*Cominciandosi poi ad appressar l'ora de l'alba*' – just before the hour of daybreak. But she masters her fear and drinks the potion '*ne l'ora che giá l'Aurora aveva cominciato a por il capo fuor del balcone de l'oriente*' (395) – at the hour of sunrise when the sun begins to show his head above the balcony of the East – *ca* 6 a.m. Her chamber woman arrives somewhat later – '*poi l'ora del levarsi*' – at the hour of rising – and finds Giulietta apparently dead. In Boaistuau's version the time of sunrise is explicitly identified. Julliette instructs her maid to wake her '*sur les six heurs*' (103) – promptly at 6 a.m. Indeed, the maid discovers Julliette's body '*comme l'aube du jour commençoit à mettre la teste hors de son Orient*' (105) – as the dawn of day begins to put his head out of the East. In Boaistuau, the maid's arrival is timely – '*comme l'aube du jour commençoit à mettre la teste hors de son Orient*' (105). In Brooke, Juliet instructs her Nurse to 'comme before the dawning light' (line 2332). But only in Brooke does Nurse arrive late; she enters Juliet's bedroom 'when that Phoebus bright heaved up his seemely hed, / And from the East in open skies his glistring rayes dispred' (lines 2403–4).

In each of the sources Giulietta is entombed on the day of her death.[33] Although da Porto's Lorenzo had promised Giulietta that he would free her from the tomb on the night of her interment, he is away from Verona when he learns of her 'suicide' – '*il quale per alcuna bigona del monasterio poco fuori della città era andato*' (37) – therefore, he cannot go to her tomb that night. But he manages to entrust a letter addressed to Romeo into the care of a brother who is on his way to Mantova. Unfortunately, the brother calls two or three times at Romeo's house without finding him at home, and keeps the letter lest it come into the wrong hands (37). In adapting da Porto, Bandello creates a more elaborate scheme to thwart the delivery of the letter. His Lorenzo officiates at Giulietta's funeral, makes room for her in the tomb by moving Tebaldo's corpse aside, and even provides a pillow for her head (399). He also writes to Romeo and entrusts the letter to a fellow friar who rides to Mantua and stops at the '*convento di San Francesco*' where he seeks a companion who knows the city. But a brother having recently died apparently of plague, the health authorities command that no one within the monastery may leave it. Bandello's brother and his letter are trapped inside for an indefinite period of time (397). In Boaistuau, Laurens writes to Rhomeo '*qu'il eust à venir la nuict suyvant par ce que l'operation de la pouldre prendroit fin*' (106) – to come on that night when the operation of the powder will end. But Laurens' courier is quarantined in a monastery '*pour ce jour*' (107) – for that one day. Brooke adopts this scheme; his quarantined friar-messenger 'differd [deferred] untill the morowe' (line 2502). This may explain why Shakespeare's Brother Anselm is held in quarantine only one day (5.2.5–14).

In each of the sources, the news of Giulietta's death is conveyed to Romeo by the servant, Pietro (in Brooke he's named Peter). The distance between Verona and Mantua is some twenty miles (33 kilometers) – eight hours by foot, but a little over two hours by post-horse relay, given stations at intervals of ten miles which was common during the Renaissance. In da Porto, Pietro observes the interment of Giulietta and then – '*la notte seguente sì verso Mantova camminò, che la mattina per tempo vi giunse*' (37) – on the ensuing night walks to Mantova, arriving there in the morning. In Bandello, Pietro delays until he has seen Giulietta on her bier and clearly recognized her. Then he mounts his horse, rides swiftly to Villafranca where he refreshes his horse and sleeps a while. Then he rises two hours before day and enters Mantova at sunrise and goes to the house of his master (398). Boaistuau follows Bandello closely, but for the change of horses substitutes a post-horse – '*print incontinent la poste*' (107) – and omits the early hour of Pietro's arrival. Brooke's Peter 'hyed away in post, / And in his house he found his maister Romeus' (lines 2532–3). Shakespeare seems to remember the early arrival of da Porta's and Bandello's messengers in Romeo's lines which open 5.1: 'If I may trust the flattering truth of sleep, / My dreams presage some joyful news at hand' (5.1.1–2). Yet, two lines later, it is late in the day: 'And all this day an unaccustomed spirit / Lifts me above the ground with cheerful thoughts' (3–4).

In da Porta, Romeo receives the news of Giulietta's death from Pietro, borrows the servant's tawny cloak as a disguise and, carrying with him a phial of '*acqua di serpe*' (38) – serpent water – returns to Verona where he awaits the fall of night. In Bandello, Pietro finds Romeo '*ancora era in letto*' (399) – still abed – which may have suggested to Shakespeare his 'false presentment of good fortune.'[34] On hearing the most cruel news – '*crudelissima nuova*' – Romeo is turned to marble and cannot weep – '*impietrato e divenuto marmo, che lagrima da gli occhi non gli poteva uscire*' (400). He orders Pietro to secure two fresh horses – '*dui cavalli freschi*' – and to return before him to Verona to secure tools to open the tomb. Romeo has in his possession a vial of poison – '*un'ampolletta piena d'acqua velenossima*' (401). After writing an explanatory letter to his father, Romeo takes horse and arrives at Verona *'ne l'ora de l'avemaria'* (401) – the hour of the Angelus. This prayer was accompanied by the sounding of the 'curfew' bell to which Shakespeare alludes at 4.4.2, and the closing of the city gates. In both da Porto and Bandello, Giulietta is laid in the tomb at night. Boaistuau alters the late hour of Julliette's burial; Rhomeo's servant, Pierre, reports that he saw Julliette buried yesterday morning – *'hier matin ma damoisle Julliette a laissé ce monde pour chercher repos en l'autre, et l'ay veue en ma presence recevoir sepulture'* (108). In Brooke, the report is 'that yesterday my lady and you wyfe' was buried (line 2539).

Boaistuau's Rhomeo buys poison of a poor apothecary – *'que l'extreme pauvreté'* – for fifty ducats – *'cinquante ducats'* (108). These details are Boaistuau's innovations and find their way into Brooke and Shakespeare. The apothecary warns Rhomeo that half the lethal draught will kill the strongest man in the world in an hour – *'la moytié pour fair mourir en une heure le plus robuste homme du monde'* (108). Brooke shortens this interval to 'lesse then halfe an howre' (line 2587). Shakespeare remembers Brooke's 'half an hour' (5.3.130), but makes the action of the poison almost instantaneous; his Romeo dies in the time it takes to speak thirteen words (5.3.119–20). After securing the poison, Boaistuau's Rhomeo departs for Verona. He arrives *'par les obscures tenebres de la nuict … avant que les portes fussent fermées'* (109) – that is, after sunset but before the city gates are shut. In Brooke, 'even with the shade of night he entred Verone towne' (line 2614).

That night when the town grows quiet, da Porto's Romeo goes to the tomb (38). Bandello is, of course, more precise about the time of night; his Romeo goes to the tomb *'circa le quattr'ore'* – about ten o'clock. Finding Giulietta apparently dead, Romeo drinks the 'serpent water' which kills a man in less than an hour. In da Porto's version, as Romeo lingers, Giulietta revives and the two exchange words of love and grief before he dies (40). In Bandello, Romeo's kiss awakens Giulietta, and the couple speak their lamentations and farewells (404–5) Overhearing their conversation, Pietro is turned to a marble statue – *'una statua di marmo'* (405). In Boaistuau and Brooke, Romeo dies before Julliette awakes.

Da Porto's Lorenzo had planned to remove Giulietta from the tomb on the same night that she was interred; being out of the city at the time of her seeming death, he could not do so. But having heard (presumably from Giulietta's maid) at what time she took the potion – and knowing the time when its effect would end, he hastened to the tomb *'innanti il giorno all'arca venne'* (41) – about an hour before daybreak. Seeing a light within, Lorenzo enters and finds Giulietta sitting up; and in her lap lay the head of her lover, almost dead (41). In Evans's translation, she demands of Lorenzo 'a knife with which I may strike my breast'; Lorenzo addresses Romeo, who rouses momentarily, fixes his eyes on Giulietta, and dies. Lorenzo urges Giulietta to come out of the tomb and enter a convent. She refuses and 'drew in her breath holding it for some time and then sending forth a great cry, upon the dead body of her loved one she expired …' At this moment the officers of the Podesta' enter and challenge the friars: 'What are you doing here at this house, Signori? Are you not practicing some witchcraft over this tomb?' When Lorenzo refuses to answer, the watchmen refer the matter to 'the Signore.'

At the time when da Porto wrote his tale the city's secular authority had limited jurisdiction over the clergy; in consequence, his *denouement* is convoluted. 'Dawn was breaking when the brothers freed themselves from the officers, and some of these men [officers] went immediately to the family of the Cappelletti with the news concerning the brothers. They [the Cappelletti], knowing perhaps that Father Lorenzo was a friend of Romeo's, directly presented themselves to the Signore, begging him if by no other means, that by force he be informed by the friar what he was seeking in the tomb.'[35] Under compulsion, Lorenzo appears before della Scala. At first, he lies about his motive for being in the tomb in an attempt to conceal his involvement in the affair. But 'many brothers who wished him [Lorenzo] badly' tell the Signore that Romeo's body was also found in the tomb. Finally, Lorenzo confesses all. He acknowledges his responsibility for the deaths of Romeo and of Giulietta 'who died thus strangely the day before yesterday.' Hearing the sad tale della Scala 'was almost moved to tears from compassion,' and punishes no one. The lovers' death ends the enmity between the two houses. The fathers embrace, and order 'a beautiful monument, on which in a few days was sculptured the cause of' Romeo's and Giulietta's deaths.[36]

In Bandello's version Lorenzo would also have removed Giulietta from the tomb on the first night had Romeo received his letter and come to Verona. Now, at about eleven o'clock on the second night – forty-one hours after Giulietta drank the potion – Lorenzo arrives with a trusty brother to discover Giulietta awakened and Romeo dying. Romeo barely has breath to gasp '*che pentito dei suoi mali a lui e a Dio ne domandava perdono*' (406) before he expires; Fr. Bandello could hardly have allowed Romeo to die without a good act of contrition. For her part, da Porto's and Bandello's Giulietta commits suicide by holding her breath – '*Ristretti adunque in sé gli spirti, con il suo Romeo in grembo, senza dir nulla se ne morì*' (407).[37] In Boaistuau's version of the catastrophe Laurens is dismayed that he has not had a response to his letter from Rhomeo. Knowing when the effect of the powder will wear off – '*qui cognoissoit le periode certain de l'operation de sa poudre*' (111) – Laurens goes to the tomb alone and encounters Pierre waiting outside. Alarmed, the friar enters the tomb and finds Rhomeo dead and Julliette awakening. After a brief conversation, Pierre warns Laurens of noises outside and the men flee. Left alone, Julliette draws the dagger which Rhomeo wears at his side, stabs herself many times in the region of the heart, speaks a welcome to death, and dies

(113).[38] The dagger and this means of death are Boaistuau's innovations which Brooke and Shakespeare adopted. At that moment passing watchmen spy a light in the tomb, find the bodies, suspect foul play, seize the friars and Pietro, and report the apparent murders to '*signor Bartolomeo.*' At dawn – '*essend giá venuta l'alba*' (408) – he views the bodies and then pardons the friars and Pietro. Romeo and Giulietta are laid in a tomb engraved with an effusive epitaph. Thus ends the story of the lovers in da Porto and Bandello. But in Boaistuau and Brooke, the sad tale has one additional, important beat.

In Brooke, on the following morning the bodies are 'set forth upon a stage' (line 2817) – in Boaistuau the phrase was '*sur un theatre*' – while '*seigneur de l'Escale*' and Magistrates convene to sit in judgment (114).[39] In his defense, Laurens admits that his presence nearby the tomb at '*l'heure suspect*' makes him appear guilty, but '*comme si les heures n'avoient pas toutes esté créées du Seigneur egales; et ainsi que luy mesmes a enseigné, il y en a douze au jour, monstrant par cela qu'on peut faire bien ou mal à toutes indifferemment, ainsi que la personne est guidée ou delaissée de l'esprit de Dieu*' (115). Painter's translation of this passage runs, 'as though all houres were not indifferently made equall by God their creator, who in his owne person declarth unto us that there be *twelve houres in the day*, shewing thereby that there is no exception of houres nor of minutes, but that one may doe either good or yll at all times indifferently, as the partie is guided or forsaken by the sprite of God …' (245 [my emphasis]).

Brooke rewrites Boaistuau as follows:

> Or els (a liker proofe) that I am in the cryme,
> You say these present yrons are, and the suspected time:
> As though all howres alike had not been made above!
> Did Christ not say the day had twelve? whereby he sought to prove,
> That no respect of howres, ought justly to be had,
> But at all times men have the choyce of dooing good or bad. (2867–72)[40]

As noted above Bandello set Giulietta's birthday and death on Saint Euphemia's day, 16 September – *which date in 1302 was the Autumnal Equinox* – one of two days in the year when there are twelve hours of darkness and twelve of light. Unless Boaistuau's '*il y en a douze au jour*' is an extraordinary coincidence, the Frenchman seems to have grasped Bandello's trope; Boaistuau certainly describes a sunrise at six o'clock on Julliette's fatal morning (103). On 16 September 1302 the sun rose at Verona at 5:58 a.m. and set *ca* 6:05 p.m.; there were twelve hours of day and twelve of night. Appropriately, Boaistua's source for Laurens' text is John 11:9–10, the tale of Christ raising the dead Lazarus.[41]

To my knowledge no commentator has ever grasped the calendrical significance of Saint Euphemia's day or Boaistuau's invented speech. Brooke, it seems, adopted Boaistuau's trope without recognizing its significance.

Metaphorically, the equivalence of day and night conveys the equinimity which the Montini and Capelletti mourners achieve when they bury their ancient grudge in the grave of their dead children.

William Shakespeare was not the first writer intentionally to link scenes in a tragedy of Romeo and Juliet to holy days and/or luni-solar events – Matteo Bandello was. There is, I suggest, persuasive evidence that Shakespeare knew Bandello's version in its 'choice Italian.' I believe this finally explains why Shakespeare described his young lovers as 'starre-crost' (Prologue 6) – that is, predestined by celestial powers to meet a tragic end. In Bandello Shakespeare found a tale in which time was not merely a passive medium but the engine driving the lovers to disaster.

Finally, I will identify the man who was Fr. Bandello's inspiration for rejigging da Porto's story so that its principal events conformed to the calendar of 1302 under the della Scala rule in Verona. Bandello was born *ca* 1480 in the duchy of Milan, Italy, and died in Agen, France, in 1561 or 1565. Educated at the universities of Milan and Padua, Bandello was a genuine Renaissance man who led careers as a soldier, monk (from 1505), and diplomat as well as a writer. He lived a colorful life and rubbed elbows with exciting personalities, serving Isabelle d'Este, Francisco Gonzaga, and Sforza. Likely, Bandello knew both Niccolo Machiavelli and Leonardo da Vinci.

In 1550 Bandello was elevated to the bishopric of Agen. He was one of a succession of Italians to serve in this post. These men brought to the French town the rich and invigorating spirit of Renaissance scholarship and learning. As luck would have it, another writer concerned with time and destiny lived in the town of Salon, some forty miles from Agen – Nostradamus (1503–1566). At the same time Agen's most illustrious citizens were another Italian family, the della Scalas or Scaligeri, a branch of the very family that had ruled Verona at the time of Romeo and Juliet. The paterfamilias of the Agen branch, Julius Caesar Scaliger (1484–1558), was an almost exact contemporary of Bandello. Likely, the two knew each other well.

In 1525 Scaliger had come to Agen as physician to Antonio de la Rovera, Bandello's predecessor as bishop. Saliger, of course, is numbered among the great Renaissance humanists for his studies of Cicero, his translation of Aristotle's *Natural History,* and his works on poetry. But Scaliger's son, Joseph Justus, born in Agen in 1540, was the greatest mathematician of his era. His monumental *De ementaione temporum* (1583), one of the most important books of the Renaissance, reconciled and corrected a multitude of calendars of antiquity and laid the first scientific basis for chronography. In a smallish town the size of early modern Agen, Bishop Bandello must have known well the distinguished Scaligers father-and-son. And Bandello would have been aware of their kinship to the line of della Scalas who ruled in Verona. Whether Bandello's interest in the calendar grew out of his association with the Agen branch of the Scaligeri – and whether to flatter them he rewrote da Porta's tale of doomed lovers who flourished under their eminent forebear – are questions which historians cannot answer. But it is certainly safe to infer that time, calendars *and destiny* were lively topics of conversation when Bandello, the Scaligers, and perhaps Nostradamus gathered before a fireplace.

Notes

1 Jesse Benton Evans (tr.) *Giulietta e Romeo* (Portland: Mosher Press, 1934), p. 7.
2 In consequence whereof daytime hours were longer in summer and shorter in winter; nighttime hours were the reverse.
3 Olin H. Moore, *The Legend of Romeo and Juliet* (Cincinnati: Ohio State University Press, 1950).
4 Lord Byron, wrote to Thomas Moore that this date (1303) was still current among the Veronese when Byron visited the traditional site of the tomb (7 November 1816).
5 In English tradition during Shakespeare's lifetime the 'Twelfth Night' celebrations were often held on the night of 6 January, i.e. 'Twelfth Day at Night.'
6 Both Rosalind and Paris are invited to the party but, apparently, neither attends.
7 Levenson, p. 201n.
8 Moore, p. 45.
9 Quadregisma Sunday is the Sunday after Shrove Tuesday, the first in Lent and the forty-second day before Easter. But in both da Porto and Bandello the phrase signifies Lent in general, i.e. the 'forty days.'
10 During this season the sun rises between 6 and 7 a.m. and sets between 6 and 7 p.m., yielding more than 12 hours of night.
11 In England, the time of shriving was Shrovetide, which engrossed Quinquagesima Sunday and the following Monday and Tuesday. This English tradition arose from the dictum of the Anglo-Saxon Abbot Ælfric (*ca* AD 1000), 'In the week immediately before Lent everyone shall go to his confessor ...'
12 The Dominicans being the other. Preaching required extensive theological education.
13 Shakespeare may remember this when his Lawrence says, 'you shall not stay alone / Till Holy Church incorporate two in one' (2.6.36–7).
14 Catholic Encyclopedia, vii.697.
15 Under canon law, Rosalind's vow of chastity was a 'diriment impediment' which permanently precluded her from marrying. Shakespeare certainly may have understood that, by continuing to court Rosalind's favor, Romeo was pursuing an illicit marriage. Catholic Encyclopedia, vii.696.
16 Perhaps the brightness of the full moonlight in Giulietta's garden is remembered in Boaistuau, where Julliette's bedroom *'estoit aussi claire que le jour à cause de trois mortiers de cire vierge que Julliette avoit faict allumer pour mieux contempler son Rhomeo'* (p. 80). Brooke renders this, 'the waxen quariers ... / Which Juliet had before prepared to be light, / That she at pleasure might beholde her husbandes bewty bright' (lines 836–8).

17 Although H.A. Kelly attributes to Geoffrey Chaucer's *Parliament of Fowles* (1382) the first association of 14 February with this feast of lovers, Bandello – who wrote in the mid-sixteenth century when the Valentine tradition was well-established – may have believed the feast was ancient and observed in the early fourteenth century. Henry Ansgar Kelly, *Chaucer and the Cult of Saint Valentine* (Leiden: Brill, 1986), pp.40–1. In correspondence 14 February 2000, Kelly writes 'I still think that the *Parliament of Fowls* was written for 3 May 1382, constituting the first of the series of Valentine Day/3 May anniversary tributes to Richard II and Anne of Bohemia, celebrating their betrothal on 3 May 1381.'

18 'Friday, subject to Venus, is widely held to be unlucky and a day when evil influences are at work – especially if it happens to be the thirteenth day of the month … [The] prejudice against the number thirteen is of obscure origins, as evidence exists of it in Roman civilisation, long before Christ and the Last Supper at which thirteen dined and one betrayed Him.' David Pickering, *Dictionary of Superstitions* (London: Cassell, 1995), pp. 80, 258–9.

19 Shakespeare heightens the lovers' desperate, scant hours together by moving the death of Tybalt to the afternoon between the marriage of Romeo and Juliet, and their night of consummation.

20 Da Porto, p. 27; Bandello, p. 384; Boaistuau, p. 85; Brooke, line 1046.

21 Catholic Encyclopedia, vii.697.

22 Evans, p. 21.

23 See Granger Ryan and Helmut Ripperger (trs.), *The Golden Legend of Jacobus de Voragine*, (New York: Arno Press, 1941), pp. 551–3.

24 On 31 July the sun set at Verona *ca* 7:40 p.m., and twilight ended *ca* 9:40 p.m.

25 Did Shakespeare recognize that allowing Juliet to wake between two dead men (Romeo and Tybault) might too closely parallel Peter's circumstances in Acts 12?

26 Da Porto, p. 29; Bandello, p. 387; Boiastuau, p. 94; Brooke, line 1882.

27 In production Old Capulet has struck his daughter, e.g., Arkangel Complete Shakespeare, *Romeo and Juliet*, Penguin Audio Books (New York: Penguin, 1998).

28 The thirteenth Sunday after Trinity in the Anglican reckoning.

29 Leduc and Baudot, *The Liturgy of the Roman Missal* (London: Burns Oates and Washbourne, n.d.) p. 400

30 *OED*. The banns were a 'proclamation or public notice given in church of an intended marriage, in order that those who know of any impediment thereto may have opportunity of lodging objections.'

31 In context '*espousailles*' means the day on which Juilliette must pledge her troth, perhaps by formal *verba de futuro* declaration followed by the signing of a marriage contract. It is necessary for Julliette to take desperate measures before the espousal which was then a binding agreement, in force nearly equivalent to actual marriage vows.

32 In the pre-Gregorian reform era the sun rose at 6:00 a.m. in Verona in mid-September, and first light (daybreak) occurred some two hours earlier.

33 Da Porto, p. 37; Bandello, p. 398; Boiastuau, p. 107; Brooke, lines 2511–12.

34 But J.W. Hales in *Quarterly Review* 134 (1873) saw a link with Chaucer's *Troilus and Criseyde*, v, 1163–9. Evans, p. 176.n.1.

35 Evans, p. 46.

36 Evans, p. 47–8.

37 Moore believes that da Porto borrowed the device of dying by holding one's breath from Boccaccio, *Il Decamerone*, Fourth Day, Eighth Tale, p. 26n.24.

38 '*Et ayant tiré la dague que Rhomeo avoit ceincte à son costé, se donna de la poincte plusieurs coups au travers du cueur, disant d'une voix foible et piteuse: "Ha, mort, fin de malheur et commencement de felicité, tu sois la vien venue: ne crains à ma vie, de peur que mon esprit ne travaille à trouver celuy de mon Rhomeo entre tant de morts."*' (Boiastuau, p. 113).

39 After consultation the magistrates determine to set Pierre free, banish Julliette's nurse for concealing the clandestine marriage, and hang the apothecary. Laurens ends his days in '*un petit hermitage à deux mille pres de Veronne*' (p. 118–19). Likewise in Brooke (lines 2987–93).

40 A pungent speech in an age when predestination versus free will was hotly debated.

41 Romeo made a good act of contrition and Juliette had been shrived on her third visit to Laurens.

SIX

Disrobing images:
Shakespeare rewrites the Holy Ghost

Even William Shakespeare's earliest plays reveal a distancing of his mind from the religious dogmas of his age. In what may be his first drama, *3 Henry VI* (1591),[1] Shakespeare parodied the Crucifixion. Though his principal historical source was Hall's *Chronicle*,[2] Shakespeare exploited Holinshed's account of the persecution and assassination of York:

> Some write that the duke was taken alive, and in derision caused to stand upon a molehill, on whose head they put a garland in steed of a crowne, which they had fashioned and made of sedges or bulrushes; and having so crowned him with that garland, they kneeled downe afore him (as the Jewes did unto Christ) in scorne, saieng to him; Haile king without rule, haile king without heritage, haile duke and prince without people or possessions.[3]

York's tormentors humiliated their captive by performing a satire of the scourging of Christ by Roman soldiers in Matthew 27 and Mark 15. Though Shakespeare certainly knew the relevant passages of Scripture he could hardly have adapted one or both to the stage whole-cloth; after 1589 London's playwrights and theaters were constrained by a Star Chamber order which prohibited players from taking upon themselves 'to handle … matters of Divinytie and of State unfitt to be suffred.'[4] In this censorious atmosphere representations of the Sacraments – including the marriage ceremony – and overtly political plays from *Isle of Dogs* (1597) to *A Game at Chess* (1624) – were driven from the stage. The ban was sufficiently stifling for one modern scholar to conclude that 'no play of consequence devoted to an avowedly religious subject was written for public performance by professional actors after Marlowe's *Dr Faustus* [*ca* 1588].'[5] As I will indicate, this conclusion is far from safe; William Shakespeare not only handled religious subjects, he examined and interrogated the dogmas of the received religions vigorously, tenaciously and phlegmatically.

In Shakespeare's rendering of the murder of York his harridan Margaret
commands,

> Come make him [York] stand upon this molehill here,
> That wrought at mountains with outstretched arms
> Yet parted but the shadow with his hand.

(1.3.68–70)

Apparently, Shakespeare's diction was sufficiently equivocal to satisfy (or scam)
the Revels Office censors;[6] York's 'outstretched arms' *could* allude to his defeated
military forces or his political overreaching. But Margaret's words powerfully
conjure the helpless Christ on His cross as York mounts his molehill-Golgotha.
'Wrought at mountains' recalls Saint Mark's metaphor for the power of faith
(11:23). The 'parted … shadow' recalls the rending of the temple veil at the
moment of Christ's mortal death (Matt. 27:51, Mk. 15:38, Lk. 23:45). By
gleaning from disparate passages, Shakespeare makes his version of York's death
scene more subtle than Holinshed and enormously more sophisticated.
Whereas Holinshed described a single moment in York's passion, Shakespeare's
version economically dispenses Jesus Christ's Crucifixion, His teaching on the
power of faith, and the fragile evidence of His godhead. When Shakespeare
wrote this passage he was, perhaps, twenty-seven years old.

These three lines tell us more about Shakespeare than they tell us about
Margaret and York. No writer can manipulate Scripture with such facility and
economy unless he possesses an absolute mastery of the New Testament. And
no writer could dispense Scripture with such phlegm without a certain
contempt for dogmatic interpretation of holy writ.

While the principal endeavor of this chapter is the identification and
enumeration of a constellation of literary devices Shakespeare adopted (or invented) for the purpose of publicly interrogating banned theological topics in
his plays, insofar as a playwright's tactics must be inseparable from his
language – and his language inseparable from ideas – this chapter will also
offer to interpret certain responses to. Scripture, doctrine, and dogma in
Shakespeare's plays.

Beginning with *3 Henry VI* Shakespeare assembled a toolbox of subversive
devices which enabled him to circumvent the Star Chamber decree of 1589.
The simplest of these devices was equivocation, as in Margaret's stage direction
for the slaughter of York. Another rudimentary device was the intentional
misquotation of Scripture. For example, in *Richard III* (1592–3) the usurper
declares on the eve of the battle of Bosworth 'the King's name is a tower of
strength' (5.3.12). But it is not the king's name but God's which is the 'strong
tower' of Proverbs 18:10. Richard's perverse misquotation foreshadows his
overthrow at the hands of the suitably pious Richmond – who, by the way,

impiously recognizes in himself God's 'minister of chastisement' at 5.5.66 – a play on Romans 13:4.[7]

Of course, the efficacy of misquotation as a mode of theological discourse depends on the audience's and playwright's mutual knowledge of an absent but familiar touchstone text. In the York and Richard instances, the touchstone is the Bible, a particularly serviceable text since Elizabethans high-and-low knew the Scriptures far better than we do. Statute required them to attend church weekly or suffer fines (as Shakespeare's father did), and their Books of Common Prayer and Bibles incorporated rubrics which prescribed Scriptural readings for each day of the year. That being said, easy access to Scripture in English was still something of a novelty when Elizabeth came to the throne in 1558. Henry VIII's decree of 5 September 1538 had, for the first time, authorized the translation, printing, and dissemination of the Bible in English. Prior to that date, the making, owning, or even reading Scripture in vernacular English had been banned by Archbishop Arundel's 'Oxford Constitutions' (1409). Those who persisted could be punished by pain of excommunication (followed by a singularly unpleasant examination for heresy) and, for persistent readers, the worst kind of death by burning. As late as 1535, the translator of the first printed New Testament in English, William Tyndale – arguably the greatest scholar in Europe – had suffered an horrific imprisonment at Vilvorde prison and an ignominious death; perhaps as a concession to educated opinion Tyndale's persecutors (mercifully) strangled him before burning his body on 6 October 1536.[8] Shakespeare chiseled a minor monument to Tyndale in *All is True* (aka *Henry VIII*, 1612–13). The translator's famous last words in Foxe's *Acts and Monuments* (1563) – 'Lord, open the king of England's eyes'[9] – are echoed by Shakespeare's ahistorical Chamberlain at 2.2.40–1: 'Heaven will one day open the king's eyes....' Shakespeare corrected 'Lord' to 'Heaven' to satisfy the Jacobean *Act to Restrain Abuses of Players* (1606) for 'the preventing and avoiding of the greate Abuse of the holy Name of God in Stageplayes, etc.'[10]

By 1597 the Bible and the popular almanacs were the most widely disseminated printed documents in England; every church was required to own and display the Scriptures along with John Foxe's monumental *Acts and Monuments*. It is certainly safe to infer that Shakespeare intended Richard III's misquotation of Proverbs 18 to be transparent to his many of his auditors. These examples of Shakespeare's rudimentary ploys – casting York as the Christ-like victim of the malevolent (foreigner) Margaret – exhibiting Richard III as an insolent hijacker of Scripture only moments before he dies by the hand of the patriarch of the reigning Tudor line – could hardly fail to be construed as political statements in London in the 1590s. But with a Tudor safely on the throne, these were safe sentiments; Shakespeare's devices are accordingly transparent.

Another of Shakespeare's devices for recondite discourse was calculated to be opaque to censors as well as the great mass of playgoers – and to reveal the playwright's *unsafe* sentiments to but the wiser few. This device was the intentional disordering of information which challenged the wiser sort to synthesize information presented in an unconventional sequence. In a primitive form this tactic makes its first appearance in the opening lines of *2 Henry IV* (as I will demonstrate below) which entails that as early as 1598 Shakespeare perceived his audience as segmented. He had recognized the possibility that speeches, scenes, even entire plays could convey an exoteric dramatic experience to the playhouse as a whole, while the playwright conducted a concurrent esoteric discourse with a small and knowledgeable coterie.

There's an elegant example of this disordering tactic in *Hamlet* (1600–1). Shakespeare requires his auditors to wait until the Gravedigger-Clown's revelations at 5.1.139–44 – almost *four hours* into his play – before they have sufficient information to deduce that, thirty years before the action began, Hamlet was born on the very day Old Fortinbras was overcome by Old Hamlet who, on the day of that combat *and* young Hamlet's birth, wore the armor Old Hamlet's Ghost bears when he confronts his son on the parapets of Elsinore (in 1.4).[11] I will show in a later chapter that this reckoning proves Hamlet's illegitimacy.

An earlier instance of the same ruse – in *Julius Caesar* (1599) – begins with a pair of Tribunes and ends with a parody of the Catholic ritual of Creeping to the Cross. As the play opens the Tribunes attempt to disabuse Rome's tradesmen of their slavish adulation of Caesar. When their castigating fails, Flavius hatches a plan to deprive Caesar's images of honors. He tells Murellus,

> Go you down that way towards the Capitol.
> This way will I. Disrobe the images,
> If you do find them decked with ceremonies.
> *Murellus* May we do so?
> You know it is the feast of Lupercal.
> *Flavius* It is no matter, let no images
> Be hung with Caesars trophies.
>
> (1.1.64–70)[12]

Shakespeare is relying on Plutarch, who recorded in his *Life of Caesar* that 'there were set up images of *Caesar* in the city with Diadeames upon their heades, like kinges.'[13] But Shakespeare also knew that Plutarch's *Life of Antony* mentions *only one* trophy and *one disrobing* of an image: that was the laurel wreath Caesar refused to accept from Antony which 'was afterwards put upon the head of one of *Caesars* statues ... which one of the Tribunes pluckt [off] ...'[14]

In contriving his Tribunes' mischief Shakespeare has merged and altered his sources. Broadly speaking, Shakespeare never alters a source by accident, but only to a purpose. Sometimes that purpose is dramatic – as when he compresses seventeen years of the tyrannous reign of the historical Macbeth into what seems a matter of days, thereby enduing the onstage action with the speed and momentum of a bullet-train. But on other occasions Shakespeare altered a source to enable his wiser sort to deduce from the discrepancy between source and playtext a secondary or tertiary meaning, one which might be forbidden free expression under prevailing law.

For example, in contradiction of his dual sources for *Julius Caesar*, Shakespeare's images of Caesar are not crowned with diadems but 'decked' with 'trophies'; the Tribunes 'disrobe' a number of these images. When Caska later describes the crime for which the Tribunes have been punished, Shakespeare reveals that these 'trophies' are not laurel wreaths but ahistorical 'scarves': 'Murellus and Flavius, for pulling scarves off Caesar's images, are put to silence' (1.2.285–6). Auditors who could follow Shakespeare's *intentionally* obscure trail of details could deduce that the 'trophies' decking Caesar's images are scarves – and, given this information, it did not require any great leap of imagination to supply the color of Caesar's scarves: *purple*. From Plutarch, Shakespeare and other Elizabethans knew that Julius Caesar had been uniquely entitled by the Senate to wear purple in perpetuity; no doubt, the actor William Shakespeare wore such a robe when he entered upon the Globe stage on the Summer Solstice in 1599 in the character of Caesar at the head of a religious procession on one of the most sacred of all Roman holy days, the Lupercal, a feast of purification.[15] He also wore purple at his death; as Shakespeare-Caesar prepares to leave for the Capitol on the Ides of March he calls out, 'Give me my robe, for I will go' (2.2.107).

Not incidentally, we can deduce that Shakespeare played Caesar (as he did Polonius in *Hamlet*) from a nexus of performers' inside jokes in these texts. When Caesar reminds Antony to touch the barren Calphurnia during the race, Antony replies: 'When Caesar says 'Do this', it is performed' (1.2.10), a smile at a playwright's godlike power to order his actors to play. Moments later, Cassius complains that Caesar 'bade the Romans Mark him, / and write his speeches in their books' (1.2.125–6) – which the historical Caesar never did but an Elizabethan playwright did routinely. When Polonius tells Hamlet 'I did enact Julius Caesar. / I was killed i'th'Capitol. Brutus killed me' (3.2.91–2)[16] the circle is complete – and very funny to those in the know – since Polonius-Shakespeare is recalling his stage-death to Hamlet-Burbage-Brutus, who also slew him. We know the latter joke *must* be a glance at Shakespeare's *Julius Caesar;* only in Shakespeare's play is Caesar killed in the Capitol. In Plutarch, the dictator was slain in Pompey's Theater.

But Shakespeare's *Julius Caesar* scarf gambit doesn't end with the color purple. The Lupercal was the Romans' spring feast of purification. In Catholic

Europe – as in England prior to the Reformation – statues draped in purple scarves were a familiar sight during the Catholic feast of purification, Passiontide. Images of the saints and the Cross were enrobed in purple on Palm Sunday, then ceremoniously uncovered on Good Friday, the day of Christ's death. The unveiling ceremony, familiarly known as Creeping to the Cross, climaxes with the disrobing of the crucifix. The ritual is performed in this manner: parishioners and clergy kneel and three times chant *Venite adoremus*. Then the principal celebrant – *barefoot* – kneels and kisses the Cross.[17] Shakespeare's Brutus will kneel and kiss the purple-robed Caesar on the morning of his murder: 'I kiss thy hand, but not in flattery, Caesar' (3.1.52). A moment later Caesar sneers, 'Doth not Brutus *bootlesse* kneel?' (1285 [my emphasis]).[18] With this luminous *double-entendre* on 'bootlesse' Shakespeare completes his parody of Creeping to the Cross. Appropriately enough, Shakespeare found his cue for this elaborate parody in an anomaly in Julius Caesar's antiquated Julian calendar which prevailed in England. From their reading of the best-selling *Legenda Aurea*, Elizabethans knew that Christ died on Good Friday and, furthermore, that the date of His death was 25 March AD 33.[19] Since England's Julian calendar was ten days behind the Gregorian, the 25 March Gregorian fell on the English 15 March Julian – the Ides of March – the date of Caesar's death in Plutarch as in Shakespeare's play.

Since there has been such a massive effort in recent years to identify Shakespeare as a recusant Catholic, I should note here that his parody of Passiontide's purple scarves and bootless Brutus creeping to Divus Julius may be the most persuasive evidence in any of the plays of Shakespeare's Catholic experience. I believe it impossible for a writer who had not actually witnessed the Creeping to the Cross to create such a nimble, edgy, meticulous parody. These passages convince me Shakespeare was an eyewitness to the Catholic Good Friday Mass perhaps more than once, perhaps many times. But this inference does not entail – or even imply – that Shakespeare kept the Catholic faith when he wrote *Julius Caesar* in 1599. Quite the contrary.

One cannot receive Shakespeare's manhandling of purple scarves and cross-creeping as anything but hard-headed debunking. The historical Julius Caesar was for twenty-odd years *Pontifex Maximus* of the Roman religion; Sir Thomas North, in his *Plutarch*, everywhere translates this addition as 'Bishoppe of Rome,'[20] an English pejorative for the pope at least since Henry VIII published *The Ecclesiastical Licenses Act* in 1534 (25 Henry VIII, c. 21). I have no doubt that, when Shakespeare-Caesar made his entrance upon stage, in addition to his purple robe he carried a bishop's crook and wore a mitre, as the historical Caesar had. Shakespeare presented a dumb-show Bishoppe of Rome. In a later chapter on *Othello* I will demonstrate that Shakespeare also debunks the Catholic dogmas of virginity and merit.

The instances of Shakespeare's recondite theological discourse so far enumerated have, for the most part, escaped the notice of commentators. Even the all-seeing Samuel Johnson and indefatigable Edmond Malone either failed to detect these esoterica or were too discreet to report them. So a word of apology for past oversights may be warranted.

Modern-day scholars, who imagine they live in an era of academic freedom and open, uncensored debate, have lost the appetite for digging out recondite levels of discourse in drama, art, and literature. So have modern audiences. Perhaps this is because, nowadays, there are few social or legal strictures other than the libel laws which compel a contemporary artist to resort to subterfuge in order to express views on controversial subjects. Like Archimedes' lever, so-called 'Freedom of Speech' has been employed to pry away the bans of law, tradition, and decency which have shielded taboo subjects, institutions, and public figures from the roughhousing of discontented writers. This is another respect in which the sixteenth-century English were utterly unlike us. In Shakespeare's era, free-speaking as well as access to printed documents – including even Scripture – was fiercely controlled by censorious civil and ecclesiastical authorities. As a consequence, Elizabethans were masters at reading between the lines. They were also heirs of the *Quadrata* tradition (then and now lively in Catholic seminaries) which taught Christians to receive the words of Jesus, the Apostles, and the Holy Ghost as symbols, signs, analogies, metaphors, topologies, and ciphers. Though the Lutherans disclaimed the *Quadrata* method and argued there was nothing arcane or symbolic about the writings of the Holy Ghost, the habit of discovering as many as four meanings in a Gospel passage, tract, sermon – or, for that matter, in a play – was nothing so alien to Elizabethans as to us. Besides, we have testamentary evidence that Shakespeare's wiser sort were keenly aware that recondite levels of discourse could (and should) be retrieved through close scrutiny of his plays. This is the subtext of Hemminges' and Condell's conspicuous admonition in the head-pages of the First Folio. Shakespeare's 'Friends' now being long dead, we must teach ourselves anew to read him closely – or neither shall we understand him.

Shakespeare's most sophisticated tactics of subversion relied on rubrics of the Elizabethan liturgy which rigidly linked verses of the Old and New Testament with particular dates in the calendar. How many individuals obeyed these rubrics is a matter of speculation. But historians accept that large numbers of Shakespeare's contemporaries, even those illiterate, committed to memory whole books of the Bible or even entire Testaments. Illiterates also had non-lexical means for remembering the numerous dates of holy days famous and obscure; in addition to practicing the *computus manualis,* they rote-learned nonsense rhymes such as the *Cisio Ianus,* in which each doggerel verse enumerated the holy days of a single month.[21]

In *Othello* (1603) Shakespeare seized on this mutual knowledge of psalmody to identify the date of the Venetians' arrival at Cyprus and Othello's revels. Iago's drinking song – the only song in the play unknown in a prior form – appears to be Shakespeare's invention:

> And let me the cannikin clink.
> And let me the cannikin clink.
> A soldier's a man.
> O, man's life's but a span,
> Why then let a soldier drink!

> (2.3.65–9)

A 'span' was a measure of extension equal to the width of an outspread human hand.[22] Iago's ditty is what Elizabethans called a 'jig' – a metrical rendering of a Psalm – in this instance of Psalm 39:6 : 'Behold, thou has made my days as an handbreadth ...' In the Book of Common Prayer, the Psalm about the handy palm was prescribed for reading on the 8th day of the month. In a subsequent chapter I will demonstrate that 1603 is the *annus praesens* of *Othello;* in that year 8 March – the day on which the Venetians land at Cyprus – was Shrove Tuesday according to the Julian calendar which prevailed in Cyprus as it did in England.

A similar calendrical marker is Hamlet's 'What a piece of work is man ...' (2.2.305–10). This speech is a refashioning of Psalm 8, which begins 'What is man,' which the Book of Common Prayer calendared for reading on the first day of the month. In a subsequent chapter I will demonstrate that this speech identifies the arrival of Rosencrantz, Guildernstern and the traveling players with the evening of first day of the month (February) – which places the playing of 'The Mousetrap' and the purification scene in Gertrude's closet ('go not to my uncle's bed. / Assume a virtue if you have it not' 3.4.150–1) on the Feast of Candlemas, 2 February, that holy day of another mother's purification upon which plays had traditionally been presented in England.[23]

Shakespeare began writing parodies of Scripture with *3 Henry VI*. Three years later, in *The Comedy of Errors* (1594) he created a far more elaborate parody of the myth of the cloistering of Saint Mary at Ephesus following the Crucifixion of Jesus. In the climax of the play, Emilia, Shakespeare's Lady Abbess, declares she has languished long in expectation of the rebirth of sons believed lost at sea:

> Thirty-three years have I but gone in travail
> Of you, my sons, and till this present hour
> My heavy burden ne'er delivered.

> (5.1.400–2)

Is it not a bitter wit that turns the lifespan of Jesus on its head and stages a mother's pregnancy *after* parturition? But the real legerdemain behind

Shakespeare's trope is that the legendary Mary who lived out her life at Ephesus *was not* Blessed Virgin Mary. It was Mary Magdalene.[24] And she was courted – and perhaps even married – to that equally legendary wanderer of the Aegean, Saint John Evangelist.[25] Like Shakespeare's Egeon, Aegean John was an émigré upon whom a dreadful sentence fell. In the *Legenda Aurea*, Elizabethans could read how, for preaching the Gospel at Ephesus, John was banished by Emperor Domitian (*ca* AD 90).[26] After supposedly writing his Apocalypse in rocky solitude on Patmos, a northern isle of the Cyclades some hundred miles from the Turkish coast, John re-crossed the Aegean to Ephesus, where he seems to have made a career of raising the dead and a living spinning twigs and sand into gold. Mary Magdalene was there, too, with her brother Lazarus whom Jesus had raised from the dead in John 11. Recognizing this aggregation of death-defiers finally recovers Shakespeare's motive for relocating Plautus' *Menaechmi* from Epidamnum to Ephesus (which *prima facie* seems like changing one's name from Smith to Jones). It also explains the constellation of allusions to birth, rebirth, and baptism ('gossips' feast') which dot Act Five of *Errors*. Shakespeare's Ephesus is the locus where the Sun (Solinus) rules,[27] where the dream of perfect love comes true (for Antipholus Syracusan at 5.1.376), and where the two halves of man rejoin, fulfilling the Book of Common Prayer's promise to all believers lost at sea that souls and bodies will be reunited at the second coming of Christ.

This being so, Shakespeare's Ephesus must be Heaven. But it is a heaven out of a Christmas pantomime – chockablock with mad coincidences, hairbreadth escapes, impossible dénouements, a hooker with a heart (and ring) of gold, and a dreaded-but-impotent Doctor Pinch who Patricks a leaky purgatory (cellar). Indeed, Ephesus is as rife with happy endings as the King of Britain's court at the instant which began 'the time of universal peace,' that *sine qua non* for the coming of the Messiah in Isaiah 39:8–40:3 – which Shakespeare glanced at in *Antony and Cleopatra* (4.6.5) and then actually performed onstage before a live audience at 5.5.461–3 of *Cymbeline* amidst a barrage of happy endings that would embarrass a Hardy Boys mystery.

The thread that weaves its way through all these instances of Shakespeare's theological discourse is a well-informed, well-formulated skepticism toward the received dogmas and documents of religion, canonical and acanonical. The ease and dexterity with which Shakespeare subverts Scripture, defrocks saints, and juggles the massive cornerstones of faith entails both a refined knowledge of the sacred texts (and their attendant, abundant potpourri of popular legends) and a keen, dissatisfied intelligence.

To find exactly these qualities collocated in a writer of Shakespeare's era is hardly surprising. The infant Will Shakespeare was born (1564) when Elizabeth's religious settlement (1559) was only just taking hold in England.

Shakespeare was not the only English person to recognize Elizabeth's contrivance wasn't a religious settlement at all but a political coup. The unbelovéd Act of Uniformity (1559) was merely the latest reformulation of a long series of draconian laws – going back at least to the time of Constantine – designed to impose this-or-that monolithic religion on the state and everyone in it. Yes, Elizabeth and her churchmen made accommodation to her loyal Catholic subjects of conscience. But the Act of Uniformity was an only slightly more civilized version of *De Haeretico Carburendo* (1401) which had been so enthusiastically exploited by Elizabeth's hallucenant half-sister, Mary, and their egomaniacal boorish father.

Had Shakespeare's own father, John, conformed throughout his life to the established religion *en vogue*, he would have been born and lived Catholic until 1533, become a Henrican 1533–47, turned Protestant from 1547 to 1553, returned to Catholicism during 1553–58, and been reborn (again) as a Protestant from 1559 to his death *ca* 1601. In other words, in sixteenth-century England the crackers and wine were just that for fifty-three years. But they were the blood and very flesh of Christ on His Cross for forty-seven years.

Not only Shakespeare's father but nearly all the leading prelates of Tudor England were sooner or later swinged with this crux. Even such great figures as Cranmer and Gardiner at one time or other served religion *à la mode*. Saint Thomas More played the hack propagandist with *The History of Richard III* (written *ca* 1513, published 1557) and obfuscated the meanings of *agape, charis, ekklesia, metanoeo, poterion* and *presbuteros* in his *Dialogue Concerning Heresies* (1529).[28] To find an exemplar of untainted conscience Elizabethans had to ponder the deaths and lives of martyrs, which perhaps accounts for the popularity of John Foxe's martyrology, by law ubiquitous, but also widely admired and read. Somewhere in this compost of *cuius regio, eius religio* William Shakespeare's skepticism took root. And its early phase reached its climax in a defining moment in *The Merchant of Venice* (1596). In Act Four, the ducal court is seated. Portia enters disguised as Balthazar, namesake of that pagan whose epiphanous discovery of Christ brought down the wrath of Herod on the children of Israel. Among the assembled Venetians, Shylock must have been more than conspicuous to the audience in his 'Jewish gabardine' and pointed Jewish hat. But Shakespeare's Portia surveys the assembly and delivers a stunning indictment of sanctimonious Venetian society: 'Which is the merchant here? and which the Jew?' (4.1.171). Then again, every great work of literature is an indictment of society.

In his second historical trilogy, *1–2 Henry IV* (1597–8) and *Henry V* (early 1599),[29] Shakespeare ruthlessly interrogated the lip-servers of England's shreds-and-patches state religion. Two contrasting aspects of Henrys father-and-son drew the playwright. In Henry Bolingbroke that quality was prevarication; he was peerless in saying one thing and doing another.[30] His son, Henry of Monmouth, inherited these skills. But Hal's fascination for Shakespeare lay in the prince's variegated epiphanies and conversions.[31] No commentator has recognized that Shakespeare's Hal-Henry V undergoes *two* epiphanies and *two* conversions – one feigned, the other one real (of which more below).[32] With the writing of his Henriad during 1597–99 Shakespeare's theological discourse – of necessity – sublimated to a new and more rarified level. In this trilogy the target of Shakespeare's pen is no longer religious dogma *solus* as it was in *The Comedy of Errors*. In the Henriad Shakespeare takes up his pen against religion-*cum*-politics, a writer's game infinitely more perilous.

In 1597 Shakespeare commences to write for two audiences; in the same playhouse – at the same time – he produces both an exoterically entertaining play for casual playgoers *and* simultaneously engages in tense esoteric discourse with a handful of *cognoscenti*, Gabriel Harvey's wiser sort. Shakespeare continues to use (and intentionally misuse) familiar touchstone texts. To the casual playgoer (and censor), Shakespeare's Henriad appeared to rehash Holinshed's hoary history, long in print and widely read, hardly liable to the label of subversive document. But Shakespeare makes minute alterations to Holinshed's tale – recisions noticeable only to the keen-eared and – eyed – such as shuffling the deathbed encounter between Henry and Hal from the room called 'Jerusalem' to the king's bed chamber. This is the physical equivalent of Richard III misquoting Scripture on the eve of Bosworth. In the tension between source and playtext of *2 Henry 4* the wiser sort could discern Shakespeare's mordant assessment of Henry Bolingbroke's life and death. A death in 'Jerusalem' would have ironically fulfilled Henry *pere's* erstwhile pledge to lead a crusade (*1H4* 1.1.22–6), and would have figuratively placed his death on the holy soil where Jesus walked and bled. Instead, Shakespeare gives Henry a death amidst his dirty linen.

But to his familiar undertext – Holinshed – Shakespeare conjoined a second, far less well-read text: Niccolò Machiavelli's *Il Principe* (written *ca* 1513, published 1557). Though Shakespeare's Henrys pre-deceased the Italian by generations, the playwright fashions father and son as Machiavelli-devotees. In so doing, Shakespeare engages a familiar tactic of esoteric discourse: anachronism. This long-established theatrical convention invited an audience to relate the onstage action set in a remote time and place to contemporary events in England.[33] In a play written *ca* 1410, the First Shepherd of the Wakefield Cycle's *Second Shephard's Play* laments,

> we simple shepherds that walk on the moor,
> Are soon by richer hands thrust out of door;
> No wonder as it stands, if we be poor,
> For the tilth of our lands lies as fallow as the floor,
> As you know

> We are so lamed,
> Overtaxed and maimed,
> And cruelly tamed,
> By our gentlemen foe.[34]

Though this scene is set in Bethlehem on the night of the birth of Christ, fifteenth-century English auditors could hardly have failed to recognize an assault on the then-contemporary Enclosures Controversy. Likewise, in the opening lines of *1 Henry IV* Shakespeare announces the Machiavellian basis of the Bolingbrokes' piety as the usurper-king declares

> So shaken as we are, so wan with care,
> Find we a time for frighted peace to pant
> And breathe short-winded accents of new broils
> To be commenced in strands afar remote.
>
> (1.1.1–4)

This is double-speak. We are to have peace *and* new wars in foreign destinations. Henry seems to promise an immediate crusade:

> Therefore, friends,
> As far as to the sepulchre of Christ –
> Whose soldier now, under whose blessèd cross
> We are impressèd and engaged to fight –
> Forthwith a power of English shall we levy,
> Whose arms were moulded in their mothers' womb
> To chase these pagans in those holy fields
> Over whose acres walked those blessèd feet
> Which fourteen hundred years ago were nailed,
> For our advantage, on the bitter cross.
>
> (1.1.18–28)

With words pious and picturesque Henry sets the stage for a glorious quest to wrest the holy land from the hated infidels. But Henry's next breath produces an abrupt volte-face:

> But this our purpose now is twelve month old,
> And bootless 'tis to tell you we will go.
> Therefore we meet not now.
>
> (1.1.28–30)

One moment we are to have a crusade – and the next, not have it. An instant later we learn that reports of several battles had arrived *the previous night* (1.1.36ff); this eradicates any lingering doubt that Henry's pietistic promise of foreign adventures was anything more than stagecraft.[35] Crusadoes, not crusades, are Henry's immediate object.

With his usurper-king's linguistic sleight-of-hand Shakespeare is preemptively staking out the throughline of his Henriad: the road to Jerusalem not taken. This tactic – announcing a play's theme in its opening lines – was another familiar Elizabethan stage convention. No glossy programs pronouncing a play's 'argument' greeted an audience entering the playhouse. As a consequence, a playwright often opened a play by announcing what M.M. Mahood calls a 'governing idea' of the drama. The opening line of *Measure for Measure* bluntly declares the intention, 'Of government the properties to unfold' (1.1.3). *Lear* opens with the theme of fickle favoritism: '*Kent*. I thought the King had more affected / the Duke of Albany than Cornwall. *Gloucester*. It did always seem so to us; / but now, in the division of the kingdom …' (1.1.1–3). *Hamlet* proceeds from a simple-seeming but all-consuming question of identity: 'Who's there?' (1.1.1). By opening *1 Henry IV* with an exemplar of Bolingbroke's feigned piety Shakespeare articulates the governing idea which compasses his entire Henriad. These three plays are a long interrogation of what Mahood called 'a question … which can only be answered mimetically,' that is, via the performance of a play. The question Shakespeare is asking in his Henriad was, perhaps the great question of his age. And it is one he found in Machiavelli: *In What Mode Should Faith be Kept by Princes?*[36] Under this chapter head the Italian wrote

> one sees by experience in our times that the princes who have done great things are those *who have taken little account of faith* and have known how to get around men's brains with their astuteness, and in the end they have overcome those who have founded themselves on loyalty.[37]

This is the question Machiavelli poses in *Il Principe* which Shakespeare answers mimetically in his Henriad. As Henry and his northern earls fall to squabbling over their ransom-rights in prisoners held by Hotspur Percy (1.3), we are abruptly thrust into a commerce which reduces the value of human life to shillings and pence. We are worlds away from a crusade to liberate the Holy Sepulcher. And yet – as Shakespeare and his wiser auditors knew from their reading of Holinshed – both Henrys *have* begun a journey to Jerusalem. Henry Bolingbroke is destined to die in Jerusalem, as readers of Robert Fabyan's *Chronicle* (1516) and Holinshed knew.[38] It was in the Jerusalem chamber of Westminster Abbey that these sources laid the bizarre scene in which Hal lifts the crown from his father seemingly dead, only to have Henry revive long enough to chastise him. In depicting this incident in *2 Henry 4* 4.2, Shakespeare removes the scene to the king's bedchamber. Only at its conclusion does Henry ask to be carried to Jerusalem to die (4.2.365–9). Scholars have noticed that by this tactic Shakespeare voids Henry's Christlike resurrection in Jerusalem in his source.[39]

Shakespeare also characterizes the outwardly affable Hal by exploiting touchstone Machiavelli:

> Sirrah, I am sworn brother to
> a leash of drawers, and can call them all by their
> christen names, as 'Tom', 'Dick', and 'Francis'. They
> take it already, upon their salvation, that though I be
> but Prince of Wales yet I am the king of courtesy, and
> tell me flatly I am no proud jack like Oldcastle, but a
> Corinthian, a lad of mettle, a good boy by the Lord,
> so they call me; and when I am King of England I shall
> command all the good lads in Eastcheap ...
> To conclude, I am so good a proficient in one
> quarter of an hour that I can drink with any tinker in
> his own language during my life.
>
> (*1H4* 2.5.6–19)

Shakespeare's undertext for this speech is the epistle dedicatory of *Il Principe*. 'For just as those who sketch landscapes place themselves down in the plain to consider the nature of mountains and high places and to consider the nature of low places place themselves high atop mountains, similarly, to know well the nature of peoples one needs to be prince, and to know well the nature of princes *one needs to be of the people*' [my emphasis].[40]

To emphasize the Bolingbrokes' affinity for Machiavelli, Shakespeare contrives a scene in which Henry IV lectures Hal on Machiavelli's precept '*What a Prince Should Do to Be Held in Esteem*' by the people; Machiavelli writes that the prince should 'give rare examples of himself,'[41] which in Bolingbroke's mouth becomes

> My presence, like a robe pontifical,
> Ne'er seen but wondered at; and so my state,
> Seldom, but sumptuous, showed like a feast
> And won by rareness such solemnity.
>
> (3.2.50–9)

As the audience already knew, Henry Bolingbroke might have saved his breath; in guile his heir precedes him. Below stairs in an Eastcheap public house Hal has already declared his 'loose behaviour' a disguise, and predicts that when he throws it off

> My reformation, glitt'ring o'er my fault,
> Shall show more goodly and attract more eyes
> Than that which hath no foil to set it off.
> I'll so offend to make offence a skill,
> Redeeming time when men think least I will.
>
> (1.2.205–14)

'Reformation' and 'redeeming time' are heavy-handed clues to Shakespeare's undertext (he was still young), which is Saint Paul's injunction to Masters to treat their servants with respect: 'Walk in wisdom toward them that are without, redeeming the time. Let your speech be always with grace, seasoned with salt, that ye may know how ye ought to answer every man' (Col. 4:5–6). Hal has read both Machiavelli *and* Saint Paul – and has gleaned from both the same advice.

This speech marked the first appearance in the Shakespeare canon of a new tactic of theological discourse. Whereas in *3 Henry VI* (1592) Shakespeare borrowed details from the Crucifixion to comment on Margaret's murder of York, now in *1 Henry IV* (1596) Shakespeare inverts his device. Hal's borrowing of parallel advice from Machiavelli and Saint Paul is certainly a comment on the duplicity of Shakespeare's prince. *But it is also a comment on Paul.* And this moment marks a turning point in Shakespeare's skepticism toward the received documents of religion. No longer is he merely harnessing Scripture to comment on his characters; now, *he begins to enlist his characters to comment on Scripture.* By mid-1599, this tactic will blossom to full flower in *Julius Caesar.*[42] Before *2 Henry IV* ends the Prince's gift for knowing how to answer every man will work a fakir's miracle. In Act Five the newly anointed Henry V's magnanimity toward his brothers and the Lord Chief Justice (5.3) – the first (and false) of his two conversions – and his callous disavowal of Falstaff (5.5) coupled with his newfound modesty in speech – create in his new subjects the desired effect which his father commended to him: awe.[43]

Here one needs to recognize that Shakespeare's skepticism was not monolithic, but bifurcated. His attitude toward the *documents* of religion is evidenced by York's 'crucifixion,' his lampoon of Saints John Evangelist and Mary Magdalene in *Errors* along with his deadpan parody of the reunion of body with soul promised by the Book of Common Prayer. But like the Jesus of Matthew 23, Shakespeare was also deeply skeptical of *ostensibly religious men.* Henry V's Archbishop of Canterbury and Bishop of Ely are crass politicians who recognize that Hal's (apparent) conversion to goodness ironically threatens the privileges of the Church. Indeed, they dread a bill pending in Commons which would cost the clergy 'half of our possession' (1.1.8) were the young king to countenance it. They needn't worry; by dangling the glittering wealth of the church they distract Henry V from his pietistic reforms and excite him to bloody adventurism in France (1.1.78–82). Canterbury caps the offer with a preposterous explication of Henry's rights under Salic law (1.2.33–100) concluding, 'For in the Book of Numbers is it writ, "When the son dies, let the inheritance Descend unto the daughter."' This is another of Shakespeare's intentional misquotations of Scripture. The actual passage reads, 'If a man dye *and have no sonne*, then ye shall turne his inheritance unto his daughter' (Num. 27:8, [my emphasis]). The wiser sort could hardly have missed this trope and what it entails for Shakespeare's judgment of the character of Canterbury; the War of Roses had been fought over *this very principle* of inheritance. To the same equivocator, Shakespeare gives the memorable speech on divine order; in

Canterbury's dry mouth the parable of the bees (1.2.183–213) becomes an unmistakable send-up of the lesson 'Concerning Good Order' from the Book of Homilies, by statute declaimed in English churches three times each year.

Henry IV's momentary resurrection – pointedly *not* in Jerusalem – was a false resurrection. And the seeming epiphany this event produced in Hal was an equally false conversion. In the opening act of *Henry V* Shakespeare's Machiavellian hypocrite proclaims himself 'a Christian King' (1.1.242) while cheerfully enlisting as Canterbury's cat's-paw.[44] Henry leads a ragtag army into France. Horrifying bloodshed ensues. But events prove that Henry's principal endowment isn't soldiership. It's *language*. At Rouen, we have Fluellen's expert word that Henry's mines are improperly dug and 'not according to the disciplines of the war' (3.3.4–5). And Henry's siege proves futile; after his celebrated 'once more into the breech' oration (3.1.1–34) the English trumpet sounds not victory but retreat (3.3.33). In the aftermath, what Henry has failed to achieve by arms he merely (but grandiloquently) threatens (3.3.84–126). And he conquers the town by mere coincidence; the Governor capitulates after receiving word the Dauphin's forces are unready and unable to raise the siege (3.3.127–30). Minutes later, the king who subsidized his French exploits with the extorted wealth of the English Church condemns to death his ancient friend, Bardolph, for stealing a pyx from a French church. This is bitter, biting irony.

But there's more of Hal's flummery yet. Shakespeare knew from his reading of Holinshed (552) that the battle of Agincourt took place on 25 October, 'being then fridaie, and the feast of Crispine and Crispinian [two French saint], a day faire and fortunate to the English, but most sorrowfull and unluckie to the French.' On the prior night Henry first disguises himself, then reveals himself as an obfuscator who double-talks his common soldiers out of moral compass (4.1.85–184). Alone, apart, and wrapt in an old cloak, Henry cribs the Book of Common Prayer's rite of the Visitation of the Sick, bargaining chantries to God in return for a pardon from the guilt of his father: 'Not today, O Lord, O not today, think not upon the fault / My father made in compassing the crown, etc.' (4.1.286–302). In fact, Shakespeare mined two sources to produce this memorable speech. From the BCP he drew on 'Remember not, Lord, our iniquities nor the iniquities of our forefathers,' etc.[45] The other, previously unrecognized source of Henry's prayer on the night of the *twenty-fourth day* of October is the Old Testament book of Nehemiah, which begins with a startling reference to the date:

> Now in the *twenty and fourth day* of this month the children of Israel were assembled with fasting, and with sackclothes, and earth upon them. And the seed of Israel separated themselves from all strangers, and stood and confessed their sins, and the iniquities of their fathers.
>
> (Neh.9:1–2. [my emphasis])

Surely, it's no coincidence that Shakespeare gave Henry's prayer this particular shape on the night of the twenty-fourth day of October.

On the following morning Henry fought the battle of Agincourt; it was 25 October 1415, the feast day of Saints Crispin and Crispianus. And the outcome of the battle works a double-miracle. After Henry's savage order to murder the French prisoners – after the roll of the French dead is read aloud and the awesome scale of the English victory is known – Shakespeare's Henry *finally* experiences a true epiphany. The extraordinary moment comes as Exeter gasps, '''Tis wonderful' (4.8.112). In Shakespeare's lexicon, 'wonderful' implies something miraculous, as when Hamlet reflects upon his encounter with his father's ghost –'O wonderful!' (1.5.122) – or Pandolph detects God's hand sewing disarray among his English enemies (*King John* 3.4.178). In each instance 'wonderful' characterizes 'a deed performed or an event brought about by miraculous or supernatural power; a miracle.'[46] In at least one production of *Henry V* at the Royal Shakespeare Company the English powers went to their knees at the fall of Exeter's wonderful word. This concords with Holinshed's report (following Hall) that 'Henry caused 'his prelates and chapleins to sing this psalme: *In exitu Israel de Aegypto,* and commanded everie man to kneele downe on the ground at this verse: *Non nobis, Domine, no nobis, sed nomini tuo da gloriam.* Which done, he caused *Te Deum,* with certeine anthems to be soong.'[47] Rising, Shakespeare's Henry humbly declares 'God fought for us' and prescribes 'all holy rites: Let there be sung 'Non nobis' and 'Te Deum'' (4.8.120–3). And here we encounter a tantalizing shred of evidence that Shakespeare was not a Catholic at all, but a practicing Protestant.

In Holinshed's version of events Henry orders the singing of a psalm which begins *In exitu Israel* and the passage beginning *Non Nobis, Domine* is referred to as a 'verse.' In the Catholic Vulgate Psalter – the one Henry and English recusants knew – *In exitu Israel* and *Non nobis, Domine* were two parts of a single psalm, Psalm 113.[48] Shakespeare appears not to be aware of this. Despite a loud cue in Holinshed, Shakespeare's Henry orders 'Let there be sung 'Non nobis' – equivalent to ordering his followers to begin singing Psalm 113 from the middle without its eight opening verses. One might argue, I suppose, Shakespeare simply wished to dispense with an irrelevant reference to Israel's exodus from Egypt. But the Psalter which was companion to the Great Bible (1539) and the Book of Common Prayer (1549) was Miles Coverdale's 1535 translation of the psalms which reverted to the Hebrew forms and numbering system, and included *Non nobis, Domine* as the separate Psalm 115.[49] This is the version which a Protestant Shakespeare would have known.[50] Not incidentally, in the Book of Common Prayer Psalm 115 was calendared for reading on the 23rd day of the month. A keen-eared Elizabethan would note that Henry called for the wrong psalm.

Before Shakespeare's play has ended Henry's agile tongue will climax a hypersonic courtship of Princess Katherine and the French king will (coolly) declare Henry his most dear son and heir of France (5.2.333–6). The nobles on both sides will agree to swear an oath to the alliance. Though amiable to modern audiences, this scene must have rung melancholy-hollow for Elizabethans who knew that Henry's French exploits, full of sound and fury, came to nothing. Indeed, the scene is redolent with Machiavelli's caustic advice on casuistry in making and breaking oaths.[51] Years before, in the opening scene of *1 Henry VI*, Shakespeare had already assessed the very little gain Henry V's French escapades had brought England; a Messenger interrupts the dead king's obsequies with news that 'Guyenne, Compiègne, Rheims, Rousen, Orléans, Paris, Gisors, Poitiers, are all quite lost' (1.1.60–1) – and this before Henry's body is in the ground.

Regrettably, an aspect of *Henry V* little-considered by scholars is the human cost of Henry's conquests, not least to his Eastcheap friends. Machiavelli wrote in Chapter 20 of *Il Principe* that a conquering prince must, in the flush of victory, emasculate and destroy his friends.[52] In *Henry V*, Hal fulfills this instruction – to the last man. Falstaff dies of a broken heart. Hostess, too. Nym dies robbing the dead. Bardolph, he of the flaming venereal nose, steals a French pyx – an apt pun on 'French pox' – and is hanged for it at Henry's order. Alone, the bitter realist Pistol survives. But he harbors no expectation of enjoying the bounty, brotherhood and gentility promised so eloquently by Henry before the battle.[53] Pistol perceives his fate is to return to England and live a pimp and thief. And Henry – for all his famous victories – well, Shakespeare's audience hardly needed reminding good King Harry died of diarrhoea.

Into the balance with Hal-Harry-Henry V Shakespeare counterpoises the impious prevaricator-opportunist Sir John Falstaff who sold his soul to the devil 'on Good Friday last, for a cup of Madeira and a cold capon's leg' (1.2.114–15). In the first version of *1 Henry IV* to reach the London stage this character's name was Sir John Oldcastle (of his name-change more in a later chapter). To Falstaff honor is a scutcheon, the law a hurdle, truth an inconvenience, and mortal men cannon fodder merely. But Shakespeare contrives for Falstaff to experience a true and pious conversion. Unlike Harry's epiphany after a great victory, Falstaff's cue to reform – like Cardinal Wolsey's in *Henry VIII* (3.2.351–460) – appears out of the depth of adversity.

With Falstaff's very first words Shakespeare affixes an emblem to the man.

Sir John   Now, Hal, what time of day is it, lad?
Prince   Thou art so fat-witted with drinking of old sack, and unbuttoning thee
             after supper, and sleeping upon benches after noon, that thou hast
             forgotten to demand that truly which thou wouldst truly know. What a

devil hast thou to do with the time of the day? Unless hours were cups of
sack, and minutes capons, and clocks the tongues of bawds, and dials
the signs of leaping-houses, and the blessed sun himself a fair hot wench
in flame-coloured taffeta, I see no reason why thou shouldst be so
superfluous to demand the time of the day.

Sir John   Indeed you come near me now, Hal, for we that take purses go by the
moon and the seven stars, and not 'By Phoebus, he, that wand'ring
knight so fair.' And I prithee, sweet wag, when thou art a king, as God
save thy grace – 'majesty' I should say, for grace thou wilt have none –

(1H4 1.2.1–18)

Falstaff is a man out of his time, but seeking time. Moments earlier, in the first
scene of the play, Henry Bolingbroke had articulated his own quest: to make
his way to Jerusalem where it had been foretold he must die. Likewise,
Shakespeare's Falstaff enters proclaiming his quest: he must find time. He is a
man of the past who reckons by the moon as did the antique Etruscans and
early Britons in the ages before the solar calendar. But Falstaff is also a man of
the future – as Sir John Oldcastle was. An early proponent of Lollardry,
Oldcastle died for his reforming faith and won a name-day in Foxe's
martyrology. More than a century before the neologism was coined during the
protests against the Diet of Speyer (1529), Oldcastle was what Elizabethans
would call Protestant. And Shakespeare's Oldcastle-Falstaff *does* find time.[54]
Hostess tells us 'A made a fine end, / and went away an it had been any christom
child. / A parted e'en just between twelve and one, / e'en at the turning o'the
tide' (2.3.10–13). That is, Falstaff died in that liminal hour when ghosts are
wont to walk and at tide-turn, the traditional time of leave-taking. In a later
chapter in this book I will closely examine Falstaff's death and what it tells us
about Falstaff-Oldcastle, William Shakespeare, and a Lord Chamberlain
named Henry Brooke.

Shakespeare's counterpoised portraits of Hal and Falstaff represent a
pinnacle in his tactics of theological discourse. The historical John Oldcastle
died a martyr, burnt at the stake in 1417 on the warrant of *Henry V.*
Shakespeare's Hal-Henry-Harry wins only transitory *gloria mundi*; before his
body cools his French empire has crumbled to dust. And like that other pagan
conqueror of Gaul, his soul is destined to burn – to burn like a star in the
firmament (*1H6* 1.1.55–6).[55] But meek Oldcastle-Falstaff finds time and
heavenly peace – unshrived, without ceremony, without ritual intercessors –
and his soul sleeps forever in the embrace of God.

Why, we must ask, did Shakespeare counterpoise Hal and Falstaff this way?
The answer, I think, is this. In the Spring of 1599, as he completed his Henriad
and achieved the age of thirty-five, William Shakespeare entered upon a period
of profound religious doubt. This cast of mind would shape his indictment of all
things Roman (i.e. Catholic) in *Julius Caesar*, haunt the dour comedies *Measure*

for Measure (1603) and *All's Well That Ends Well* (1604–5), and persist until the playwright had drained human experience of honor, hope, meaning – and even carnal desire – in *Othello* (1603), *Macbeth* (1604), *King Lear* (1605), and *Antony and Cleopatra* (1606).[56] The triumph of the bloodless man-god and *Pontifex Maximus* Augustus was for Shakespeare the catastrophe of the human soul.

But William Shakespeare's four great tragedies did not mark the end of his spiritual journey. In his future lay the magical landscape of the romances – with their promises of the redemption of sin and their knee-slapper happy endings. The most extraordinary of these is surely *Cymbeline*, written 1610–11. From his reading of Holinshed Shakespeare knew that Kymbeline (or Cimbeline) had been king in Britain during the reign of the Roman Emperor Augustus at the time of the birth of Christ – and precious little else. Holinshed recorded that

> This man (as some write) was brought up at Rome, and there made knight by Augustus Cesar, under whome he served in the warres, and was in such favour with him, that he [Kymbeline] was at libertie to pay his tribute or not. Little other mention is made of his dooings, except that during his reign, the Saviour of the world our Lord Jesus Christ the onelie sonne of God was bourne ...' (3.32)

Beyond this statement Holinshed vacillates about whether or not Kymbeline paid the tribute which his predecessors had promised to Rome under Julius Caesar. The invasion of the Roman duns – a pivotal event in Shakespeare's romance – is the playwright's invention; the historical Romans came in force for their money only under Claudius (reigned AD 41–54), by which time Kymbeline was long dead.

In his *Cymbeline* Shakespeare turns a dim and distant chapter of Britain's history into an age of miracles. Nosworthy captures the spirit of the piece when he writes:

> Puppet characters, usually of royal or noble birth, actuated by motives which, whether good or bad, are wholly impossible, are made to undertake fantastic adventures, often to distant parts. Exhausting journeys through woods and wildernesses are a commonplace ... [until] the whole contorted pattern yields to poetic justice, which effects the conventional happy ending. (xlvii)

But that is *not quite* what happens; the denouement of *Cymbeline* is more than mere poetic justice. It is miraculous – and intentionally epiphanous.

In Act Five, as the ghosts of his dead parents and brothers hover over Posthumus, Jove – father of gods – descends and imparts to the young man a book of holy writ (5.4.133) in which, waking, he reads this prophecy:[57]

> When as a lion's whelp shall, to himself unknown, without seeking find, and be embrac'd by a piece of tender air: and when from a stately cedar shall be lopp'd

branches, which, being dead many years, shall after revive, be jointed to the old stock, and freshly grown, then shall Posthumus end his miseries, Britain be fortunate, and flourish in peace and plenty. (5.4.138–45)

Shakespeare has conjured here two images – the lion and the cedar – both charged with Biblical symbolism. A Jacobean audience would certainly have recognized the lion as the emblem of the tribe of Judah, of which King David was a member as was his descendent, Jesus. Cedar trees, which Jacobeans knew to have been planted by God Himself (so says Psalm 104), are alien to Britain and favor warmer climates such as the holy land. One gloss to this passage could run: Britain will not flourish in peace and plenty until the restoration of that foreign old religion associated with cedars. Having read this prophecy, Posthumus himself falls to prophesying:

> 'Tis still a dream: or else such stuff as madmen
> Tongue, and brain not: either both, or nothing,
> Or senseless speaking, or a speaking such
> As sense cannot untie
>
> (146–9)

Dr Johnson found the meaning of this speech 'too thin to be easily caught.'[58] But surely some of Shakespeare's auditors would have recognized that Posthumus is describing (and enacting) the speaking in tongues described by Saint Paul in 1 Corinthians 12–14. Though Paul was skeptical of the practice, this gift of tongues had been bestowed by the Holy Ghost upon Peter and the brethren at the Pentecost (Acts 10:44–6) in order to enable them to preach the Gospel to a whole world of foreign speakers.

Posthumus believes he has had a dream – but we have seen the business actually happen – *and the book in his hands is real.* Jacobeans knew that throughout the Old and New Testaments God's chosen – Daniel, Joseph Husband, Peter and Paul, to mention only a few – were visited in dreams by divine entities. Moments later the Gaolers mock Posthumus' newfound vision of his heavenly destiny (180–6) as he exits – carrying his book. In the aftermath the First Gaoler delivers – as many of Shakespeare's minor characters have done – a judgment of events recently passed:

> … for all he be a Roman; and there be some of them too, that die against their wills; so should I, if I were one. I would we were all of one mind, and one mind good: O, there were desolation of gaolers and gallowses! I speak against my present profit, but my wish hath a preferment in't. (203–8)

There's another marvelous wordplay here; Shakespeare is bandying with the local meaning of 'Roman.' If one said the word 'Roman' to a typical Jacobean, the hearer was far more likely to think 'Catholic' than associate the world with the Rome of antiquity. To the Jacobean ear 'Roman' *meant* Catholic – which is why, when Horatio moves to share Hamlet's poisoned goblet he declares himself an 'antique' Roman (5.2.292) to make clear to his auditors he does not mean Roman Catholic.

In my view, Shakespeare is playfully flitting between these loci. And his tactic is subtle, tantalizing, and shrewd. The wiser sort among his audience would have remembered that, like the antique Romans, Catholic Rome had exacted tribute from pre-Reformation England through a variety of mechanisms associated with the ordination of bishops and cardinals. While these sums were paid from the Church's treasury, Rome also exacted a tax from the crown itself – the annual tribute of two hundred pounds called 'Peter's pence.' Henry VIII put a stop to these payments in 1534.

Cymbeline can be read, as Maurice Hunt has done, as Christian revelation[59] – or as a Catholic statement of faith as Peter Milward would have it[60] – or it can be read as an anti-Catholic statement. But from Posthumus' revelation and exegesis one could as readily argue that Shakespeare was calling for a return to Old Testament Judaism. Reading into the divine scenes of *Cymbeline* a Catholic (or anti-Catholic) testament is to deny the dramatic structure of the play.[61] Shakespeare has written a fantasy – as we now call it, a *romance* – a genre recognized from at least the thirteenth century as an improbable yarn 'embodying the adventures of some hero or chivalry … of which the scene and incidents are very remote from those or ordinary life … an extravagant fiction, invention, or story; a wild or wanton exaggeration; a picturesque falsehood' (*OED*).[62] In *Cymbeline* we are in a realm of fable. Shakespeare's Roman Britain is pagan, not Christian. Jove is a Roman god, not the God of the Jews or early Jewish Christians. Act Five of *Cymbeline* depicts an archetypal noble youth (Posthumus) freed from imprisonment by a convenient *deus ex machina* (Jove) animated by pleas of the ghosts of the boy's kin. If this were read as anything but fantasy its effect would be laughable. To drive this point home, as Posthumus in confusion wanders offstage (clutching his book), all heaven breaks loose.

In the tent of Cymbeline in machine-gun rapid succession: a wicked queen dies; Romans sue for peace; a boy turns out to be a woman; a villain confesses his misdeeds; a wife believed a harlot is revealed as chaste; a manslaughter of an incivil prince is confessed (and forgiven); a husband thought dead is discovered alive; two long-lost sons of a monarch are found, and a wicked villain pardoned. Most important to understanding Shakespeare's perspective on his material, his Posthumus is revealed as the lion-born of Jove's book's prophecy (*Leo-natus*) and Cymbeline as its lofty cedar – demonstrating that a prophecy which, on first hearing may have had a perfectly clear meaning to a Christian audience … can have an entirely different and equally sound meaning to a roomful of pagans. This is Shakespeare's grand trope. One can almost hear his Cicero in the 'tiring house muttering, 'men may construe things after their fashion, / Clean from the purpose of the things themselves'

(*JC* 1.3.34–5). Shakespeare has lured us into *thinking Christian* – and then yanked out from under us the pagan rug. *Cymbeline* is a parodic rewrite of the Christian myth which states that the coming of the time of universal peace under Augustus was the final precondition for the birth of the Messiah and His age of miracles – and that England's payment of its arrears was the act that sealed the deal. In Shakespeare's rewrite God comes down to earth (5.1.133) and scads of miracles occur (5.2.25–421) *before* Cymbeline speaks the words that bring universal peace:

> My peace we will begin: and Caius Lucius,
> Although the victor, we submit to Caesar,
> And to the Roman empire; promising
> To pay our wonted tribute ...
>
> (5.5.460–3).

If this reading of *Cymbeline* is sound, two great questions arise: why did Shakespeare do it? and how on earth did he get away with it? The answer to the first question must be sought in Shakespeare's profound and wonderfully well-informed skepticism. A writer himself, he deplored the notion that any book written by men – even the Bible – could be infallible. He had disdained men who slavishly believed the written word – even the written Word – as early as 1599 in *Julius Caesar*.

Then again, English Christians believed theirs was the true religion because the events described in the New Testament actually happened. In his *Arte of Rhetorique* (1553), Thomas Wilson wrote: 'The Historie of God's booke to the Christian is infallible' (Muir *Arte* 190). Shakespeare was certainly not the only Englishman who found this statement paradoxical; Protestants who rejected the infallibility of the pope – a man – were expected to believe that *a book* was infallible? A book which had gone through countless drafts and translations was infallible? A book written, transcribed, copied, typeset, and printed by men was infallible? If a man is fallible, how can a book created by a man be infallible? The Christian's answer in Shakespeare's day (as in ours) is *this book is the word of God*. And this, I believe, was the sticking point for William Shakespeare: according to the received religions, believing in the divinity of Christ is inseparable from the belief that the Gospels are infallibly, literally true. But in Shakespeare's era, just as there were two rival calendars, there were two Bibles – the Protestant Geneva New Testament (1560) and its successors, and the rival Catholic Rheims (1582). While the variations between the two texts may seem trivial to modern readers, they certainly weren't for William Tyndale and Saint Thomas More, who blasted thousands of words at one another over a handful of definitions. For almost a hundred years English Protestants and Catholics had butchered each other over variations in the rival holy texts and interpretations thereof.[63]

During Shakespeare's working lifetime the Renaissance mind was struggling to digest the new vernacular Bible as literal history. But it was also grappling with fundamental questions of historiography. Through the essays of Montaigne (1580, 1588) to Machiavelli's *Florentine Histories* (tr. 1595) to Raleigh's *History of the World* (1614), we can trace the growing dissatisfaction of the wiser sort with the Christian interpretive historiography typified by St Augustine's *Civitas Dei* (AD 413–26) and Orosius' *History Against the Pagans* (AD 417). In 1599, Shakespeare's *Julius Caesar* represented a blunt rejection of Christian historiography. '*Julius Caesar* exploits for dramatic purposes the growing awareness among Renaissance historians and others that the past is difficult to retrieve, and that the ends of history are best served by scrupulous objectivity.'[64] According to Saint Augustine it was God's will which brought Augustus to the empery of Rome. According to Shakespeare's *Julius Caesar*, it was Marc Antony's speech in the Forum.

But Shakespeare's rejection of Christian historiography did not end with the writing of *Julius Caesar*. And this brings us to the reason why – perhaps – he took up *Cymbeline* as his subject in 1610. In that year the rival calendars again presented the playwright – for the last time during his active life in the theater – with *precisely* the same bizarre concordance of holy days which had occurred in 1599 and may have inspired *Julius Caesar*. In 1610 the English St Valentine's Day fell on the Catholic (and correct) date of Ash Wednesday. The English Ides of March fell on the Catholic (and correct) Annunciation to the Blessed Virgin Mary. The Jacobeans' date of the Annunciation fell on the Catholic Palm Sunday. And true Easter, 11 April 1599 Gregorian, fell on the date the English observed April Fools' Day.

J.R. Simmons believed Shakespeare's discontent with Christian historiography underlay his decision to take up the story of Kymbeline:

> Perhaps the most impressive evidence that Shakespeare was preoccupied with the crucial factors of Christian historiography lies … in the complex of motivations that led Shakespeare, uniquely, to fix his attention upon the reign of King Cymbeline. Once more Shakespeare turns to Holinshed … [where] the only unequivocal evidence about Cymbeline to be picked up … was that 'during his reign, the Saviour of the world our Lord Jesus Christ the onelie sonne of God was borne of a virgine, about the 23 yeare of the reigne of this Kymbeline … after the building of the citie of Rome 750 nigh at an end.' There again, even in a single phrase anticipating the fall of Rome, history is shaped in the way that most captured Shakespeare's imagination.[65]

Whereas Shakespeare's *Julius Caesar* was an inquisition against revelation as history, his *Cymbeline* romances history as revelation.

The writer Shakespeare knew that writers can't be trusted. One can see this idea at work in his treatment of 'writers' in *Julius Caesar*. Caesar, who hopes to be king, 'bad the Romans Marke him, / and write his Speeches in their Bookes'

(223–4); instead he became a corpse and a god. Cassius tries to use anonymous letters to whet Marcus Brutus against Caesar (669), but succeeds only in ruining the republic and sealing his own awful death. Brutus loses the war by writing a 'bille' which calls his armies down to defeat (2476). Artemidorus alone writes truth (1213); he is ignored. Cinna, a benign poet, is murdered for bad verses (1843). The Cynicke Poet who brings the Gospel of John is reviled and kicked off the stage (2115). In Shakespeare's *Julius Caesar* the legitimate chroniclers of history are slain, silenced, or dismissed. In their place, Antony, Octavius, and Lepidus use pen-and-ink to murder the innocent (1853). Another poet's namesake, Pindar(us), is a flatterer who proves blinder than Cassius (2488). Caesar's only true believers are Cassius – a forger who stoops to writing letters on behalf of an extortionist (1970) – and the suggestible Brutus, the slave of the proverbial idiom and slave of the book. In the end, the writing of the history of Caesar and his 'honorable' murderers is left to ruthless Octavius and the great liar-priest, Antony.

If this is why Shakespeare took up the story of Kymbeline in 1610, the better question is: how did he get away with *Cymbeline*? The answer is that when Shakespeare's romance was on the boards – in 1610/11 and succeeding years – the Catholic menace to the kingdom from without – and the anti-Catholic paranoia within – were much declined since Elizabeth's time. Recusants were, for the most part, domesticated; rather, it was the Puritans who vexed the king and drew his ire. Besides, some Catholics would have taken comfort that James had been baptized in the Roman rite by his ultra-Catholic mother, Mary Queen of Scots (1542–87). The persistence of this inference accounts for James' repeated denials that his baptism made him a Catholic. As he complained in *Basilikon Doron*, 'I was never of their [Catholic] church' (15), and 'I am sure none will condemn for an heretic save such as make the pope their God' (36). Like Elizabeth, James was tolerant of the religious consciences of his subjects so long as they neither impugned nor threatened his throne. In his *Papal Opposition* James noted he had barely time and paper to enumerate the instances of forbearance he had shown to English Catholics. Whether or not this is entirely true, the published writ of the king certainly set a clear tone of toleration:

> How many did I honor with Knighthood of known and open Recusants? How indifferently [evenhandedly] did I give audience, and access to both sides, bestowing equally all favors and honors on both professions [confessions]: How free and continual access had all ranks and degrees of Papists in my Court and company? And above all, how frankly and freely did I free Recusants of their ordinary payments [see below]? Besides, it is evidence what strait order was given out of my own mouth to the judges to spare the execution of all Priests ... (19)

The 'ordinary payments' to which James refers were fines imposed upon non-conformists for failure to attend Anglican services by Elizabeth's Act of Uniformity (1559); in 1592 Shakespeare's father was tolled for missing church, though it was alleged that he did so to avoid duns. As Elizabeth had done before him, James was determined to show his subjects (and the world) he was no bloody tyrant *ala* Mary Tudor, under whose brief and traumatic reign (1553–8) hundreds of Protestants – including genuinely great men Nicholas Ridley, Hugh Latimer and Thomas Cranmer – burnt at the stake.

It is certainly true that, by modern standards, Catholics received ungentle treatment under the Tudors and Stuarts and for a long time thereafter; an act of 1563 had imposed the death penalty on priests for saying mass. James showed intolerance only to those who were intolerant – the Puritans, after all, would not have landed on Plymouth Rock had James acceded to their demands. After the reign of James and Charles (and the Glorious Revolution), certain professions were closed to Catholics by the Corporation Act (1660) and Test Act (1672) which prevented Catholics from becoming government or military officers, lawyers, teachers or university members. As late as the eighteenth century Catholics were suspect of disloyalty merely because they could not accept the monarch as head of the English Church – a notion risible today. Elizabeth's conformity laws and her fines – in one form or another – remained in force until the so-called 'Toleration Act' of 1689, and the Pipe Rolls are filled with instances of their enforcement. Genuine Catholic emancipation arrived in England only in 1829. Notwithstanding this ugly history, James I – by his own account as well as others' – treated his (reliably loyal) Catholic subjects with remarkable toleration. In this atmosphere Shakespeare's *Cymbeline* passed muster.

Notes

1 Wells and Taylor, *Textual Companion*, pp. 109–34, posit that *3H6* followed *TGV* (1590) and *Shrew* (1591).

2 Edward Hall, *Chronicle; Containing the History of England, etc.* (London, 1548).

3 Holinshed, 659.1.63, cited in Geoffrey Bullough (ed.), *Narrative and Dramatic Sources*, ii.210. The misattribution of the scourging of Christ to 'the Jews' is spiteful anti-Semitism.

4 Minutes of the Privy Council, 12 November 1589, cited in E.K. Chambers, *The Elizabethan Stage* (Oxford: Oxford University Press, 1923), 4.306.

5 G. Wickham, *Early English Stages* (London: Routledge and Kegan Paul, 1981), 2.94. In particular, it has been held that *Julius Caesar* has little or nothing to do with the Bible. 'There are hardly any direct reference to Biblical texts or subjects in the play.' T. Carter, *Shakespeare and Holy Scripture* (London: Hodder and Stoughton, 1905), p. 343.

6 Some scholars have suggested that the Revels Office was a lacuna of benign

tolerance. This is naïve. Virtually every significant Elizabethan writer was at one time or another fined, jailed, banned, exiled, broken, or murdered, including Kyd, Lily, Marlowe, Jonson, Nashe, Middleton, etc. But see R. Dutton, *Mastering the Revels* (Iowa City: University of Iowa Press, 1991).

7 Naseeb Shaheen, *Biblical References in Shakespeare's History Plays* (Newark: University of Delaware Press, 1989), p. 91.

8 *Dictionary of National Biography.*

9 But see Foxe's expanded, more sensational version of Tyndale's martyrdom in his edition of 1570.

10 Chambers, *Stage*, 4.338–9.

11 Sohmer, *Mystery Play*, pp. 234–40.

12 Text and lineation from David Daniell (ed.), *Julius Caesar* (London: Methuen, 1998).

13 North, p. 792.

14 *Ibid.*, p. 976.

15 Sohmer, *Mystery Play*, pp. 29–31 and 45–8.

16 Text and lineation from Philip Edwards (ed.), *Hamlet* (Cambridge: Cambridge University Press, 1985).

17 'What these details imply is a practice like the one condemned in the Elizabethan homily *Against perill of idolatries, and superfluous decking of churches* ... The corollary to this is that Caesar-worship is something akin to Roman Catholic worship.' David Kaula, 'Let Us Be Sacrificers': Religious Motifs in Julius Caesar,' *Shakespeare Survey* 14 (1981), 198–9.

18 Shakespeare plays on the same pun in *1 Henry IV* (3.1.63–6).

19 W. G. Ryan, *The Golden Legend* (Princeton: Princeton University Press, 1993), 1.119.

20 See for example North, p. 766.

21 C. Wordsworth. The *Cisio Ianus* appears on 166–8.

22 *OED on CD-ROM* (Oxford: Oxford University Press, 1993), span n.1.

23 S. Sohmer, 'Certain Speculations on Hamlet, etc.,' *Early Modern Literary Studies* (EMLS) 2:1 (April 1996), 5:5–31.

24 Various legends supported Magdalene's presence in Ephesus. See Gregory of Tours, *De miraculis* i.xxx. Others, including de Voraigne, place her at Marseilles; see Ryan, 1.378ff.

25 For a terse précis of Magdalene myths see D.L. Jeffrey, *A Dictionary of Biblical Tradition, etc.* (Grand Rapids: University of Michigan Press, 1992), pp. 486–9.

26 Ryan, 1.51–5.

27 With the absolute power of life-and-death; a set of sun is to cue the execution of Aegean Egeon.

28 Richard III died in 1485, and More wrote only twenty-eight years later (1513). Perhaps his *Richard* long lay unpublished (until 1557) because there were many still living who could put the lie to it. See the (partisan but) scholarly discussion of the Tyndale-More exchange in David Daniell, *William Tyndale* (New Haven: Yale University Press, 1994), pp. 250–80. Some may find profound irony in Pope John Paul II naming More the Patron Saint of Politicians on Halloween 2000.

29 Wells and Taylor, *Textual Companion,* suggest 1598–99.
30 In *2 Henry IV* his son, John of Lancaster, carries on that family tradition when he equivocates Archbishop Scroop and Lords Mowbray and Hasting to death (4.1).
31 See, for example, Hugh Dickinson, 'The Reformation of Prince Hal,' *Shakespeare Quarterly* 12 (1966), 33–46.
32 But see the providential reading of J. H. Walter (ed.), *King Henry V* (London: Methuen, 1954), xvii–xxi.
33 There are many such time-shift signals, e.g. the blather of the grumbling Porter in *Macbeth* 2.3 being one.
34 Rose, *Wakefield Mystery Plays,* p. 207.
35 But see James Black, 'Henry IV's Pilgrimage,' *Shakespeare Quarterly* 34 (1983), p. 26.
36 Playing on the title of Chapter 18 in Harvey C. Mansfield (tr.), *Niccolò Machiavelli: The Prince* (Chicago: University of Chicago Press, 1985), p. 86. Also see Mahood, *Wordplay,* p. 48. 'In a really great play ... this governing idea is never a thesis to be expounded, but an issue to be explored.'
37 Mansfield, p. 87. [My emphasis].
38 Bullough, 4.276–8.
39 I am indebted to Professor Richard Wilson for calling this detail to my attention.
40 Mansfield, p. 4. This text, written *ca* 1513 (pub. 1532), circulated widely in Italian and French manuscript in sixteenth-century England. Machiavelli himself – boasting of many friends among the English – appeared on the London stage in Christopher Marlowe's *Jew of Malta* (*ca* 1590).
41 Mansfield, pp. 87–9.
42 As in Shakespeare's searing send-ups of baptism and confirmation in *Julius Caesar* 3.1.111–90. See Sohmer, *Mystery Play,* pp. 138–41.
43 For a kinder, gentler view see G.K. Hunter, 'Shakespeare's Politics and the Rejection of Falstaff,' *Critical Quarterly* 1 (1959), 229–36.
44 For an alternative perspective see David Evett, 'Types of King David in Shakespeare's Lancastrian Tetralogy,' *Shakespeare Survey* 14 (1981), p. 61.
45 The Book of Common Prayer, etc. (Cambridge n.d.), p. 312.
46 *OED,* wonder *n* 2.
47 Walter, p. 135n.
48 In the Vulgate Psalter, Psalm 113 is a compound of the Hebrew Psalms 113 and 114 (just as the 23rd Psalm appears as Psalm 22). Henry would have known Psalm 113 in the form below. Note that *Non nobis* begins at verse 9 [my emphasis]:

> *In exitu Israhel de Aegypto domus Iacob de populo bar baro*
> *Facta est Iudaea sanctificatio eius Israhel potestas eius*
> *Mare vidit et fugit Iordanis conversus est retror sum*
> *Montes exultaverunt ut arietes colles sicut agni ovium*
> *Quid est tibi mare quod fugisti et tu Iordanis quia converseses retrorsum*
> *Montes exultastis sicut arietes et colles sicut agni ovium*
> *A facie Domini mota est terra a facie Dei Iacob*
> *Qui convertit petram in stagna aquarum et rupem in fontes aquarum*
> **Non nobis Domine non nobis** *sed nomini tuo da gloriam, etc.*

49 Rudyard Kipling wrote a version, the *Templar Hymn,* in 1934. Kenneth Branagh used Patrick Doyle's version in his film.

50 The Catholic Douay psalter, published 1609 and in use today, keeps the Vulgate form.

51 'Alexander VI never did anything, nor ever thought of anything, but how to deceive men … And there never was a man with greater efficacy in asserting a thing, and in affirming it with greater oaths, who observed it less; nonetheless, his deceits succeeded at his will …' Mansfield, p. 70.

52 Mansfield, pp. 83–5.

53 'For he today that sheds his blood with me / Shall be my brother; be he ne'er so vile, / This day shall gentle his condition' (4.3.61–3).

54 Peter J. Seng recognized Falstaff/Oldcastle's liaison with Time in 'Songs, Time, and the Rejection of Falstaff,' *Shakespeare Survey* 15 (1962), 31–9.

55 The star speech by Bedford is intentionally over-the-top and the interruption of the Messenger from France a welcome relief. Then again, though in 'heaven,' Henry is 'burning' – whereas Falstaff sleeps in Arthur's bosom.

56 The tragicomedy *Troilus and Cressida* (1602) also fits this somber profile with its savage debunking of Homer, Helen, Hector, heroic war and heroic sex – as does *Coriolanus* (1608), which does as much for mother-love and *Timon of Athens* (1605) which lampoons the overarching Christian virtues of *philadelphy* and *caritas.* One play usually dated to this period seems out of character, i.e. *Twelfth Night.* But I have shown elsewhere that *TN,* dated 1601 in most modern editions, was performed at court on the night of 2/3 February 1600/01 and may have been commissioned or written even earlier. Sohmer, *Mystery Play,* pp. 199–216.

57 Shakespeare wasn't nearly the first English playwright to create such a scene. See Henry Hitch Adams, *English Domestic or, Homiletic Tragedy, 1575 to 1642* (New York: Columbia University Press, 1943).

58 J.M. Nosworthy, *Cymbeline* Arden (London: Routledge, 1988), p. 161n.146–51.

59 Maurice Hunt, 'Visionary Christianity in Shakespeare's Late Romances,' *CLA Journal* 47 (2003–4), 212–30.

60 Peter Milward, 'Providential Discovery in Shakespeare's Plays,' *The Mutual Encounter of East and West* (Tokyo: Renaissance Institute, 1992), pp. 125–36.

61 See Margaret Jones-Davies, '*Cymbeline* and the Sleep of Faith,' in *Theater and Religion: Lancastrian Shakespeare,* Richard Dutton, Alison Findlay, and Richard Wilson (eds), (Manchester: Manchester University Press, 2003), pp. 197–217.

62 For a contrary view see John S. Pendergast, '*Cymbeline* and the Question of Genre,' *Journal of the Wooden O Symposium* 2 (2002), 127–35.

63 For another perspective see Jeffrey Knapp, *Shakespeare's Tribute: church, nation, and theater in Renaissance England* (Chicago: University of Chicago Press 2002).

64 Joseph S.M.J. Chang, '*Julius Caesar* in the Light of Renaissance Historiography,' *Journal of English and Germanic Philology* 69 (1970), p. 63.

65 J.R. Simmons, *Shakespeare's Pagan World* (London: Harvester 1973), p. 165.

SEVEN

The 'double time' crux
in *Othello* solved

In 1992 Graham Bradshaw wrote, 'Although it is factitious and distracting, the theory or myth of 'double time' is still respectfully trundled out in every modern scholarly edition of *Othello* … It has been as long-lived as Nahum Tate's adaptation of *King Lear* which held the stage for a century and a half and, like that adaptation, deserves to be firmly laid to rest.'[1] But the formidable Professor Bradshaw underrated the resilience of the 'double time' phoenix (it survived his sally) as he understated its longevity by half; *Othello's* obscure time-scheme has remained the greatest crux in Shakespeare for 400 years.[2]

As early as 1693 Thomas Rymer fulminated over Othello's irrational fantasy that he had been cuckolded by his lieutenant and bride:[3] 'Michael Cassio came not from Venice in the ship with Desdemona, nor till this Morning [3.3] could be suspected of an opportunity with her … this is very hasty.'[4] Forty years later, Lewis Theobald noticed the untimely arrival of Lodovico in 4.1: 'Othello is … but just arriv'd at Cyprus … [therefore] the Senate could hardly yet have heard of the *Ottoman* Fleet being scatter'd by Tempest.'[5] In 1788, George Steevens reasoned that Cassio could not 'have kept away, for the space of a whole week, from Bianca … unless they had been longer at Cyprus than is represented in the play'[6] since, as Edmond Malone observed in 1821, Cassio 'had only been one day at Cyprus.'[7] In the mid-nineteenth century, John Wilson writing as 'Christopher North' offered to resolve the temporal anomalies in *Othello* via an ingenious 'double time' theory.[8] Since the appearance of Wilson's hypothesis, every editor of *Othello* from Dyce (1857) to Honigmann (1997) has attempted a response;[9] as a consequence, by 1886 Furness' selection of critical commentary on the play's 'Duration of Action' already ran to fifteen closely printed pages.[10] In the post-Einstein era (1969), Ned B. Allen insisted that 'the double time in *Othello* is not scattered throughout the play – the two times exist separately, one in Acts I and II, and the other in the rest of the play.'[11] In 1987, Lorne M. Buchman suggested a post-Freudian solution – 'Iago destroys Othello by altering his perception ... of time' – and argued that the audience's dramatic experience of the play depends on their sharing Othello's temporal disorientation.[12]

Doubtless, Shakespeare wished us to receive Othello's impossible pronouncement of Desdemona's guilt – 'she with Cassio hath the act of shame / A thousand times committed' (5.2.210–12) – as the hobgoblin of a disturbed mind. But the Moor's inclination to erotic fantasy cannot explain the speech in 3.3 which seems to jar us into 'double time,' Emilia's 'My wayward husband hath a hundred times / Wooed me to steal it [the handkerchief]' (292–3).[13] Nor can an appeal to Othello's distraction resolve Emilia's baffling '"Tis not a year or two shows us a man' (3.4.105). Iago might be lying to Cassio when he describes Othello in the throes of 'his second fit; he had one yesterday' (4.1.52); after all, Iago lies relentlessly – including his whopper 'I lay with Cassio lately' comprising a raging tooth, a shared bed, and the lieutenant wooing in his sleep (3.2.418–30). Even if Iago's preposterous tale *were* true, how could it have happened 'lately'? Iago and Cassio traveled from Venice in separate vessels, they 'had only been one day [and night] at Cyprus,' and from their dialogue in 3.1 we know that neither slept that night.[14] And exactly when does Iago execute his plan to drop the handkerchief in Cassio's lodging (3.3.324)? And how and when does Cassio come to possess it before 3.4.179? And don't we accept the nuggety particularity of Bianca's rant: 'What keep a week away? seven days and nights? / Eight score eight hours' (3.4.166–7)? Surely the over-speedy arrival of the Venetian ambassadors (4.1.203) is no hallucination.[15] To resolve these and other temporal inconsistencies Emrys Jones advised 'we must think of time in terms of a more illusionist and mimetic system in which the prime concern is not duration but continuity.'[16] This is useful advice for a director or performer. But, as Dr Johnson noted dryly, 'A little longer interval [on Cyprus] would increase the probability of the story.'[17]

To apologize for Shakespeare's (apparent) chronological howlers, Ned B. Allen suggested the playwright composed *Othello* in two tranches – the latter first (!) – then carelessly stitched the lobes together: 'It may be hard to picture a playwright of Shakespeare's ability as having joined two parts of *Othello* not originally intended to go together.'[18] It is hard. On the other hand, in the Q's and F's of *Hamlet* and *Lear* we have plentiful evidence that Shakespeare continued to revise his plays long after they had entered the repertoire of The King's Men. Balz Engler neatly articulates the case for an authorial revision of *Othello* to account for the numerous variances between the 1622 Quarto and 1623 Folio;[19] Kenneth Muir enumerates Shakespeare's before-and-after-thoughts,[20] and Nevill Coghill demonstrates how Shakespeare elaborated his portraits of Roderigo and Emilia when he revised the Q text.[21]

But *Othello's* abundant manifestations of shifty time can't be explained away by a cobbled first draft or a rewrite gone adrift. Their stubborn insistence and the pressure they exert on reader and audience to reconcile the irreconcilable are *per se* evidence that the subversion of time is a principal strategy in Shakespeare's design for *Othello*. As Ernst Honigmann concluded in 1997, the 'double time scheme is intricately bound up with Shakespeare's reshaping of [Cinthio's] material. Despite attempts to deny its existence or to explain it as the result of exceptional methods of composition, I see double time as important in *Othello*.'[22]

Given the attention commentators have lavished on the play's 'double time' it is remarkable none has noticed that two asynchronous, rival clocks were ticking in Europe throughout Shakespeare's working lifetime, one in Venice, another on Cyprus. After the promulgation of the Gregorian calendar reform of 1582 Europeans lived and worshipped by not one, but two antithetical time-reckoning systems: the Gregorian 'New Style' calendar which prevailed in Catholic nations, and the incongruent Julian 'Old Style' calendar which persisted in Sweden until 1696, in parts of Germany and Holland until 1700, in Denmark (1700), Switzerland (1701), and in England until Lord Chesterfield's reform took effect in September 1752.[23]

The reader will already know how, in 1583, Elizabeth's plan for an English calendar reform was derailed by Archbishop Grindal. But they were not only Protestant states who rejected the Gregorian reform in all or in part. Catholic Florence continued to observe 25 March as New Year's Day until 1751.[24] The proud republicans of Venice, though generally acceding to the Gregorian reform, insisted on perpetuating their unique local calendar, the *More Veneto* (annotated in their books and documents as '*MV*') which recognized 1 March as New Year's Day, just as the Roman republic had done prior to Julius Caesar's reform of 45 BC.[25] Furthermore, lettered Jacobeans certainly knew that the Eastern Orthodox Church wholly rejected the Roman reform and continued to live by the Julian calendar.[26] As a consequence, the Old Style calendar which prevailed in England also prevailed in (of all places) Cyprus.[27] And therein lies the key to the most long-lived crux in Shakespeare. The reason we sense two clocks running on Cyprus is that Shakespeare knew that Venetians and Cypriots reckoned time by different calendars.

Scholars variously date the writing of *Othello* to 1603–4. The date *ad quem* is set by the performance of the play by The King's Men on 1 November 1604.[28] If, as Emrys Jones has suggested, Shakespeare borrowed details of the maneuvers of the Turkish fleet in *Othello* 1.3.34–40 from Richard Knolles' *General Historie of the Turkes*,[29] then the date *a quo* must be the publication of that book;[30] Knolles' manuscript was entered in the Stationers' Register on 5 December 1602 and could have appeared in print early in 1603. In this chapter I will suggest that Shakespeare undertook the writing of *Othello* in 1603, incorporating that year as the *annus praesens* of the play and linking the dramatic action to certain dates on which holy days in the rival Protestant

Julian and Catholic Gregorian calendars conflicted ironically.[31] Following Maurice Hunt, I'll propose that Shakespeare contrived the death-struggle between Iago and Cassio to personify the conflict between the Catholic doctrine of works and the Protestant dogma of election.[32] I'll also suggest that Jacobeans recognized Cyprus as the penultimate way-station for pilgrims to the Holy Land and that Shakespeare, although he followed Cinthio in setting the action of his drama on Cyprus,[33] construed Othello's journey as an unconsummated pilgrimage. Finally, I'll suggest that Shakespeare painted with the colors of Marian idolatry the convert Catholic Othello's obsession with the chastity of his bride.

In 1961 Emrys Jones noticed the correlation between the date of the writing of *Othello* – 'probably the first of Shakespeare's tragedies to be written for the King's Men'[34] – and the reprinting in 1603 of King James' epic poem, *Lepanto*, which had first appeared in 1591.[35] James' opus describes the triumph of united Christian forces under Don Juan of Austria over a Turkish fleet 'at the Gulf of Lepanto (near Corinth) on Sunday 7 October 1571.'[36] Jones infers that a Jacobean audience would have linked the wreck of the fictional Turkish fleet in *Othello* with the glorious deliverance of Europe from the threat of Muslim invasion. This may be so. But Lepanto (modern: Navpaktos, Greece) is over 800 nautical miles from Cyprus and closer to Venice than to Famagusta. And despite the Europeans' famous victory at sea, a concurrent Turkish land siege of Famagusta was successful. As lettered Jacobeans knew, Cyprus fell to the Turks on 1 August 1571 – more than two months *before* the battle of Lepanto.[37]

It was also well known that the Cypriots received their new Turkish overlords as a welcome change from their hated Venetian occupiers. The Venetians were the last in a long line of Roman Catholic invaders who had oppressed Greek Orthodox Cyprus under a cruel feudal system. In ancient times Cyprus had become an Egyptian fiefdom under Ptolemy I (323 BC) and a province of Rome (58 BC). Early Christians fleeing Judea after the execution of Saint Stephen (*ca* AD 35) proselytized their religion to Cyprus. One of Saint Paul's traveling companions, Barnabas, was a converted Cypriot Jew. On the division of the Roman Empire in AD 395 Cyprus fell under the hegemony of the Eastern branch and the Byzantine wing of Christianity. Then in 1191, the conquest of Cyprus by the English crusader King Richard I ('Lionheart') initiated a second period of oppressive foreign occupation that would last almost 800 years. By then the Byzantine church had broken with Rome (AD 1054) and had begun its evolution into the Greek Orthodox Church of today. Richard used Cyprus as a staging area for his crusade to the Holy Land, then sold the island to Guy de Lusignan (*ca* 1129–94), erstwhile king of Jerusalem. That transaction brought Cyprus – which was Greek in culture and language, and fervently Orthodox in religion – under the harsh rule of an aristocracy French in culture and speech, and adhering to the Roman Catholic rite.

Compared to the French, the Venetians were recent arrivals at Cyprus; they came by way of love, murder, and *coup d'etat*. In 1472, Cypriot King James II unadvisedly married a Venetian, Caterina Cornaro. She seems to have poisoned him at the instigation of the Venetian Senate, which quickly dispatched a force to occupy the island.[38] After the coup Queen Caterina shipped home to Italy where the grateful senators settled upon her the fiefdom of Asolo with an annual stipend of 8000 ducats.[39] In her wake Cyprus remained an unhappy vassal of the Venetian state for the next 100 years. In 1508, a German visitor, Martin von Baumgarten (1473–1535), wrote that 'the inhabitants of Cyprus are slaves to the Venetians, being obliged to pay to the state a third part of their increase or income ... [and] there is yearly some tax or other imposed on them, with which the poor common people are so flayed and pillaged, that they hardly have the wherewithal to keep soul and body together.'[40] Economic slavery was coupled with the brutal suppression of the Orthodox rite by the Roman Catholic hierarchy so that 'not only the Venetian rulers but also the Latin Church [became] the enemy' of the common people of Cyprus.[41] 'Centuries of oppression and contumely had so embittered the [Orthodox Cypriot] Greeks against their Latin tyrants that ... [they] resolved to be satisfied with nothing less than the complete removal from the island of the Roman Church, whose presence they regarded as an insult to their own communion and a sign of their servitude ... To this of course the Venetians ... could not consent.'[42] A Cypriot resistance movement led by a shadowy figure named James Diassorin was ruthlessly suppressed by the Venetians in 1562.[43]

Small wonder the Cypriots received the conquering but tolerant Turks as deliverers. Through his Vizier, Sultan Selim II assured an anxious Cypriot delegation to Constantinople that 'no oppression should be exercised against the Greek Christians of Cyprus.'[44] 'Feudalism was abolished. The serfs were freed after centuries of slavery ... Freedom of worship was granted to the people, the Orthodox Church was officially recognized and the ... Greek Church was given the right to repurchase monasteries' which had been alienated by their Venetian oppressors.[45] The Turks utterly expunged the Roman Church.[46]

There is evidence in the text of *Othello* that Shakespeare was aware Cypriots considered the Venetians unwelcome occupiers. On the night of his arrival Othello's mind is troubled with thoughts of 'this warlike isle' (2.1.44); although Iago already has the watch, as a double-caution Othello co-assigns Cassio to the guard (2.3.1–5). Meanwhile, Iago resolves to exploit the uneasy peace on Cyprus and its sullen native gallants:

> Three else of Cyprus noble swelling spirits
> That hold their honours in a wary distance,
> The very elements of this warlike isle
> Have I tonight flustered with flowing cups,

And the watch too. Now 'mongst this
flock of drunkards
Am I to put our Cassio in some action
That may offend the isle.

$$(3.3.51–7)$$

Moments later Roderigo enters pursued by Cassio. Iago cries: 'Away I say. Go out and cry a mutiny' (3.3.150). When the alarm bell sounds Iago shouts, 'Diablo, ho! / The town will rise' (3.3.154–5). This is no jape. The fear of mutiny is palpable among the occupiers and their women; when Othello's temper turns, Desdemona speculates the cause is 'some unhatched practice / Made demonstrable here in Cyprus' (3.4.142–3).

The Cypriots' status as vassals also provides a previously unrecognized overtone in Cassio's extraordinary command at the entrance of Desdemona in 2.1, 'You men of Cyprus, let her have your knees!'(2.1.84). It is incredible that the Venetian nobles who are present – particularly the serving governor of the isle, Montano – would kneel to the incoming general of the garrison, much less to his wife. Perhaps as a senator's daughter Desdemona might have commanded some demonstration of respect for her father's position. But under then-prevailing law her marriage had reduced her to the social rank of her husband, a black former-pagan mercenary commoner. Through Brabantio, Shakespeare has already expressed what the Venetian nobility *really* thinks of Othello, i.e. that his marriage to Desdemona deserves 'a general mock … / For if such actions may have passage free / Bond-slaves and pagans shall our statesmen be' (1.2.69, 98–9). On the other hand, a Venetian occupier might have expected (or demanded) a crooked knee as a sign of submission from native 'men of Cyprus.' What has not been recognized is that the assembly in 2.1 comprises Venetian nobles and soldiers *and* Cypriot gentlemen (who may have been recognizable by Eastern touches to their wardrobe), and that when Cassio commands men's knees *only the Cypriots* kneel. This tableau would emphasize the Venetians' status as an occupying force.

It is a testament to the faith and valor of the Cypriots that through centuries of foreign occupation they withstood repeated efforts to eradicate their Orthodox religion (and their sacred Julian calendar). When plans for the Gregorian reform were underway (1572–82), the Vatican dispatched emissaries to the Patriarch of Constantinople seeking concurrence between the Orthodox and Roman Churches on a new calendar.[47] Constantinople rejected these overtures – as it would later reject Gregory's reformed calendar; the bitter calendar dispute deepened the schism between the branches of Catholicism.[48] Only in 1923 did Greece (including Cyprus) become the last country in Europe to adopt the Gregorian calendar. Even then the adoption was for civil purposes only; the Greek Orthodox church stubbornly revised its old Julian calendar, dropping thirteen days and altering its leap year rule so that there would be no difference between the Gregorian civil and Greek Orthodox liturgical calendar until AD 2800.[49]

While the Turkish occupiers were welcomed on Cyprus in 1571, the loss of the island to Islam had a chilling effect on one important aspect of the religious life of Europe. Cyprus was Christianity's *Ultima Thule*, the farthest outpost of the Faith in a vast Muslim-dominated region. Throughout the Middle Ages and the Renaissance an enormous number of Europeans – certainly many hundreds of thousands – undertook religious pilgrimages. Although there were several great pilgrim centers in Europe – among them pre-Reformation Canterbury and Santiago de Compostela, Spain – the most exalted pilgrim destination was the Church of the Holy Sepulcher in Jerusalem. Since overland travel via the Balkans and Turkey was time-consuming and dangerous, the majority of Jerusalem-bound pilgrims traveled by sea, so the course of these voyages was well-established. A common point of departure was Venice, and pilgrim vessels routinely re-provisioned at Corfu, Crete, and at Rhodes before that island was conquered by the Turks in 1522. The pilgrims' final safe harbor was Cyprus, lying only seventy miles off the coast of Lebanon (a day's sail), and 200 miles from the principal pilgrim port in the region, Jaffa (now Tel Aviv-Yafo, Israel). Cyprus was a destination for the majority of seagoing Jerusalem pilgrims, the last-save-one harbor on their journey to the Holy Land. But once both Rhodes and Cyprus had fallen into Turkish hands, pilgrim vessels had no safe haven between Crete and Jaffa – a distance of more than 500 nautical miles.[50]

Throughout the canon – from *1 Henry IV* to *Hamlet* – Shakespeare repeatedly associates pilgrimage with his Catholic characters. Henry Bolingbroke makes an unexpected 'pilgrimage' to die in 'Jerusalem.' Falstaff refers to Gad's Hill as a junction for 'pilgrims going to Canterbury with rich offerings, / and traders riding to London with fat purses' (*1 Henry IV* 1.2.125–6). Italian Catholics Romeo and Juliet woo with the language and kisses of pilgrims (1.5.92–101), and French Catholic Helena writes that she is 'Saint Jaques' pilgrim' (*All's Well That Ends Well* 3.4.4). In *The Merchant of Venice* Antonio styles n'er-do-well Bassanio's quest for a fortune, 'Well, tell me now what lady is the same / To whom you swore a secret pilgrimage' (1.1.119–20). Would Shakespeare have allowed Ophelia to sing, 'How should I her true love know … / By his cockle hat and staff, and his sandal shoon' (4.5.23–6) if he weren't confident his audience would recognize this description of a pilgrim?[51] His Othello flatly declares his life history 'my pilgrimage' (1.3.154).

Although pilgrimages had been dismissed as foolishness in the Protestants' *Augsburg Confession* (1530) and suppressed in England under Henry VIII, Jacobeans had access to a wealth of pilgrim literature including *The Book of Margery Kempe* (1501) which contains a detailed description of a voyage from

Venice to the Holy Land. An English friar, William Wey, also undertook the journey from Venice in 1458 and again in 1462, and left a detailed manuscript guidebook, *Informacion for Pylgrymes*, which was printed by de Worde in 1498 and ran through many editions.[52] In his colorful journal Wey records that a bed for the journey could conveniently be rented in Venice 'besyde saynt Markys chirche' for one and a half ducats net.[53] By contrast, Wey warned his countrymen to avoid Famagusta, 'For many englysshe men & other also have deyed [there] for that ayre is so corrupt there aboute and the water there also.'[54] In Wey's guidebook, Kempe's journal, hundreds of extant Jerusalem pilgrims' memoirs and innumerable contracts for conveyance, Shakespeare and the Jacobeans had access to information that a voyage from (Gregorian) Venice to (Julian) Cyprus was expected to last four or five weeks.[55] And this change of place and time could create the most remarkable calendrical anomalies. During the age of rival calendars, travelers between Protestant and Catholic areas of Europe *routinely* experienced temporal anomalies we would find both startling and perplexing. For example, an England-bound traveler who departed from Gregorian France on the morning of Shrove Tuesday 11 February 1603 and enjoyed favorable winds could arrive at Julian Dover on Candlemas Eve 1 February 1602, one year and ten days before leaving Calais. Though alien to us, such calendrical quirks were familiar to Renaissance travelers. Which brings us to an intriguing hypothesis.

Let us suppose that a super-subtle Venetian and a swarthy barbarian marry in Venice on the night of Shrove Tuesday 11 February 1602/3 *More Veneto*. And let us further suppose that, on the instant, he's called to the wars, falls to his preparations for departure, and embarks early the following morning, 12 February *MV*, Ash Wednesday – without consummating his marriage. Now husband and wife make for Cyprus in separate vessels. They arrive exactly five weeks later; according to their calendar, the date is Tuesday 18 March 1603 *MV*. But according to the Julian calendar prevailing on Cyprus the date is 8 March 1602, the Julian Shrove Tuesday. That evening amid the island's general gaiety the reunited couple prepare to celebrate their nuptial, to consummate their union, and make wanton the night. But as bride and groom divest themselves for bed a crash of swords and cries of 'Mutiny!' intrude. He shoos her back to their boudoir while he surgeons the wounded. Day breaks. According to the local Julian calendar it is now 9 March 1602 – Ash Wednesday – the onset of Lent and the season of abstinence – and the marriage debt's become unpayable for the next forty-six days.

Isn't this the curious journey Shakespeare contrived for Othello and Desdemona? Doesn't the prevalence of Julius Caesar's calendar on Orthodox, mutinous Cyprus explain why Othello chooses as his lieutenant a man 'who never set a squadron in the field' (1.1.21)? The man is Cassio, a Veronese (as I will prove below) 'framed to make women false' (1.3.397) – a man almost damned *not* in a fair 'wife' but in a fair 'wise' (1.2.20) – meaning his visage, face, and particularly his manners. It's Cassio's *manner* of welcoming Emilia (and paddling with Desdemona's hand) that cues Iago's deadly gambit. 'I extend my *manners*; 'tis my breeding' says Cassio 'That gives me this bold show of courtesy' (2.1.98–9) while Iago darkly swears 'I will gyve thee in thine own courtesies' (2.1.169–70). Foppish Cassio is 'a great arithmetician' (1.1.18) – a sobriquet that in Shakespeare's time entailed the study of the calendar and, perhaps, the mathematics of warfare. Shakespeare may have personally known an Elizabethan arithmetician 'who never set a squadron in the field' (1.1.21) but was Her Majesty's sometime Muster-Master in the Lowlands, and whose son Leonard contributed an awful doggerel to the Folio. As noted above, Thomas Digges (d.1595) published the first defense of Copernicus in English. He also authored an *An Arithmeticall Warlike Treatise named Stratioticos … teaching the Science of Numbers … with Modern Military Discipline, etc.*[56] This book includes seventy-seven pages of impenetrable math which the title page declares 'requisite for the profession of a Souldier.' Why is Othello fixated on Iago's honesty? Perhaps there's a clue in Digges' description of a proper Ancient: let him be 'a man of good account, *honest* and virtuous [and] have … two or three assistants … *most honest* … [and let him be] no less careful of his charge … then every *honest* … gentleman … of his wife.'[57] Does the latter phrase account for Iago's suspicion that Othello 'twixt my sheets … has done my office' (1.3.386–7)? Why is Cassio so concerned with his reputation? Digges describes a proper lieutenant as a man 'of credite and *reputation* … of great toils and paine, the which he ought willingly to suffer … for his own *Reputation*.'[58] Digges instructs the lieutenant to 'oftentimes with his owne person … aide in setting the watch'[59] just as Othello orders Cassio to do (2.3.1). Digges would also forbid the lieutenant on pain of dismissal not to 'have [quarrel] with any [man], nor suffer any … to commit the like disorder …' Cassio is drawn into just such a disorder and justly dismissed.[60] Are these parallels coincidental? Or is there is a doctoral thesis waiting to be written on 'Digges' *Stratioticos* as a Source of Shakespeare's *Othello*'?

Iago ridicules Cassio for possessing only 'the bookish theoric, / Wherein the togaed consuls may propose / As masterly as he' (1.1.23–5). Scholars have inferred that Iago is referring to the theoric of war; that inference is not safe. In *Stratioticos* Digges remembered one togaed warrior-consul, Julius Caesar, who 'was … singularly Learned … about the Theoricke of … reformed years … called *Anni Juliani*.'[61] Is this the basis for Iago's strange declaration that Cassio, who 'never set a squadron in the field,' is notwithstanding 'a soldier fit to stand by Caesar' (2.1.118)? Like Caesar, Pope Gregory XIII had reformed the year; both had eradicated the 'old gradation, where each second' – each tick of time – 'was heir to th' first' (1.1.36–7). If you were leading a troupe of hated occupiers to a 'warlike isle' where Greek Orthodox gallants were tetchy-proud and mutinous 'unhatched practice' lurked in every shadow, wouldn't you engage an officer who understood the locals' bloody sacred calendar?

Doesn't Iago accuse his rival of an ungovernable passion for chronography? Isn't Cassio a man who'll 'watch the horologe a double set' unless he drinks himself to sleep (2.3.126–7)? Isn't the wretch a 'finder-out of occasions' (2.1.240) whose moods are equinoxes (2.2.120)? Wasn't this 'counter-caster' (1.1.30) Cassio casting horoscopes on the voyage from Venice? Isn't that why he anticipates the arrival of Iago and Desdemona 'se'nnights' hence (2.1.77)? If you doubt my portrait of a calendrical Cassio, listen to his mistress: 'What, keep a week away? Seven days and nights, / Eightscore-eight hours, and lovers' absent hours / More tedious than the dial eightscore times!' (3.4.173–5). Isn't Bianca's cunning calculation a calculated chastisement for a calendrically-calculating man? And how does Cassio excuse his absence? He'll make it up, he claims, 'in a more continuate time' (3.4.178). In counterpoint, Iago proclaims his mischief works by 'dilatory time' (2.3.368). Is it Cyprus' discontinuate and dilatory time which scholars and auditors of *Othello* have sensed shifting beneath their feet?

Not incidentally, Cassio is no wily Florentine *ala* Machiavelli as the compulsive liar Iago sneers at 1.1.19; nor is he a dissolute Roman as Othello fears at 4.1.117. (On the other hand, when at 3.1.39 Cassio says Iago's a Florentine we believe him.) In fact, Cassio is Veronese – as the 3 Gentleman, who has no reason to lie, reports in the Quarto:

> The Ship is heere put in: A *Veronessa, Michael Cassio*
> Lieutenant to the warlike Moore, *Othello,*
> Is come ashore.
>
> (2.1.25–8)

In the Folio, '*Veronessa*' becomes the wholly unintelligible '*Verennessa.*' But the Quarto's 'A *Veronnessa, Michael Cassio*' is simply a typographer's misreading of what Shakespeare wrote and 3 Gentleman said:

> The Ship is heere put in: A *Veronese, a Michael Cassio*
> Lieutenant to the warlike Moore, *Othello,*
> Is come ashore.
>
> (2.1.25–8)

As Shakespeare does in his alliterative *Moor of Venice*, in *The Merchant of Venice* he exploits the *MV*. (Is his arch alliteration mere coincidence?) Don't Jessica and Lorenzo elope on Shrove Tuesday amid 'Christian fools with varnish'd faces' and 'the vile squealing wry-neck'd fife' (2.5.33, 30)? Isn't Shrove Tuesday the day when Shylock and Antonio mask their mutual contempt and conclude their lethal joke-bond while Jessica elopes in disguise and Bassanio and Gratiano ship for Belmont after Antonio chides 'No masque [for you two] tonight' (2.6.63)? Didn't *Merchant's* links with Shrovetide provide the motive for Shakespeare and Company to resurrect the twelve-year-old play before King James on Shrove Sunday 1605, and motivate the king to command a reprise two nights later on Shrove Tuesday?[62] As Jessica and Lorenzo did, Othello and Desdemona elope on Shrove Tuesday night. This inference would be a slam-dunk if Iago and Roderigo were masquers. But aren't they? Iago proclaims – 'I am not what I am' (1.1.64) – and Roderigo will soon defeat his favor with 'an usurp'd beard' (1.3.341). With *Othello* Shakespeare has moved beyond the varnish'd faces of *Merchant* to portray a deeper, darker masquing of the soul.

In the opening scenes of *Othello* Francois Laroque detects the subversive energy of carnival.[63] The same spirits recrudesce at Cyprus, first in Iago's seamy quibbling with dissembling Desdemona (2.1.117–60), then in the Venetians' jubilation at the Turks' destruction, and finally in Iago's drinking songs. In all these episodes Laroque detects a carnival of license. And what a carnal carnival it is. Othello's Herald declares for bonfires, dancing, sport (2.2). Iago pronounces it 'a night of revels' (2.3.40). A masquer, Roderigo, wreaks havoc. The officers and watch are drunk. Everywhere, the night on Cyprus rings with insistent echoes of Act One's fateful night in Venice: Iago and Roderigo again conspired to affront authority; darkness swarms again with angry shouts; swords flash on the court of guard as they did before the Sagittary; Othello and Desdemona again fail to consummate their marriage; in the aftermath, the supreme authority again conducts an inquest.

Why these determined echoes of the Venetian Shrovetide on Cyprus? Because Shakespeare is signaling that he has set *both* sequences on Shrove Tuesday night. Act One of *Othello* begins in Venice on Shrove Tuesday *MV*. Act Two unfolds at Cyprus on Shrove Tuesday *Julian*. That is why Othello's Herald orders the revels to end when 'the bell have told eleven' (2.2.10) – because Lent begins at midnight.[64]

Shrove Tuesday on Cyprus was 8 March Julian. Shakespeare pinpoints that date in the text of *Othello* with a calendrical marker which anyone who knew her psalmody might recognize. Every song in *Othello* is known in a prior form save one:

> And let me the cannikin clink.
> And let me the cannikin clink.
> A soldier's a man.
> O, man's life's but a span,
> Why then let a soldier drink!
>
> (2.3.65–9)

Cassio cries: ''Fore God, an excellent song!' (2.3.71). Iago brags, 'I learned it in England' (2.3.72) – no doubt from William Shakespeare, who improvised this jig of Psalm 39:6, 'Behold, thou has made my days as an handbreadth …' In the calendar of The Book of Common Prayer, the 39th Psalm was prescribed for reading on the eighth day of the month. Recovering 8 March as the date of the Venetians' disembarkation at Cyprus also reveals the calendar joke in Emilia's lament, ''Tis not a year or two shows us a man' (3.4.104). The Venetians observed New Year's Day on 1 March *MV*. They left Venice in 1602 but arrived at Cyprus in 1603.

Recognizing the Venetians arrive on the 8 March Julian / 18 March *MV* also explains why Shakespeare's Cassio anticipates the arrival of Iago and Desdemona 'se'nnights' hence (2.1.77). Seven nights after the Julian 8 March is the 15th, the Ides of March, a date vividly associated with betrayal. Seven nights after 18 March *MV* is the 25 March, the Feast of an Annunciation to another wife who died a virgin, Blessed Virgin Mary. This explains Cassio's extravagant blazon: 'Hail to thee, lady, and the grace of heaven, / Before, behind thee, and on every hand / Enwheel the round' (2.1.85–7). In Renaissance painting as in literature the Lady enwheeled by the grace of heaven was the Blessed Virgin Mary.

The dual subtexts of Cassio's se'nnights calculation is Shakespeare's signal the dual calendars have kicked in – which explains why he endowed this play with two awful clown-scenes. In the morning-after-scene 3.1, the music's 'i'th' nose' (3.1.4) and the jokes are stale because Shrovetide's been-and-gone. It's the morning of 9 March, the Cypriot Ash Wednesday. And what a solemn day it is. First, Cassio prays to Desdemona for help. Then Desdemona prays to Othello to forgive Cassio. Then Iago preys on Othello's jealously inclining mind. Before the day is out, Desdemona fumbles her handkerchief, Emilia laterals it to Iago, and Othello swears the death of Desdemona and Cassio. But if this is the 9 March Julian, then the day is Wednesday. So why does Desdemona think it's Sunday? Recall her badgering Othello: 'Shall 't be tonight at supper?' – No? – 'Tomorrow dinner, then?' – if not – 'Why then, tomorrow night, or Tuesday morn, / Or Tuesday noon, or night, or Wednesday morn' (3.3.60–1). If tomorrow precedes Tuesday, tomorrow must be Monday and today must be Sunday, not Wednesday. So what's going on here? Desdemona's *lapsus linguae* is another of Shakespeare's jibes at the rival calendars. The Julian 9 March was Wednesday. But in the *More Veneto* the 9 March was a Sunday. Like many travelers, Desdemona is confused by a time-change. She's suffering the Jacobean equivalent of jetlag and, like Lancelot Gobbo remembering his nosebleed, Desdemona is conflating two calendars.[65]

There's more calendar mischief yet. The 9 March Julian was 19 March *MV*, the Feast of Joseph Husband – the archetype of a groom with good reason to fret his bride's chastity. As Saint Matthew remembered it,

> When … Marie was betrothed to Joseph, before they came together, she was founde with childe of the holie Ghost. Then Joseph … was minded to put her away. But while he thoght on these things, beholde, the Angel of the Lord appeared unto him in a dreame … (Mt. 1:18–21)[66]

This is the Gospel for 19 March, the Feast of Joseph Husband. Furthermore, 'Joseph, being raised from slepe, did as the Angel … injoyned him' and knew Mary not (Mt. 1:24–5). Is the parallel between the circumstances of Joseph and Othello, two bridegrooms who can't enjoy their brides, mere coincidence? The nasal strains of Cassio's ill-timed *aubaude* are Shakespeare's signal that it is Lent on Cyprus. And like Joseph, the convert Othello must abstain. Which explains why he's so desperate for the sight of a strawberry-dotted handkerchief – Shakespeare's oh-so-heavy-handed emblem for bed linen flecked with ruddy telltale spots.[67] When Othello roars 'Would I were satisfied!' (3.3.396) the sexual irony is deafening. But the Christian convert bridegroom who declared, 'We must obey the time' (1.3.300) *can't* be satisfied until the Lenten proscriptions lapse on the Julian Holy Saturday.[68]

Is it only coincidence Shakespeare jigs the 39th Psalm, glances seven nights ahead to the Ides and the Annunciation, intentionally writes his worst Clown scene for Ash Wednesday morn, and stages Othello's temptation on the feast day of that other anxious husband? Or did Shakespeare plan the scenic form of *Othello* with a dual-calendar almanac at hand? And was he alert to the Feast of Joseph Husband (long suppressed in England) because he was – or had been – Catholic? I will respond to this question at the close of this chapter.

There's another Joseph who figures prominently in the annals of the New Testament – and he has a specific connection with Cyprus. Like Shakespeare's Roderigo, this man sold all his land, altered his identity, and journeyed to the Greek island. 'And Joses, which was called [renamed by] the Apostles, Barnabas … Whereas he had land, solde it … Then departed … to Tarsus to seke Saul: And … sailed to Cyprus' (Acts 4:36, 11:25–6, 13:4). Which brings us to the second Clown scene (3.4) and the fool who tells Desdemona he 'will catechize the world … and be edified' (3.4.16) by the report. Who was the fool who visited Cyprus and went on to catechize and edify the world if not Saint Paul?[69]

Othello's clown-scenes are so arid directors often cut them. They shouldn't. These scenes have a critical dramatic purpose: they denote the passage of time. After Desdemona's parlay with the Clown in 3.4 the action will run seamlessly to the play's catastrophe. But how much time has elapsed before Desdemona and the Clown encounter for the second time? Twice in the play there are references to what we might call 'the passion of Cassio' lasting three days. In 2.1 Desdemona pleads that Cassio may not languish in Othello's displeasure more than three days: 'i' faith, he's penitent' (3.1.63). Othello pledges to find the nearest way 'to bring [Cassio] in' (3.3.75–6). But he doesn't. In 3.2 Othello orders Iago to murder Cassio 'within these three days' (3.2.475). Iago swears he will, but doesn't. We can be certain more than three days have elapsed when Desdemona encounters the Pauline Clown again in 3.4 because the Venetian embassage arrives on the same day (4.1). How much time, then, has passed? The entire season of Lent. How do we know? Not only because 'the messengers of Venice stay the meat' (4.2.172)[70] but because Desdemona asks Emilia to lay her wedding sheets on the bed (4.2.106–7), an unambiguous signal the Lenten proscriptions are at an end. And we know Desdemona's sheets are unspotted (proving her persistent virginity) else she wouldn't ask Emilia to shroud her in one if she died (4.3.22–3). A shroud had to be unspotted.

The Lenten proscriptions lapse on Holy Saturday. Shakespeare drops a series of heavy hints to this holy day. The most prominent is Othello's puzzling

> Put out the light, and then put out the light:
> If I quench thee, thou flaming minister,
> I can again thy former light restore,
> Should I repent me; but once put out they light,
> Thou cunning'st pattern of excelling nature,
> I know not where is that Promethean heat
> That can they light relume.
>
> (3.2.7–12)

The candle Othello carries is the light of which he first speaks, his 'flaming minister.' Desdemona's life is the second light. The central moment of the Holy Saturday ritual is the extinguishing of all candles within the church, at which point the building becomes the cold and dead body of Christ. Then, outside the church, a new light is struck by the priest and carried inside to signify the revivification of Christ. With that new flame the pure white Paschal Candle is lighted, 'signifying the figure of Jesus Christ 'appearing on earth after his glorious Resurrection.'[71] In passage 3.2.7–12 above Shakespeare has written a poetic epitome of the Holy Saturday rite from the quenching of the candle to the need for divine heat to revivify a corpse.

In 1603 Holy Saturday on Cyprus was 23 April Julian – 3 May in the *More Veneto* – a dual date with tremendous overtones. In the Julian calendar it is Holy Saturday and the eve of Easter Sunday. It is also the Feast of Saint George (and Shakespeare's putative birthday). But in the *More Veneto* it is the feast of the Invention of the Cross, that annual commemoration of the excavation at Calvary of the True Cross by that redoubtable English explorer-saint, Helena, mother of Constantine. In the widely read *Golden Legend* Helena sallies to Jerusalem, unearths the three crosses used at the crucifixion of Jesus, and proves the miraculous power of His Holy Cross by restoring a dead man to life.[72] Homebound in AD 327, Helena lands on Cyprus, bringing with her the cross of the Good Thief, which she installs at a monastery erected on the island's highest peak. We know the tempest that destroyed the Turkish fleet in 2.1 was Shakespeare's invention. But was he inspired by the valiant Helena, who tossed a nail from the True Cross into Cyprus' Satalia Bay to calm a raging storm? Does this account for the play's several references to 'bay' and 'embayed' and for Cassio's observation that the roiling sea made way for 'divine' Desdemona (2.1.73)?

Into the text of *Othello* Shakespeare drops a series of calendrical markers to indicate that Holy Saturday and the murder of Desdemona occur on the night of 23/24 April Julian – that is, 3/4 May *MV*. The first is Othello's 'It is the cause, it is the cause, my soul' (5.2.1). E.A.J. Honigmann refers us to the 16th Psalm: 'O my soul, thou has unto the Lord: thou art my Lord, *etcetera*.'[73] The 16th Psalm was the prescribed reading on the 3rd day of the month. Scholars have endlessly debated whether Shakespeare wrote of 'the base Indian (or was it 'the base Judean'?) who threw away a pearl richer than all his tribe' (5.2.345–6)? And does this allude to Judas who bestowed a fatal kiss on Jesus as Othello does on Desdemona, 'I kissed thee ere I killed thee' (5.2.356)?[74] The solution to this crux can be found in the Gospel for 4 May, Matthew 2, which begins 'in the dayes of Herod the King ...' In this chapter Saint Matthew describes the Magi's visit with Herod and his subsequent massacre of the infants. But Herod not only murdered babes. Like Othello, he put to death a pearl of a wife, Mariamne. And like Othello, he did so in the false belief his wife had been unfaithful. And like Othello, Herod ran mad with love and remorse thereafter. And, not incidentally, Mariamne's name shares a common root with Mary and Margaret – which means 'pearl' (*OED* margarite[1] 1). Not to flog a galloping horse but, like Othello, Herod was a commoner descended from pagan slaves whereas Mariamne was the granddaughter of two kings, a Hasmonean princess of Maccabeean blood – which certainly stamped her a pearl richer than all Herod's tribe which, by the way, wasn't Judean. Herod was Idumean.[75] And his mother's name was Cypros.

Finally, there is the Gospel for 3 May, Desdemona's fatal night, which will sound familiar: 'When ... Marie was betrothed to Joseph, before they came together, she was founde with childe of the holie Ghost, *etcetera*.' This is Matthew 1, the same Gospel prescribed for 19 March, the feast of anxious Joseph Husband. All these citations are drawn from Scripture prescribed for reading on 3/4 May *More Veneto*. In 5.2, more than anywhere else in *Othello*, Shakespeare un-tunes the music of the spheres. He infuses the action with the spirit of the *Protestant* Julian Holy Saturday and Easter Sunday ... while suffusing the dialogue with Psalms and Gospels prescribed for the *Catholic* 3/4 May *MV*.

Holy Saturday turns at Midnight to Easter Sunday. And Shakespeare made the most of this connection, too. On *Othello's* catastrophic night Roderigo, Desdemona, Emilia, and Othello die – and Iago exits condemned to a worse fate. But as Holy Saturday turns to Easter Sunday Shakespeare raises the dead. Desdemona revives long enough to deny Othello's guilt (5.2.115–23). Roderigo, too, speaks 'After long seeming dead [to say] Iago hurt him' (5.2.326). And Cassio, who believed his offence a 'mortal kind' (3.4.116), declared his 'immortal part' lost (2.2.257), and prayed to Desdemona that by her intercession he 'may against Exist' (3.4.112–3) – Cassio is resurrected on a wooden frame and hauled onstage as ruler of Cyprus (5.2.330) while his Magdalene hovers in the 'tiring house.

Cassio's unlooked-for good fortune fulfills the promise of his name, which Shakespeare derived from 'Cassia,' the cinnamon bark that scented the anointing oil of the priests of the Jews since Aaron (Exodus 30:24–6). *His name* identifies Cassio as 'the anointed,' 'the chosen,' 'the elect.' And Cassio's startling, unprepared exaltation is the apotheosis of the play's great theme, the triumph of inscrutable election over earthly merit – which Shakespeare articulates with uncharacteristic bluntness, though he wraps the statement in Cassio's drunken slurring: 'God's above all, and there be souls must be saved, / and there be souls must not be saved' (2.3.98–100).[76]

By contrast, Cassio's *other* – Iago – bears a name which, as Barbara Everett observed, echoes Sant*iago* Matamoros, the renowned Moor-killer.[77] The patron of Spain, Saint James Apostle, earned this sobriquet by appearing on a white charger to lead the Spanish to victory over the Moors at the battle of Clavijo in the eighth century. But Jacobeans might also have associated a soldier named Iago with the Order of Santiago, a Templar-like foundation whose knights battled the Moors in Spain during the Middle Ages. After the expulsion of the Moors in 1492, the Order's estimated 700,000 members[78] were principally concerned with protecting the routes to Santiago de Composetela, the repository of the Apostle's bones and the foremost pilgrim destination in Europe.[79] Dr Everett speculates that by assigning Spanish names to Iago and Roderigo Shakespeare is implying that Othello is more Spanish than African, more tawny than black. But if the playwright imagined a Spanish Othello why doesn't he merely say so? By christening his villain with the Spanish cognate of his king, Dr Everett acknowledges Shakespeare was flirting with *lèse-majesté*. Why would he have taken such a risk in naming Iago 'Iago' when 'Carlos,' 'Manuel' or 'Juan' would have achieved the same effect? Because, I suggest, the Spanish saint-name 'Iago' – with its potent associations with pilgrimage to Santiago de Compostela – was intrinsic to Shakespeare's framing of Othello's journey to Cyprus as an unconsummated pilgrimage. Shakespeare made Cassio the darling of providence. He fashioned Iago as the repository of the rival doctrine of merit. Though Iago has proven his valor 'At Rhodes, at Cyprus and on other grounds' (1.1.27–8) – despite 'Three great ones of the city ... [who] Off-capped' to Othello 'In personal suit' to make Iago his lieutenant (1.1.7–9) – Othello chose Cassio. In his rival from Verona, the Florentine Iago perceives only the outward man, the dandy 'almost damned in a fair wise' who 'Hath a daily beauty in his life / That makes me ugly' (5.1.19–20). Behind Cassio Iago does not see the moving hand of the puppeteer whom Maurice Hunt memorably epitomizes as 'The somber Calvinistic God of *Othello*, the God of double predestination.'[80]

Iago is a wilful sinner who makes love to his own damnation. Shakespeare's true counterpoint to the election of Cassio is the reprobation of Desdemona. 'Repeatedly Shakespeare conveys the possibility that God's grace has not preferred Desdemona. Her good deed ... (taking Cassio's cause as her own), directly leads to her death.'[81] Unconsciously, Desdemona identifies the engine driving her personal tragedy: 'In reply to Iago's question concerning Othello's rage – 'How comes this trick upon him?' – Desdemona replies, 'Nay, heaven doth know' (4.2.131). Ironically, it is through Iago's mouth that Shakespeare articulates the specialness of Cassio, though he wraps the statement in smoldering anger; the speaker (Iago) has no clue how true he speaks when he says of Cassio, 'he, sir, had th'election' (1.1.26).

The pilgrim of Shakespeare's tale is Othello. And his pilgrimage from pagan darkness to the True Religion is a 'travailous history' of 'disastrous chances ... hair-breadth scapes ... being ... sold to slavery' and redeemed, wandering 'antres vast and deserts idle, Rough quarries, rocks and hills,' encounters with 'cannibals ... Anthropophagi, and men whose heads / Do grow beneath their shoulders' (1.3.135–46) – all a journey toward Christian conversion and the arms of Desdemona, to whom 'I would all my pilgrimage dilate' (1.3.154). On Cyprus, the uttermost outpost of Christianity – a tiny island awash in a turbulent, rebellious sea barely seventy miles from the shore of the Holy Land – Othello's pilgrimage climaxes. The victim of Iago's deceit, Othello succumbs also to his Ancient's conceit of merit. All Othello's victories, all the 'Pride, pomp and circumstance of glorious war' (3.3.567), 'the big wars / That makes ambition virtue!' (3.3.352–3), even his conversion to Christianity signify nothing. And Othello achieves a numbing epiphany when he declares, 'I have done the state some service, and they know't' and in his next breath snarls at his own hollow vanity, 'No more of that' (5.2.337–8).

Above, I offered to identify one other important way in which Shakespeare construed *Othello* as a sequel to *Merchant*. The central action in both plays concerns a contract sealed at Shrovetide, a debt which goes unpaid, and the dire consequences ensuing. In *Merchant*, the contract is a loan. In *Othello* the contract is a marriage contract, and chaos ensues when the marital debt goes unpaid. Desdemona, according to the dying testimony of her intimate servant, lived and died 'chaste,' meaning as chaste as the Portia of *Merchant*, 'as chaste as Diana' (*Merchant* 1.2.103), a virgin enwheeled by the grace of heaven, before, behind, and on every hand (2.1.85–7).

Those who would discover in Shakespeare the soul of a Catholic could, with warrant, construe *Othello* as a metaphor for England, that other island nation where a band of Roman Catholics dwelt amidst another religion, another calendar, another time. Just as we could readily justify Shakespeare's knowledge of the *More Veneto* if we could say with certainty that he had visited Venice, we could reconcile his alertness to the Gregorian calendar and Catholic holy days long disused in England by inferring the inward man was Catholic. But to do so would ignore the play's rejection of the Catholic doctrine of works and the cult of virginity. Desdemona's lying deathbed confession makes her, in Emilia's words, 'more Angell' (5.2.128), and not 'a lyer gone to burning Hell' (127) as Othello declares with the unconditional, blind conviction of the convert. The exultation of the foppish-foolish-whoremongering and yet anointed, inexplicably elect Cassio is a resounding triumph of *sola gratia*. And the Moor's veneration of a virgin brings his world and faith to ruin.

Notes

1 Graham Bradshaw, 'Obeying the Time in *Othello*: a Myth and the Mess it Made,' *ES* 73:3 (1992), 211.
2 An earlier version of this chapter appeared in *English Literary Renaissance* (Spring 2003).
3 At 3.3.343–6: 'What sense had I of her stol'n hours of lust … / I found not Cassio's kisses on her lips.' Text and lineation from E.A.J. Honigmann (ed.), *Othello* (London: Methuen, 1997).
4 Thomas Rymer, *A Short View of Tragedy* (London: 1693), pp. 121–2.
5 Lewis Theobald (ed.), *The Workes of Shakespeare*, (London: 1733), 7.461.
6 Sam. Johnson and Geo. Steevens (eds), *The dramatick writings of Will. Shakspere, etc.* (London: 1788), 19.141.
7 Edmond Malone (ed.) *The Plays and Poems of Shakespeare* (London: 1821), 9.220.
8 *Blackwood's Magazine* (November 1849, April 1850, May 1850).
9 Sadly, Michael Neill has not in *Othello* (Oxford: Oxford University Press, 2006).
10 Horace Howard Furness (ed.), *The Variorum Othello* (Philadelphia: Lippincott, 1886), pp. 358–72.
11 Ned B. Allen, 'The Two Parts of *Othello*,' *Shakespeare Survey* 21 (1969), p. 16.
12 Lorne M. Buchman, 'Orson Welles's *Othello*,' *Shakespeare Survey* 39 (1987), p. 59.
13 Prior to leaving Venice, or during the voyage, Iago may well have importuned Emlia many times to steal the handkerchief.
14 Iago: 'You have not been a-bed then?' / Cassio: 'Why no, the day had broke before we parted' (3.1.31–2).
15 See M.R. Ridley, *Othello* (London: Methuen, 1958), lxvii–lxx; Karl P. Wentersdorf, 'The Time Problem in Othello,' (Bochum, *Jahrbuch der Deutschen Shakespeare-Gesellschaft West*, 1985), pp. 63–77; Thomas M. Rayso, 'The Aesthetic Significance of Shakespeare's Handling of Time,' *Studies in Philology* 32 (1935), 197–209.
16 Emrys Jones, *Senic Form in Shakespeare*, (Oxford: Oxford University Press 1971), p. 41.
17 Samuel Johnson (ed.), *The Plays of William Shakespeare* (London: 1765), 8.416.
18 Allen, p. 25.
19 Balz Engler, 'How Shakespeare Revised *Othello*,' *English Studies* 57:6 (1976), 515–21.
20 Kenneth Muir, 'The Text of *Othello*,' *Shakespeare Studies* 1 (1965), 227–39.

21 Nevil Coghill, *Shakespeare's Professional Skills* (Cambridge: Cambridge University Press 1964), pp. 162ff.
22 Honigmann, *Othello*, p. 71.
23 For a concise discussion of the history of calendar reform in Europe 45 BC–AD 1752, see John J. Bond, *A Handy-Book of Rules and Tables, etc.* (London: 1869), pp. 8–19 and pp. 91–101.
24 Bond, p. 98.
25 Bond, p. 98. The *More Veneto* remained in use in Venice until the Napoleonic conquest in 1789.
26 Until the twentieth century.
27 Cyprus was a Roman province when the Julian calendar was imposed by Augustus *ca* 15 BC. Sir George Hill, *A History of Cyprus* (Cambridge: Cambridge University Press, 1949), 1.235.
28 '1604. Hallamas Day … A play in the Banketing house att Whithall called the Moor of Venis.' *The Revels Accounts* cited in Chambers, *Stage*, 4.171.
29 Emrys Jones, '*Othello, Lepanto*, and the Cyprus Wars,' *Shakespeare Survey* 21 (1961), p. 51.
30 Unless Shakespeare had access to the manuscript.
31 Alvin Kernan believes *Othello* was 'new' play when The King's Men performed it before James on 1 November 1604. *Shakespeare, the King's Playwright*, (New Haven: Yale University Press, 1995), p. 60.
32 Maurice Hunt, 'Predestination and the Heresy of Merit in *Othello*,' *Comparative Drama* 30:3 (Fall, 1996), 346–76.
33 Bullough, pp. 242–3.
34 Jones, *Lepanto*, p. 49.
35 Norman Sanders suggests that Shakespeare may have written *Othello* to flatter King James' interest in the history of Cyprus. *The New Cambridge Othello* (Cambridge: Cambridge University Press, 1984), p. 2.
36 Jones, *Lepanto*, p. 48.
37 Venice formally ceded Cyprus to Ottoman rule on 7 March 1573. Doros Alastos, *Cyprus in History*, (London: Zeno, 1955), pp. 258–9.
38 J. Hacket, *A History of the Orthodox Church of Cyprus* (New York, 1901), pp. 163–9.
39 Alastos, pp. 214–19.
40 Awnsham Churchill (ed.), *A Collection of Voyages and Travels, etc.* (London: 1704), I, 489–91. Rpt. Claude Delaval Cobham (ed.), *Excerpta Cypria*, (Cambridge: Cambridge University Press, 1908), p. 55
41 Alastos, p. 232.
42 Hackett, p. 172.
43 Alastos, p. 233.
44 Alastos, p. 261.
45 Alastos, p. 260.
46 F.L. Cross and E.A. Livingston (eds), *The Oxford Dictionary of the Christian Church*, (Oxford: Oxford University Press, 1997), p. 442.
47 August Ziggelaar, S.J., 'The Papal Bull of 1582, etc.' in G.D. Coyne, S.J. and M.A. Hoskin, and O. Pedersen, *Gregorian Reform of the Calendar, etc.*, (Città del Vaticano, Speculo Vaticana, 1983), pp. 228–30.

48 Michael Hoskin, 'The Reception of the Calendar by Other Churches,' in Coyne *et al.*, pp. 261–2.
49 Calendrists regard the Orthodox formulation as more sophisticated and accurate.
50 By the 1590s Christian vessels could again provision at Limassol but only after payment of a bribe to the local Basha. Onshore, Christian visitors were regarded with suspicion. See Girolamo Dandini, S.J., and Joannes Cotovicus in Cobham, pp. 181–8.
51 Returning pilgrims brought home scallop shells to prove they had visited Galicia.
52 Bodleian MS. 565. Reprinted by E. Gordon Duff (ed.), *Information for Pilgrims unto the Holy Land by William Wey* (London: 1893).
53 Wye, fol.b.v^r.
54 Wye, fol.b.iiii^r.
55 John Tiptoft, Earl of Worcester, sailed from Venice to Limassol in 31 days in R.J. Mitchell, *The Spring Voyage* (New York: Murray, 1964), pp. 65–84. John Locke required 27 days in Richard Hakluyt, *The Principal Navigations, etc.* (London: 1599), xi.51.102–3. Cf. Sidney Heath, *Pilgrim Life in the Middle Ages*, (London: T.F. Unwin, 1911), p. 162; Margaret Gallyon, *Margery Kempe*, (Norwich: Canterbury Press, 1995), p. 161.
56 (London: Richard Field, 1590). On Shakespeare's association with Digges see Leslie Hotson, *I, William Shakespeare* (London: J. Cape, 1937). On his possible reliance on *Stratioticos* see Charles Edelman, *Shakespeare's Military Language* (New York: Athlone Press, 2000), pp. 11, 202, 357–8.
57 Digges, p. 93 [my emphasis].
58 Digges, p. 95 but misnumbered 93 [my emphasis].
59 Digges, p. 96 but misnumbered 94.
60 There may be a clue to Iago's complaint that he is 'be-leed and calmed / By debitor and creditor' (1.1.29–30) in the rate of pay for an Ancient, which was half the allowance for a Lieutenant according to Digges, p. 73.
61 Digges, p. 308.
62 E.K. Chambers, *William Shakespeare* (Oxford: Oxford University Press, 1930), ii.330–2.
63 Francois Laroque, '*Othello* and Popular Traditions,' *Cahiers Elisabethains* 32 (1987), 14–15.
64 Although the church insisted holy days began at Vespers on the previous evening, in practice Midnight was the hour more commonly observed. Edith Cooperrider Rodgers, *Discussion of Holidays in the Later Middle Ages* (New York: Columbia University Press, 1940), pp. 72–3.
65 Like Gobbo's joke, Desdemona's harrying of Othello functions on two levels. Auditors can enjoy the young bride's near-comic doggedness even if they do not guess she is conflating two calendars.
66 Citations throughout from the Bible (Geneva, 1560).
67 But see Lawrence J. Ross, 'The Meaning of Strawberries in Shakespeare,' *Studies in the Renaissance* 7 (1960), 255–40.
68 T.G.A. Nelson and Charles Haines, 'Othello's Unconsummated Marriage,' *Essays in Criticism* 33 (January 1983), 1–18.
69 Paul repeatedly refers to himself as 'fool' in 2 Cor. 11–12.

70 Meat was forbidden during Lent. However, Shakespeare's phrase 'the meat' may have been idiomatic for a meal generally.

71 Leduc and Baudot, p. 268.

72 William Granger Ryan (ed.), *The Golden Legend of Jacobus de Voragine* (Princeton: Princeton University Press 1993), I.277ff.

73 Honigmann, *Othello,* p. 305n.

74 For example: Arthur Freeman, *'Othello's* 'Base Indian': v.ii.347,' *Shakespeare Quarterly* 13:2 (1962), pp. 256–7; Robert F. Fleissner, 'The Three Base Indians in *Othello,' Shakespeare Quarterly* 22:1 (1971), 80–2; Naseeb Shaheen, 'Like the Base Judean,' *Shakespeare Quarterly* 31:1 (1980), 93–5.

75 Isn't the word which Shakespeare wrote (and which confounded the typesetters) 'the base *Idumean*'?

76 Hunt, p. 346.

77 Barbara Everett, 'Spanish Othello,' *Shakespeare Survey* 35 (1982), 103.

78 *Encyclopaedia Brittanica on CD-ROM* (1999).

79 Cross and Livingston, p. 1454.

80 Hunt, p. 346.

81 Hunt, p. 359.

EIGHT

'Who's there?':
The men behind the masks of Falstaff, Faulconbridge, Lamord, and Hamlet

Scholars have closely examined William Shakespeare's relations, real and imagined, with those dedicatees of his poems and sonnets, the Earl of Southampton and elusive Mr. W.H.[1] By contrast, Shakespeare's literary monuments to his Lords Chamberlain have gone largely unnoticed. This chapter identifies three of these postmortem tributes: the first for William Brooke, Lord Cobham, in *Henry V*; a second for Henry Carey, first Baron Hunsdon, in *King John*; the third for Carey and his son, George, in *Hamlet* Q2. In recovering these lost encomia this chapter reveals the historical figures behind some of Shakespeare's most remarkable, memorable characters.

When Henry Carey died on 23 July 1596 he had been patron of Shakespeare's acting company and Lord Chamberlain to Queen Elizabeth for more than a decade.[2] Carey's elder son, George, inherited the former distinction and politicked hard for the latter; he was disappointed. On 8 August 1596 Elizabeth gifted the lucrative and influential post to William Brooke, 10th Baron Cobham, member of the Privy Council and Warden of the Cinque Ports.[3] But young Carey did not brood long; Brooke died after only seven months in office and George received the white wand on 14 April 1597.[4] In the interim, so we're told, Shakespeare leveled two broadsides at Brooke.

The first appears in *1 Henry IV* (1596) wherein Shakespeare imprudently lampooned Brooke's illustrious ancestor, Sir John Oldcastle, who had married Joan, Baroness Cobham, in 1409.[5] Shakespeare may have found license for exploiting Oldcastle's famous name in the old play, *The Famous Victories of Henry the fifth* (*ca* 1588), in which Sir John is cast as the misleader of Prince Hal's youth. Shakespeare's knight is an old, fat, irreligious, manipulative, thieving, loveable prevaricator.[6] By contrast, the historical Oldcastle was a doughty fellow-in-arms to both Henrys IV and V, a courageous convert to

Lollardry who inspired an abortive insurrection and rode a hurdle to the flames at St Giles's Fields in December 1417. Oldcastle's exploits were familiar to Elizabethans via John Foxe's ubiquitous *Acts and Monuments* (1563); the hagiographer had honored the martyr with an elaborate testimonial and a name day (7 December) in his martyrology.[7]

Apparently Shakespeare's caricature of Oldcastle created a flap at court; we know that some months after the debut of *1 Henry IV* Shakespeare altered the name 'Oldcastle' to 'Falstaff' and appended an Epilogue to its sequel, *2 Henry IV* (1597),[8] vouching that 'Oldcastle died martyr / and this is not the man' (31–2).[9] In his edition of 1709 Nicholas Rowe explained Shakespeare's disclaimer: 'some of the [Oldcastle/Cobham] family being then remaining, the Queen was pleased to command him to alter it; upon which he made use of Falstaff.'[10] Though this explanation seems plausible enough, we have only Rowe's word for it, and his single-source intelligence is viewed by some with skepticism.[11] Even so, scholars generally receive Shakespeare's *2 Henry IV* epilogue as his 'apology' to Brooke for buffeting Oldcastle.[12]

But if one considers what the epilogue says – rather than what we have been told it says – it's impossible to find in it an apology to Brooke, or to anyone other than the original John Oldcastle.[13] Below I'll demonstrate that Shakespeare *did* pay his debt to Brooke – but not until 1599.

What is held out as Shakespeare's second swipe at Brooke appears in *The Merry Wives of Windsor* (1597) via the character of foolish Ford, a husband who cloaks himself in the alias 'Brooke' while soliciting his own cuckolding (2.2.152–3).[14] This play is thought to have been purpose-written for the occasion of new Lord Chamberlain George Carey's induction as a Knight of the Garter in 1597.[15] If so, the merrymaking lords might have received Ford's alias as a tidbit of fun at the expense of Carey's late rival.[16] Curiously, the name 'Brooke' also underwent an Oldcastle-like transformation; when *The Merry Wives of Windsor* appeared in the Folio of 1623 the impertinent 'Brooke' had become an everyday 'Broome.' Below I'll suggest why this may have transpired.

Despite the estimable scholarship which has been lavished on Shakespeare's supposed slights to Brooke[17] these instances remain naggingly out-of-character for Henry Chettle's man of 'civill' demeanor and Jonson's 'Sweet swan of Avon.'[18] One cannot but wonder why a man of Shakespeare's admired discretion would intentionally – and so very publicly – twit a powerful court official upon whose good will his own career and the fortunes of his acting company depended. On Brooke's side there is no evidence that his attitude toward plays or players was other than benign; though as Lord Chamberlain Brooke was not at pains to shelter the players from the antagonism of London's Puritans, he did *not* subscribe the notorious petition of Blackfriars residents which prevented Burbage from operating a lucrative playhouse in that district (whereas George Carey did sign).[19]

A more likely explanation for Shakespeare's 'Oldcastle' gaffe is that *1 Henry IV* was written and staged prior to Henry Carey's death on 23 July 1596. And Brooke's appointment as Lord Chamberlain was as awkward a surprise for Shakespeare as it was to George Carey. Regarding the 'Brooke' alias in *The Merry Wives of Windsor*, if – as we've been told – this play was written in haste (in a fortnight?)[20] for performance on Saint George's Day, 23 April 1597 – well, by that date Brooke had been dead six weeks, i.e. no harm, no foul.

Far from being Brooke's antagonist, in 1599 Shakespeare wrote into *Henry V* a sentimental memorial for his late Lord Chamberlain which scholars have never recognized. In 2.3, Bardolph, Pistol and their Eastcheap brothers-in-arms are preparing to join the king's expedition to France when Hostess brings word that Sir John Falstaff has died. On hearing this Bardolph declares, 'Would I were with him, wheresome're he is, either in heaven or in hell.' To which Hostess responds,

> Nay, sure he's not in hell. He's in Arthur's bosom if ever man went to Arthur's bosom. A made a finer end, and went away an it had been any christom child. A parted ev'n just between twelve and one, ev'n at the turning o'th' tide – for after I saw him fumble with the sheets, and play with flowers, and smile upon his finger's end, I knew there was but one way. For his nose was a sharp as a pen, and a babbled of green fields. (2.3.9–16)[21]

This speech has two thrusts. First, Hostess assures us that Falstaff – after a death as decorous as any innocent child's – has been saved. His soul has flown directly to 'Arthur's bosom' – that is, Abraham's heavenly bosom.[22] Given that Hostess is speaking on the eve of Henry V's departure for France – 11 August 1415 – Falstaff's is a remarkably (early) Protestant death-and-salvation.[23] Then again, Foxe and the Elizabethans admired Lollard Sir John Oldcastle as an archetypal Protestant.[24]

The second thrust of Hostess' speech is a minute description of the circumstances surrounding Falstaff's death. Hostess is precise about the hour, telling us Falstaff 'parted ev'n just between twelve and one,' i.e. between Midnight and 1 a.m. Further, Hostess noticed Falstaff died 'ev'n at the turning o'th' tide.' This is the traditional hour of leave-taking, when ships left harbor and sailors bade loved ones farewell; tide-turn became, thereby, a commonplace for the final leave-taking, death.[25] Remarkably, the circumstances of Falstaff's death parallel exactly those surrounding the death of William Brooke.

Brooke died on the night of 5–6 March 1597. We know this from a letter of Rowland Whyte to Sir Robert Sidney. On Sunday 6 March Whyte wrote to Sidney, 'About midnight my Lord Chamberlain [Brooke] died.'[26] So Brooke and Falstaff died at the same hour of the night. Brooke's place of death was a well-known venue, the Cobhams' London seat in Blackfriars near the confluence where the Fleet River enters the Thames. With modern oceanographic computer software it is possible to recover the time at which the tide in the Thames turned at this location on the night Brooke died. In fact, on the night of 5–6 March 1597, the Thames tide turned at 12:19 a.m. – that is, at nineteen minutes after Midnight.[27] So *both* Falstaff and Brooke died about Midnight at the turning of the tide. Furthermore, there is evidence that Shakespeare placed the death of Falstaff immediately after Henry's discovery of the conspiracy of Richard, Earl of Cambridge (*H5* 2.2), but before the king embarks for France because of a reference to the historical Oldcastle-Cobham which Shakespeare found in his principal source for the play, Raphael Holinshed's *Chronicle.*

In his Epilogue to *2 Henry IV* Shakespeare had promised that Falstaff would die on campaign with Henry in France: 'our humble author will continue the story with Sir John in it, and make you merry with fair Katherine of France, where, for anything I know, Falstaff shall die of a sweat' (Epilogue 21–3). But Falstaff doesn't live to make the voyage to France; he dies in Eastcheap on the eve of the sailing. Commentators have attributed this anomaly to the departure from the Lord Chamberlain's Men of the company's clown, Will Kemp, who likely had played Falstaff in *1–2 Henry IV* and *The Merry Wives of Windsor,*[28] which inference may be correct. But an entry in Holinshed's *Chronicle* may explain why Shakespeare set the scene of Falstaff's death on the eve of Henry's sailing and, in particular, between Chorus' report of the Earl of Cambridge's conspiracy and the king's embarkation for France.

The death scene sequence begins with Chorus' report of the conspiracy of Richard, Earl of Cambridge, Henry Lord Scroop, and Thomas Grey (20–6). Then the Boy reports Falstaff's illness (2.1.81–5). Shakespeare next takes us to Southampton where Henry confronts the conspirators and pronounces sentence upon them (2.2). But before Henry embarks for France Shakespeare shifts us back to Eastcheap for Hostess' report of the death of Falstaff (2.3). Only after Falstaff's mates receive this news do they shift to join the king's armada before it sails. For this interleaving of the illness and death of Falstaff with the Cambridge conspiracy Shakespeare found his model in Holinshed's *Chronicle.*

Holinshed recounts the Cambridge conspiracy at 3.345–8. He describes Henry's departure for France at 3.349. But between these two events the chronicler abruptly brooks his narrative of the drama in Southampton to recount a sidebar story concerning the activities of Sir John Oldcastle, the fourth Lord Cobham. According to Holinshed, while Henry was dealing with Cambridge *et al.,*

> About the selfe same time the Lord Cobham with his friends, whether as one of the counsel in the conspiracie with the earle of Cambridge, or not, was determined to have made some attempt against the lord of Aburgevennie, who

being advertised thereof, got for his defense ... to the number of five thousand archers, and other armed men ... whereof when the lord Cobham was advertised, he withdrew againe to such secret places about Malverne, as he had provided for his surety ... Unto that place the lord Aburgevennie went ... but the lord Cobham and his folks were withdrawne into some other place, after they once heard that the earle of Cambridge and the lord Scrope were executed (3.349).[29]

Holinshed's Oldcastle sidebar appears at *precisely* the same point in the narrative – after the discovery of the conspiracy but prior to Henry's embarkation – at which Shakespeare interleaves the illness and death of Falstaff in *Henry V*.

In sum then, Shakespeare contrived for Falstaff to die between Midnight and 1 a.m., just as the tide turned – exactly as did William Brooke. Furthermore, Shakespeare placed his accounts of Falstaff's illness and death at the exact juncture in the narrative where Falstaff's and Brooke's mutual namesake, Sir John Oldcastle, appears in Holinshed. Given the history of the Oldcastle/Falstaff/Cobham flap of 1596, this correlation of time, tide and text can hardly be coincidental.

Recovering Shakespeare's links between the deaths of Falstaff and Brooke casts a new and dark light on the curiously bitter rivalry that erupts between Pistol and Nym in 2.1–3. As Falstaff lies dying the pair come near to violence over the hand of prostitute/madam Nell Quickly and the lordship of her tavern-whorehouse – two doubtful prizes. Their incessant, ugly squabbling may have been inspired by events surrounding the death of Brooke. The Lord Chamberlain's last illness was bruited from at least 18 February;[30] London society – certainly including Shakespeare and his company – were keenly aware that as Brooke lay dying swarms of noblemen and arrivistes shamelessly politicked and jockeyed to succeed to his offices and emoluments. These opportunists included the Earl of Essex, young Brooke, George Carey, Sidney, Whyte, and others. Whyte's letters amply convey their ugly machinations. Shakespeare's Eastcheap rivals embody their venality.

If Hostess is describing the deaths of both Oldcastle-Falstaff and Brooke – and their mutual instantaneous salvation – clearly, few Elizabethan playgoers could have recognized this correlation; *Henry V* appeared in Spring 1599, two years after Brooke had passed. Indeed, it's hard to imagine *any* auditor – except those who were present when Brooke died – who could have detected Shakespeare's gentle memorial.[31] But isn't this tiny coterie precisely those persons whom Shakespeare's memorial for Brooke was intended to touch? Gabriel Harvey told us 'The younger sort takes much delight in Shakespeares *Venus, & Adonis*: but his *Lucrece*, & *his tragedie of Hamlet, Prince of Denmarke*, haue it in them to please the wiser sort.'[32] If this new reading of Shakespeare's portrait of the death of Falstaff – and its meditation upon his late Lord

Chamberlain is valid – some of the coteries for whom Shakespeare wrote were *very* small coteries, indeed – even so few as the deathwatchers of William Brooke.[33]

From what we know of Brooke the man, Shakespeare's Hostess' promise of his salvation was entirely fitting. Though an influential and powerful grandee, Brooke was a man of learning, modesty, charity – and a Christian who believed in forgiving trespasses. He may well have requested that Shakespeare alter the name 'Oldcastle' out of respect for his eminent forebear. Or one of Brooke's adherents or dependents may have asked (or demanded) the alteration on the family's behalf. But Hostess' insistence that Falstaff-Brooke made a fine end and flew to Abraham's bosom is a genuine and an affecting tribute – and appropriate. In his will, Brooke endowed an almshouse and refuge for the poor of Kent which still serves today. He refused burial in Westminster Abbey, and called for no lavish monument to be raised above his grave; indeed, his resting place near the tomb of his father in the rural village of Cobham was soon overlooked and its location lost. But Shakespeare's monument to William Brooke has been recovered. And it will last the ages.

By the time George Carey died in 1603 he and his father had been Lords Chamberlain and patrons of Shakespeare's company for two decades. Shakespeare and his colleagues were deeply beholden to these noblemen for cachet, opportunity, exposure at court, advancements financial and social, and – when necessary – protection from a perilous political environment. Shakespeare's debt to the Careys ran deep. So it should hardly be surprising that the playwright honored father and son with substantial memorials, one of which appears in *Hamlet* Q2.

Though commentators generally concur that *Hamlet* Q1 is a reconstructed text based on the recollections of the actor(s) who played the parts of Marcellus, Lucianus, and Voltemand,[34] there is no consensus as to the pedigree of Q2. To judge from its printer's claim on the frontispiece, Q2's appearance may have been occasioned by the pirated version of the play (Q1) which appeared in 1603. (There has been speculation about an earlier play based on Saxo Grammaticus' chronicle of Amleth – a so-called *Ur-Hamlet* – perhaps written by Thomas Kyd and extant prior to 1600.[35] But that subject is beyond the purview of this chapter.)

In fact, we know that a play associated with the Lord Chamberlain's Men entitled 'The Revenge of Hamlett Prince Denmarke' was extant by 26 July 1602; a 'blocking entry' designed to prevent publication by anyone but the entrant, James Roberts, appears in the Stationers' Register on that date. The entry did not, however, prevent the publication in 1603 of Q1, which Gregg describes as 'a "Bad Quarto," the text of which runs to no more than 2220 type-lines, whereas there are almost 3800 in the "Good Quarto" of

1604–05.'[36] The latter, 'printed for I.R. (James Roberts) for N.L. (Nicholas Ling)' claims to be 'Newly improved and enlarged to almost as much againe as it was, according to the true and perfect Coppie.'[37] Even so, there is disagreement as to the pedigree of Q2. Is this text, as G.R. Hibbard and others allege, 'Shakespeare's first draft ... [while] the Folio text is essentially his revision of that first draft, together with some additions'?[38] Was Q2 written shortly before its publication in the winter of 1604–5?[39] Or did Shakespeare's *Hamlet* exist full-blown as early as 1599/1600 as Harold Jenkins, Andrew Gurr and others believe?[40]

By parsing a handful of passages – some of which appear in Q2 only – I will suggest Q2 was purpose-written late in 1603 to embody an elaborate memorial for Henry and George Carey. Further, I will offer evidence that Q2 is a rewrite of a pre-existing, full-blown *Hamlet*. And I will propose that Shakespeare's Q2 revision was occasioned by three events which occurred in 1603: the death of Queen Elizabeth during the night of 23/24 March 1603; the death of George Carey on 9 September of that year; and the 'seven-years' day' anniversary of the death in 1596 of Henry Carey, first Baron Hunsdon. Elizabethans considered the 'seven years' day' anniversary of an individual's death a significant milestone; I have long suspected that Hemminges and Condell published the Folio in 1623 to commemorate the seventh anniversary of Shakespeare's death in 1616. Shakespeare certainly noticed the seven years' anniversary of the death of colleague Christopher Marlowe. Marlowe died on 1 June 1593; in 1600 Shakespeare commemorated Marlowe's seven years' day with his 'Dead Shepheard' couplet in *As You Like It*.[41]

A central element of Shakespeare's memorial for the Careys in *Hamlet* Q2 is the appearance in 4.7 of a mysterious Frenchman not in Q1. Suborning Laertes to Hamlet's murder, Claudius recalls:

> some two months since
> Heere was a gentleman of *Normandy*.
> I have seene my selfe, and serv'd against, the French,
> And they can well on horsebacke, but this gallant
> Had witch-craft in't, he grew unto his seate,
> And to such wondrous dooing brought his horse,
> As had he beene incorp'st, and demy natur'd
> With the brave beast, so farre he topt me thought,
> That I in forgerie of shapes and tricks
> Come short of what he did.

> *Laertes*   A Norman wast?
> *Claudius* A Norman.
> *Laertes*   Upon my life *Lamord*.[42]
> *Claudius* The very same.
> *Laertes*   I know him well, he is the brooch indeed
> And Jem, of all the Nation.

Claudius He made confession of you,
          And gave you such a masterly report
          For art and exercise in your defence,
          And for your Rapier most especiall,
          That he cride out 'twould be a sight indeed,
          If one could match you; the Scrimures[43] of their nation
          He swore, had neither motion, guard, nor eye,
          If you oppos'd them; sir this report of his
          Did Hamlet so envenom with his envy,
          That he could nothing doe but wish and beg
          Your sodaine coming ore [from France] to play with him.

                                              (Q2 4.7.69–91)

The genesis of Shakespeare's mysterious Norman and the proper spelling of his name have eluded and tantalized scholars for generations. Both mysteries can be resolved by reference to a long-ignored incident that was a turning point in the fortunes of the Carey family.

Henry Carey (1526?–96) was the nominal son of Mary *nee* Boleyn and her husband William Carey, sometime Master of the Horse to Henry VIII.[44] The pair married on 4 February 1520; Mary was then fourteen, Carey twenty-four.[45] Thereafter, Mary lived at court; her first child, Catherine, was born in 1524 – after which she embarked on an affair with the King for which her husband was richly compensated.[46] Mary's royal tryst ended in July 1525, perhaps when she realized she was pregnant. Eight months later on 4 March she gave birth to Henry Carey. Since it was common knowledge that King Henry had enjoyed Mary as well as her sister Anne[47] – and since the boy Carey strongly resembled the king – and since the child was baptized Henry (as was the king's acknowledged bastard, Henry Fitzroy [1519–37]) – it was then as now suspected that Henry Carey was King Henry's bastard son.

But if Carey were Henry's natural son, why didn't he acknowledge him as he had Fitzroy, whom he named Duke of Richmond in 1524? Because had the king done so the impediment of consanguinity (his coitus with Mary) would have rendered his marriage to her sister Anne nugatory.[48] Even so, on William Carey's death (23 June 1528) the king seized two year-old Henry from his mother's care and appointed Queen Anne his guardian.[49] Once at court the boy was well-educated and popular.[50] Henry was Elizabeth's favorite cousin; shortly after coming to the throne she created him Baron Hunsdon (1559) and Knight of the Garter (1561).[51] She also named him Master of the Hawks (which may explain Q2 Hamlet's expertise in hawks and handsaws [2.2.397]). Carey patronized a company of players of which James Burbage was a member. Like son Richard, carpenter James was an actor;[52] in 1584 he claimed to be 'Lord Hunsdon's man.' During the following year Elizabeth named Carey her Lord Chamberlain.[53]

As to the pedigree of Henry Carey's quasi-father, William, he was a descendent of an old Norman family. From their ancestral home in Lisieux, France, the Carreys [sic] had migrated to the island of Guernsey[54] and to England ca 1066.[55] But by the reign of Henry V the English Carys [sic] had apparently fallen on hard times. Then, suddenly, their line was ennobled by the remarkable feat of arms which was a defining event in the family's fortunes. This encounter is recorded in an obscure chronicle entitled *Remarkable Antiquities of the City of Exeter* (1681). It is a tale uncannily parallel to Shakespeare's anecdote of *Lamord*:

> [In] AD 1413 a Knight named Argonise, who in divers Countries for his Honour had performed many noble Achievements, at length visited England, and challenged many persons of his Rank and Quality to make trial of his skill in Arms, which the said Sir Robert Cary accepted, between whom was waged a cruel encounter and a long and doubtful combat in Smithfield, London; where this Mars vanquished this Argonise, for which he was by the King knighted and restored to part of his Father's inheritance.[56]

So William Carey's forebear, Robert, won his spurs and redeemed his family's fortunes by defeating a French champion at Smithfield under the eye of Henry V.[57] There is every reason to believe the Careys of Shakespeare's era cherished the memory of this ancient victory. As the Exeter chronicler records, 'by the Law of Heraldry, whosoever fairly in the Field conquered his Adversary may fortify the wearing and bearing of his Arms … and accordingly he [Sir Robert Cary] takes on him the Coat Armoury of the said Argonise, being Argent on a bend Sable, Three Roses of the First, and ever since born by the name of Cary …'[58] As a consequence, the arms of Argonise were a familiar sight to Shakespeare and Elizabeth's courtiers. Could the successors of Robert Carey fail to recognize Shakespeare's tale of *Lamord* as a retelling of their family's ennoblement by Henry V? I think not.

Having established this concordance between the historical Argonise and the fictional *Lamord*, it is finally possible to confirm the correct spelling of the fictitious Frenchman's name, a conundrum long debated by scholars. This difficulty arose from variants in Q2 and the Folio; whereas Q2 gives us *Lamord,* the Folio has *Lamound* – which latter spelling Rowe adopted in his edition of 1709.[59] In 1726, Pope opted for *Lamond.*[60] In 1821, Edmond Malone speculated Shakespeare wrote *Lamode* to suggest the Frenchman was fashionable (*a la mode*).[61] In the Victorian era *Lamond* was preferred.[62] Our contemporary editors embrace *Lamord* unanimously, beginning with Bevington (1980), and Wells and Taylor (1986).[63] In 2002 Orgel and Braunmuller footnoted with finality, '*Lamord* i.e. "the death" (French: *la mort*),' and there the matter has rested.

But in 1899 Edward Dowden produced this curious reading of *Lamord*: 'I retain the Q form of the name,' he wrote, 'having noticed in Cotgrave, "*Mords,*

[Fr.] a bitt of a horse."' Then he added, 'Several of Shakespeare's names for minor characters are significant.'[64] Jenkins – unaware of the Exeter chronicle – also suspected a hidden significance: 'The excessively elaborate introduction of the fencing stratagem suggests ... it had for the dramatist some ulterior significance ... many suspect a personal allusion.'[65] In fact, Dowden and Jenkins came within a hair's breadth of truth;[66] as we have seen, *Lamord's* identity *is* a personal allusion which honors the Careys whose line was ennobled by the defeat of a French champion.

But if this is so, how is Shakespeare's fictitious name *Lamord* analogous to the name Argonise? Certainly, Shakespeare must have recognized the historical champion's name implied that he came from the woodsy Argonne region of France. Does Shakespeare's *Lamord* also have a geographical etymology? I suggest it does.

Dowden's curious reading was nearly correct; *Lamord* is related – tangentially – to the French word for the equine bitt or bit, *mords*. But the playwright's translation was not literal; rather, he is indulging in a typical Shakespearean wordplay – on the French *mordre* = bite, and its homonym, byght (modern: bight). A bight is an indentation in a coastline – a body of water cupped between two headlands (*OED*) – of which there are several in Europe, including the Egmont Bight in Dorset and the Helgoland Bight where the British claimed a famous victory over the German navy on 28 August 1914. *Lamord's* Norman background identifies his bight with the Seine Bight – that bay where the River Seine empties into the Channel, hard by Harfleur where Shakespeare's Henry V delivered his memorable 'Once more ....' exhortation to his reluctant English tigers.[67] But another nearby Norman town is at the fulcrum of Shakespeare's *Lamord* gambit: Lisieux.[68] In 1066 the cathedral town of Lisieux was home to the Carrey family, whose descendant Henry was patron of Shakespeare's company and Lord Chamberlain. If this inference is valid, an obscure event in Carey family history finally certifies the spelling of Shakespeare's Frenchman's name as *Lamord*.

Another passage unique to Q2 recalls a second and more contemporary – but no less defining – event in the Carey family's fortunes: Henry's illegitimate birth. Had Henry Carey's father married his mother rather than her sister, Henry would have been King Henry IX of England and his son King George I. Carey's illegitimacy deprived his bloodline of royal hope, and in Q2 1.3 Shakespeare provided Hamlet with a long soliloquy on bastardy which appears neither in Q1 nor the Folio. Naturally enough, the occasion for Hamlet's reflection on his illegitimate birth is his anticipation of a confrontation with the Ghost of his father.

As 1.3 begins, Hamlet, Horatio, and Marcellus shiver on a platform awaiting the appearance of the Ghost. The night is shattered by the trumpets and ordnance of the king's rouse. Horatio asks, 'Is it a custom?' and Hamlet replies,

Ay marry is't,
But to my mind, though I am native here
And to the manner born, it is a custom
More honoured in the breach than the observance.[69]

(Q2 1.3.13–38)

In Q1 and F Hamlet's speech ends here and 'observance' provides a weak cue for the Ghost's entrance. But in Q2, Hamlet continues with a speech about the curse of illegitimate birth:

So oft it chaunces in particuler men[70]
That for some vicious mole of nature in them
As in their birth wherein they are not guilty,
(Since nature cannot choose his origin)
By the ore-grow'th of some complextion
Oft breaking downe the pales and forts of reason,
Or by some habit, that too much ore-leavens
The form of plausive manners, that these men
Carrying I say the stamp of one defect
Being Natures livery, or Fortunes starre,
His vertues els be they as pure as grace,
As infinite as man may undergoe,
Shall in the generall censure take corruption
From that particuler fault: the dram of eale
Doth all the noble substance of a doubt
To his own scandle.

(Q2 1.4.23–36)

Hamlet alleges that 'some vicious mole of nature … in their birth' predisposes 'particuler men' to ungovernable appetite ('complextion') or ugly 'habit' which inevitably brings them to ill-repute. Incongruously, the child polluted by this 'vicious mole' is 'not guilty' since he 'cannot choose his origin' – that is, his parentage or the circumstances of his conception and birth. Notwithstanding, the 'vicious mole of nature' pollutes the innocent child with 'one defect' so virulent that, were all the man's other virtues 'pure as grace,' nevertheless he 'shall in the generall censure [the Last Judgment] take corruption [be damned by] that particuler fault.'

What form of obloquy could cause an infant *in utero* to forfeit hope of salvation? To the minds of Elizabethans there was such a stain – only one – and it is described in Deuteronomy, a book of the Old Testament that came in for a good deal of close reading in Henry VIII's England.[71] But before examining the Scripture, a word about Hamlet's 'vicious mole.'

When Shakespeare wrote this speech 'vicious' had not achieved its savage modern sense; rather, 'vicious' alluded to vice – 'depraved, immoral, bad' (*OED*). Applied to persons, it meant 'addicted to vice or immorality … profligate, wicked.' 'Mole,' of course, is a 'spot or blemish on the human skin …

a fault.' It also signifies the familiar small mammal, in which sense *OED* finds it applied to persons who exhibit 'mole-like' qualities, i.e. 'whose (physical or mental) vision is defective.' We know the identity of the 'mole' in *Hamlet*; at Q2 1.5.161 the prince addresses the ghost of his father as 'olde Mole.' Hamlet declares the stain of his bastardy unshirkable as livery, indelible as Fortune's star; Elizabethans believed bastardy could not be expunged from a newborn infant, not even by the sacrament of baptism.[72] Deuteronomy 23:2 declares: 'A bastard shal not entre into the Congregacion of the Lord: even to his tenth generacion shall he not entre into the Congregacion of the Lord.'[73]

Hamlet's meditation on illegitimacy concludes with lines Jenkins nominated 'the most famous crux in Shakespeare':

> . . . the dram of eale
> Doth all the noble substance of a doubt
> To his own scandale.
>
> (Q2 1.4.36–8)

'Dout' means 'put out, extinguish.' 'Scandale' was closely associated with sexual incontinence; *OED* cites, 'O God, that one borne noble should be so base, / His generous [engendering] blood to scandall all his race.'[74] But what about the mysterious 'dram of eale'?

To parse this phrase one needs to remember that Hamlet is replying to Horatio's question about the king's rouse; his cue is excessive drinking and Hamlet's diction is drawn from associated jargon. Elsewhere, Shakespeare uses 'dram' both in its sense of avoirdupois weight and a measure of fluid.[75] He also quibbles with the word in an ethical sense: dram = scruple = compunction (*2 Henry IV* 1.2.130; *Twelfth Night* 3.4.79). But at the close of Hamlet's speech Shakespeare is using 'dram' in the sense of a fluid measure *and* quibbling on an unspoken word: 'bastard.'[76] In addition to bastard's familiar meaning 'born out of wedlock, illegitimate,' its homonym 'bastarde' identified a 'sweet kind of Spanish wine, resembling muscadel; sometimes any kind of sweetened wine' (*OED*) including Falstaff's favorite, sack.[77] Shakespeare uses the word in this sense in *1 Henry IV*: 'Score a pint of bastarde in the Half-moon'(2.4.30).[78] *Bastarde* wines differ from varietals by what the French call *dosage*,[79] wherein wine is adulterated with a foreign substance, usually sugar or honey, as an aid to fermentation.[80] A wine thus adulterated forfeits its varietal appellation, loses its 'name,' and is left nameless – i.e. a 'bastard(e).'[81]

As to the etymology of the mysterious 'eale,' the word is a variant of 'ealdren,' an obsolete dialectical form of 'elder' (*OED*) signifying the tree which produces the elderberry, from which wine has been fermented in England since ancient times.[82] Owing to the low sugar content of elderberries, winemakers 'bastardize' their juice with honey. Elderberry wine – eale – is always a bastarde.[83]

This reading of Q2's 'dram of eale' speech receives surprisingly strong support from Shakespeare's previously unrecognized source for it, *De*

Laudibus Legum Angliae by Sir John Fortescue (1394?–1476?), Chief Justice of the King's Bench under Henry VI.[84] This book appeared in 1537; over the next two centuries it became a definitive treatise on English law.[85] Fortescue explains that a child conceived out of wedlock *forever* carries the stigma of bastardy, even if the parents subsequently marry:

> [To] the childe borne out of matrimonye, the lawe of Englande alloweth no succession, affirmynge it to be naturall onely and not lawfull [because] the sinne of the firste carnal accion [premarital coitus] … is not purged by the matrimonie ensuynge … whiche doth not onelye judge the childe so gotten to be illegittimate but also prohibiteth it to succede in the parents inheritance … (fol. 90r–94r)[86]

Fortescue then asserts the intransigent stain of bastardy in language that reads like a prose paraphrase of Hamlet's 'dram of eale' speech:

> If a bastard bee good, that cometh to him by chance, that is to wytte, by speciall grace but if he be evil that commeth to him by nature. For it is thought that the base child draweth a certein corruption and stayne from the synne of his parentes, without his owne fault … Howbeit the blemish which bastards by the generation do receave … thereof is immortall: for it is knowen with god and with men … whom nature in her gyftes severeth, markynge the natural or bastard chyldren as it were with a certein privie mark in their soules. (fol. 96r–97v)

This passage shares an extraordinary run of vocabulary with Hamlet's speech: chance, grace, nature, corruption, fault, stain and blemish, without his own fault, known with God ('general censure'), 'nature … marking' ('Nature's livery'), and the notion that bastards carry 'a certain privie mark in their souls.' Indeed, Hamlet's speech reads like Shakespeare's poetical précis of Fortescue.[87] Can there be any doubt that Hamlet's soliloquy is a royal's meditation on the blemish of his bastardy? Not incidentally, the motto of the Carey family was *Sine Macula* – 'without blemish.'[88]

Recognizing Hamlet's bastardy finally explains why the courtiers of Denmark lent quick approval to Claudius' and Gertrude's hasty marriage (Q2 1.2.13–16). Since Hamlet was illegitimate – and, therefore, could not inherit the crown – that fact rendered the Old Hamlet-Gertrude marriage effectively childless. In these circumstances Deuteronomy 25:5–6 requires the widow to have sex with and marry the brother of her deceased husband – *in that order*: 'If brethren dwel together, and one of them dye & have no childe, the wife of the dead shal not mary without : *that is,* unto a stranger: but his kinseman shall go in unto her, and take her to wife, and do the kinsemans office to her.'[89] This practice is known commonly as the Law of the Levirate.

Neither Hamlet's 'dram of eale' speech nor *Lamord* appears in Q1. In the Folio the 'dram of eale' soliloquy has vanished and *Lamord* has become *Lamound*. Briefly, I would like to speculate as to why this is the case.

I have suggested that Shakespeare produced his Q2 rewrite in late 1603 to memorialize the death of George Carey and the seven-years' anniversary of the death of his father, Henry. I do not believe Shakespeare would have dared create this memorial to the Careys had not Queen Elizabeth died earlier that year. The Queen had been declared a bastard three times – by her father, by parliament, and by the pope; according to Fortescue's interpretation of England's inheritance laws, the Careys' claim to the crown was as flawed as Elizabeth's but every bit as good. But on the night of 23/24 March 1603 Elizabeth died. And by the time James VI of Scotland was crowned James I at Westminster Abbey on 25 July (Saint James' Day) the new king had already received a most extraordinary pledge of the Careys' loyalty; James had been notified of Elizabeth's death on 26 March by George Carey's younger brother, Robert, who rode with the news and a ring from London to Holyrood House in two days.[90] Then again, James had his own legitimacy issues – which may explain why the 'dram of eale' speech had vanished by the time *Hamlet* appeared in Folio. I infer that Hemminges and Condell excised the politically problematic speech – and disguised *Lamord* behind the spelling *Lamound* – on the conviction there was no sense tenting old wounds; for the same reasons they altered Ford's pseudonym in *The Merry Wives of Windsor* from Brooke to Broome.[91]

There is another passage unique to *Hamlet* Q2 which links Shakespeare's rewrite with clan Carey. And I believe this link places the matter beyond dispute. In the Folio prior to the fencing match Claudius calls out,

> Set me the Stopes of wine upon the Table:
> If Hamlet give the first, or second hit,
> Or quit in answer of the third exchange,
> Let all the Battlements their Ordinance fire,
> The King shal drinke to Hamlet's better breath …

(F 5.2.264–71)

Claudius' references to ordinance, battlements, and drinking echo the king's rouse which preceded Hamlet's soliloquy on bastardy. Claudius continues, 'And in the Cup an *union* shall he throw / Richer than that which foure successive Kings / In Denmark's crown have worn' [my emphasis]. 'Union' could mean 'marriage.' Or it could mean 'pearl.' Or it could mean both, which is marvelously *apropos* since pearls are known to dissolve in wine and Claudius' poisoned chalice will dissolve his marriage to Gertrude as it kills her; a husband's marriage to his wife ends at the moment of her death. The union/pearl in the cup is such an elegant metaphor it's difficult to accept that it could be a later addition.[92] Indeed, it appears in Q2 in a curious form which leaves no doubt the metaphor was present in a version of *Hamlet* prior to 1604 *and* suggests Shakespeare altered the metaphor in his Q2 draft in order to honor the Careys.

In Q2 the object dropped into the chalice isn't a pearl; it is an 'Onixe.' Claudius says, 'And in the cup an Onixe shall he throwe' – and, later, Hamlet says, 'Drink of this potion, is thy Onixe here?' As he worked up Q2 Shakespeare inserted 'Onixe' in the two places where the word 'union' had appeared in the pre-existing text. But Shakespeare overlooked the single appearance in the old text of the word 'pearl.' After dropping an 'Onixe' into the cup Claudius says, 'Stay, give me drinke. Hamlet this *pearl* is thine.'[93] Since the union/pearl metaphor doesn't appear in Q1, we must conclude Q2 is a flawed rewrite of another pre-1604 text which included the pearl but has been lost. Therefore, Q2 cannot be Shakespeare's first draft of the play.

Which brings us to a pair of seemingly unanswerable questions. Having created his elegant union/pearl metaphor in an earlier draft of the play, why did Shakespeare disfigure it in the Q2 text? And why did he replace his union with, of all objects, an onyx? The answer to both questions can be seen today in a small glass display case in the Elizabethan Gallery of London's Victoria and Albert museum.[94] It is a fabulous and famous gem, the gift of Queen Elizabeth to the man who headed her bodyguard during the alarm of the Spanish Armada: her favorite cousin, Henry Carey. One can imagine how proudly Carey wore this magnificent tribute, perhaps hung about his neck on a golden chain. The gem is known to historians of decorative art as 'The Hunsdon Onyx.'[95] For the coterie of persons who knew George Carey would have been King of England had Henry VIII married his mother rather than his aunt … who remembered that the Careys fetched their coat-of-arms from a French champion named Argonise … and who had seen Henry Carey wearing the magnificent Hunsdon Onyx … Shakespeare's previously unrecognized encomium in *Hamlet* Q2 rang clear.

These links in *Hamlet* Q2 could as readily connect Shakespeare's Danish prince with Henry Carey as with his son; though George may have been born in wedlock, according to Deuteronomy 23:2 Henry's heirs would carry the stain of his bastardy 'to his tenth generacion.' But Shakespeare may have also have included in Q2 a direct and trenchant reflection on George Carey's final illness and death. Although Carey died on 9 September 1603, he relinquished the Chamberlain's white wand on the prior 4 May to Thomas Howard, later Earl of Suffolk. In fact, Howard had been discharging this office since 28 December 1602 because Carey was slowly dying of sexually transmitted disease, most likely syphilis, and the pernicious effects of treatment with mercury.

Historians continue to debate whether syphilis was present in Europe in the medieval era or imported from the New World after Christopher Columbus' discoveries. In either case, by Shakespeare's time the malady the English called 'the French disease' was endemic; modern investigators speculate that syphilis carried off such luminaries as Charles VIII, Francis I, Ivan the Terrible, and

Henry VIII. The madness of the latter's daughter, Mary, is ascribed to congenital infection and/or contact with Philip of Spain. Since the disease felled heads of state and grandees as well as the poor, the progress of syphilis had been carefully observed by physicians and was well understood in Jacobean England.

Syphilis develops in four stages; the primary and secondary stages may run together during the first ninety to 120 days after infection. These stages are characterized by the appearance of sores and lesions, by fever, and by hair loss. Then, abruptly, the sufferer's symptoms vanish and the disease enters a latent, hidden phase. This hiatus may last for one year or as many as twenty. The disease's emergency from latency – its tertiary stage – is marked by virulent symptoms which may include ulceration of the skin and internal organs, cardiovascular degeneration, intense thoracic pain – which the English called 'bone-ache' – and madness. Shakespeare may be glancing at George Carey's death in a passage in Q2 which appears in neither q1 nor the Folio:

> There liues within the very flame of loue
> A kind of weeke or snufe that will abate it,
> And nothing is at a like goodnes still,
> For goodnes growing to a plurisie,
> Dies in his owne too much, that we would doe
> We should doe when we would: for this would changes,
> And hath abatements and delayes as many,
> As there are tongues, are hands, are accidents,
> And then this should is like a spend thrifts sigh,
> That hurts by easing; but to the quick of th'vlcer ...
>
> (q2 4.7.115–24)

This speech – and its delicacy of phrasing – seems wholly out of character as well as out of place; the usurper, Claudius, is addressing Laertes, and suborning Polonius' son to Hamlet's murder. Shakespeare's catalogue of ills proceeding from 'the very flame of love' includes pleurisy, death, sighs, hurts by easing, and ulcers; these could be symptomatic of any number of diseases. But they could be symptoms of tertiary syphilis. Indeed, the reference to 'abatements and delayes' – the sense of a time of opportunity missed – may refer to a syphilitic's latent stage. The Cambridge *Hamlet* editor, Philip Edwards, finds the disappearance of this passage from the Folio extraordinary.[96] But like the other emendations discussed above, discretion may have been the motive of Shakespeare's first editors; the begetter of this passage had been dead and buried twenty years when the Folio appeared in 1623.

Though opaque to us until now, the dual portraits of Henry and George Carey as Hamlet – royal bastards – winners of a valuable onyx – must have been transparent to Carey's heirs and intimates. If so, it is certainly possible that Shakespeare's Q2 occasioned a quiet sensation when it was performed in the winter of 1603. That might explain why a pirated and mutilated Q1 text was rushed into print that year in defiance of a blocking entry in the Stationers' Register and despite the play having been extant since at least July 1602. The Careys' long service as Lords Chamberlain may also explain why Hamlet takes upon himself so many of that officer's duties, e.g., engaging actors, choosing a play, vetting the argument, advising the players on decorum, and even writing a dozen or sixteen lines.

Had Queen Elizabeth lived into the winter of 1603 one can hardly imagine Shakespeare daring so blatant a portrait of a royal bastard as the Hamlet of Q2. By contrast, when Shakespeare set out in 1596 to create his encomium for the newly deceased Henry Carey, Elizabeth was very much alive.[97] She was also the focus of lively controversy and much discontent. Some of her subjects had religious grievances, some a lingering distaste for the beheading of Mary Queen of Scots (8 February 1587); many were anxious over Elizabeth's failure to produce an heir, which could presage a problematic succession that might fall upon the Catholic Infanta of Spain. On the other hand, popular disquiet was counterbalanced by the powerful English tradition of loyalty to the reigning monarch, as well as a loathing of rebellion and destabilization – witness the indifference of Londoners to the Earl of Essex's abortive *putsch* in 1602.

But while an aging Elizabeth held the throne (she turned sixty-three in 1596), a robust and manly natural son of Henry VIII had been busily and heroically defending the state from the northern marches to the Channel coast. As the son of Anne Boleyn's sister, Henry Carey was Elizabeth's first cousin, a ward of the crown and Elizabeth's friend and favorite. But Carey was no fey courtier; contemporary accounts characterize him as frank, outspoken, bluff – a warlike man. Throughout her reign Elizabeth relied on Carey's capabilities – and loyalty – implicitly. She sent him north in 1568 to quell the intrigues festering about the captive Mary Queen of Scots, and the numberless dangerous conspiracies among the northern earls and their Scots accomplices. When civil war erupted in Scotland after the assassination of the regent, Earl of Moray James Stewart, without waiting for Elizabeth's consent Carey waded in on the side of young James VI. The intrepid Carey captured Hume Castle, and then – still without Elizabeth's warrant – marched his men from Edinburgh to Glasgow to fight alongside the forces of James' new regent, the Earl of Lennox. Though his troops were vastly outnumbered, Carey won a series of startling victories; the Queen wrote to him, 'you were by God appointed the instrument of my glory.'[98] This was the stuff of legend.

By spring 1571, the northern marches were quieted. But Carey still pursued the renegade Earl of Northumberland – which led to a remarkable episode. Carey 'used the threat of force to bring about the surrender of the castle [at

Leith] but to no avail; the defenders hoped for succor from France while the king's party clamoured insistently for more money ... [finally] in May 1572 the Scots handed Northumberland over in return for £2000.'[99] Commodity, indeed.

Carey's magic touch in the north made him indispensable to Elizabeth for the next fifteen years. Though she appointed him to her Privy Council in 1577 and handed him the wand of Lord Chamberlain in July 1585, Elizabeth repeatedly sent Carey north when danger threatened. His final sally was in 1587. As the Armada crisis loomed Carey was abruptly recalled in April 1588 to raise the musters in Norfolk and Suffolk and to serve as chief of the Queen's personal bodyguard, which implies that Carey enjoyed the Queen's perfect trust. For this service Elizabeth presented Carey with the magnificent Hunsdon onyx. In his latter years Carey served as a leading and tireless member of Elizabeth's Privy Council. He died on 23 July 1596 and was buried in Westminster Abbey on 12 August at the Queen's expense – a fitting tribute to the extraordinary career of a royal bastard. His heirs erected a monument over his grave that is, even by Westminster standards, regal.[100]

Henry Carey's loyalty to Elizabeth – a queen against whom any number of rebels and pretenders, foreign and domestic had intrigued – is all the more remarkable when one considers that under prevailing English law Carey's claim to the crown was every bit as good (and bad) as Elizabeth's. This man who was widely believed to be the son of Henry VIII – who looked like Henry, bore his name, talked like Henry, swaggered like Henry, and fought like Henry – was a steadfast paradigm of loyalty to a barren queen who had been declared a bastard by father, parliament, and pope. Though rough-and-ready, Henry Carey was also the patron of the company of William Shakespeare; his offices presented to Elizabeth's court and to the world some of the greatest literature in the English language. Surely, this man was recognizable in his own time as a royal figure. Yet his ambitions were modest and his loyalty stainless. I believe that William Shakespeare honored these royal qualities in his patron and celebrated them in his greatest and most admired bastard in *King John*.[101]

Perhaps the following assessments can convey the concordance of the natures, manners, and personalities of the historical Carey and Shakespeare's fictional Philip Faulconbridge. According to *DNB*, Carey 'stood out in the estimate of his contemporaries by his plain speaking, forthrightness, and lack of guile. He had no hesitation in baldly pressing schemes, usually for strong measures, which ran counter to the wary caution of his devious [monarch]. His ambitions squared with his temperament. In Sir Robert Naunton's phrase: "He loved sword and buckler men."'[102] William Brooke's biographer, David McKeen, left this encomium for Carey:

A bluff man and a good soldier, devoted to his cousin and the interests of her state
… he amply repaid Elizabeth for her advancement of him, and for forty years
occupied with remarkable modesty and restraint the place of her nearest male
relation. [At his death] the government would miss especially his influence upon
Essex, for, himself a man of the sword, he [Carey] alone among the Councillors
had commanded the earl's respect in military matters. Though unpolished,
Hunsdon presided for more than a decade over the Household and ceremonial
life of the Court, and in its cultural pursuits took a memorable lead, both as the
licenser of plays and as the patron of the acting company that numbered
Shakespeare among its members.[103]

But the moment in Carey's life which most strikingly embodies the royalty
of spirit with which Shakespeare endued his Faulconbridge was Carey's final
hour. Henry Carey had long sought an earldom for himself and his heirs.
Perhaps because of Carey's (unspoken) claim to the crown Elizabeth denied
him this advancement. It wasn't until she was confident Carey was dying that
the queen relented. Fuller reported that 'When he [Carey] lay on his death-bed,
the Queen gave him a gracious visit, causing his Patent for the said Earldom to
be drawn, his Robes to be made, and both to be laid down upon his bed; but
this Lord (who could dissemble neither well nor sick) "Madam," said he,
"seeing you counted me not worthy of this honour whilst I was living, I count
myself unworthy of it now I am dying."'[104] If there is truth to this tale, Carey's
words must have been whispered among his intimates and retainers – and
more widely – within moments after they fell on the chastened ear of the
Queen.

It is, I suggest, Henry Carey's fault that *King John* is considered Shakespeare's
most unsatisfying play; '[its] stage history in the twentieth century is a
melancholy record of fewer and fewer productions.'[105] Even the handful of
scholars who have written at length about *King John* find themselves pressed to
appreciate (or defend) its curiously hollow structure and lack of a central hero-
figure.[106] Sigurd Burckhardt wrote that 'Even bardolaters have little good to say
about the last two acts … And I strongly suspect that Shakespeare himself
knew that he was not bringing the thing off.'[107] The play's most admired
Shakespearean creation is dismissed as a supernumerary: '*King John* with
Faulconbridge as hero is a play without form and void, signifying nothing. He
is outside the structure of the play as he is outside it historically.'[108]
Furthermore, there is no consensus as to whether the anonymous *The
Troublesome Reign of King John* (published 1591) was Shakespeare's source for
King John or vice-versa. Formidable scholars have queued on both sides of the
question; one has even mounted an argument that Shakespeare wrote both
plays.[109]

Rather than engage in the precedence debate I will address two nagging
questions which have pursued *King John* through the twisting annals of

Shakespearean scholarship. First, if the majority opinion as to the date of *King John* (1595 or 1596) is correct, why would Shakespeare take up and rewrite the creaky old play *The Troublesome Reign of King John* (1591)? Burckhardt wondered aloud, 'Why did he [Shakespeare] choose the subject at all?'[110] Second, why is there no reference in Shakespeare's play to that event for which John's reign is best remembered, the signing of *Magna Carta*?

I will demonstrate that the version of *King John* we have – first printed in the Folio of 1623 – was purpose-written in 1596 to commemorate the death of Henry Carey. I will also suggest why *King John* – as scholars have noticed – exhibits pre-echoes of *Hamlet*. Finally, I will demonstrate that Shakespeare does recognize (and lament) *Magna Carta* in a way appropriate to the censorious era in which he lived, a time when issues of domestic and foreign policy were banned from the stage as were enactments of the sacraments.[111]

Our principal dissatisfaction with *King John* comes with the final act, when Prince Henry makes his sudden appearance and we find ourselves convinced that the wrong man (boy) possesses the throne. In 1962, William Machett identified the root of our discontent:

> The plot of *King John* is built around the question of who should be King of England and thus of what constitutes a 'right' to the throne. In the first act, three characters are shown to have particular claims to the crown [John, Arthur, and the Bastard Faulconbridge]. With the death of Arthur, the failure and eventual collapse of John and ... the growth of the Bastard ... it would appear that the Bastard is being groomed to take over as rightful king. The final scenes, however, with their surprising introduction of a new claimant of unknown character and ability [Prince Henry], defeat this expectation ....[112]

I believe this disconcerting denouement is *precisely* the effect Shakespeare was driving at when he took up *The Troublesome Reign* in order to commemorate the death of Henry Carey.

In the months immediately following Carey's death it would not have taken much coaxing to encourage the wiser sort among Shakespeare's audience to correlate his dashing Faulconbridge with the late-great, larger-than-life Henry Carey. Shakespeare's character's royal bastardy, outspoken manner, heroism, and selfless honor could have been sufficient. But Shakespeare was not an allegorist; the playwright adopted two subtle strategies to forge links between Carey and the Bastard. First, through a series of time-shift devices he refocused his auditors' attention from the thirteenth to the sixteenth century. Then, with near-invisible brushstrokes he painted the Carey crest into his canvas.

As I've noted, time-shift devices were a playwright's innovations – usually comprising topical allusions and anachronisms – cues well-understood by Tudor audiences. These device enabled playwrights and auditors to delve into contemporary subjects which were banned by the censors. One obvious time-shift device which Shakespeare employed in *King John* is his reference to a

French 'armado' (1384–5).[113] Shakespeare's loaded word, 'armado,' does not appear in *The Troublesome Reign;* it is also Spanish in form, 'armada' being the French. When Shakespeare's *French* King Philip announces his 'armado' has foundered an Elizabethan audience could hardly fail to link his speech with the fate of the *Spanish* King Philip's Armada of 1588.[114] Henry Carey had raised the muster and commanded Elizabeth's personal bodyguard during that emergency just as the Bastard will emerge to lead the armies of King John.[115]

Another series of Shakespeare's time-shift signals – obscure to us but loudly resonant to Elizabethans – appears in King John's diction as he defies the papal legate, Pandulph:

> What earthie name to Interrogatories
> Can tast the free breath of a sacred King?
> Thou canst not (Cardinall) devise a name
> So slight, unworthy, and ridiculous
> To charge me to an answere, as the Pope:
> Tell him this tale, and from the mouth of *England,*
> Adde thus much more, that no *Italian* Priest
> Shall tythe or toll in our dominions:
> But as we, under heaven, are supreme head,
> So under him that great supremacy
> Where we doe reigne, we will alone uphold
> Without th'assistance of a mortall hand.
>
> (1074–85)

In this speech Sigurd Burckhardt hears an apotheosis of the 'Elizabethan world order'[116] and Lily B. Campbell detects 'the voice of Elizabeth' speaking through John.[117] Though attractive, these inferences miss the mark. It is not Elizabeth speaking but her father, Henry VIII. John's order of discourse was meticulously crafted by Shakespeare to convey the voice of the late king. A careful reading of these lines will demonstrate that John's words are not so much dialogue but a litany of the principal Henrican attacks on the power of the papacy in England.

To begin, 'interrogatories' are legal questions, generally in writing, demanded of a witness or litigant. Saint Thomas More notes in his *Apology* that it was common practice to question suspected heretics from a written list of interrogatories; many of the questions were cleverly designed to trip the interrogatee and/or entrap him in heresy.[118] But it was also common practice for a sitting court, when witnesses or litigants were distant, to send written interrogatories to be answered under oath in the presence of an officer of a local court secular or clerical. In 1533 the practice of sending interrogatories from Rome to England was outlawed by *The Act in Restraint of Appeals* (24 Henry VIII, c. 12).

John's next lines ridicule the name 'pope' and exchange it for 'Italian priest,' a common epithet in Shakespeare's time. But the pope's title was officially denounced in *The Ecclesiastical Licenses Act* (25 Henry VIII, c. 21) of 1534, which makes repeated references to 'the Bishop of Rome, called the Pope.'

John next dismisses the pope's power to 'tythe or toll in our dominions.' Tithing and tolling are two distinct activities. In 1532, Act 23 Henry VIII, c. 20 placed a moratorium on the payment to the Pope of those tithes known as 'first fruits,' i.e. the first year's revenues of a newly appointed English bishop. This ban became permanent in 1534 under the *Act Restraining the Payment of Annates* (25 Henry VIII, c. 20). As to the pope's power to 'toll' – i.e. to levy a tax upon the kingdom of England itself by exacting an annual tribute of two hundred Pounds known as 'Peter's pence' – this facility was suppressed in 1534 by *The Ecclesiastical Licenses Act*.

Finally, we come to John's/Henry's proclamation that 'we, under heaven, are supreme head' of the Church in England. The historical King John could not have said this. The words derive from the opening sentence of *The Act of Supremacy* (26 Henry VIII, c. 1) 1534, which finally made official the break with Rome. In its opening sentence this act states that 'the King's Majesty justly and rightfully is and oweth to be the Supreme Head of the Church of England'.[119]

Considered in this light, John's speech to Pandulph is not merely a regurgitation of the Protestant propaganda in England under Elizabeth. Shakespeare has written a point-by-point iteration of the anti-papal statutes of Henry VIII – and Shakespeare's John very nearly ticks through Henry's statutes in exact chronological order. By so doing, Shakespeare contrives to make his King John thunder with the voice not of Elizabeth but of Henry VIII, father of Henry Carey. Elizabethans would not have confused the voice of Henry VIII with Elizabeth as even our leading scholars have done. Shakespeare's auditors knew that only Henry had been 'supreme head' of the English church; Elizabeth became merely its 'supreme governor' in 1559.[120]

Shakespeare's source, *The Troublesome Reign*, begins with Queen Elinor importuning the barons to recognize John as a worthy successor to late King Richard (1.1–8). When Shakespeare took up the old play he deftly restructured the drama to focus attention on *acts of recognition;* these occur at critical junctures in his drama.[121] Shakespeare's first act of recognition may have preceded his first line of dialogue; some commentators and directors argue that Shakespeare's *Actus Primus* should open with a dumb-show coronation of John.[122] I agree, and believe Shakespeare's company offered a coronation pantomime preceding John's preemptory, '*Now* say *Chatillion* what would *France* with us?' (5 [my emphasis]). The coronation dumb-show may have been repeated prior to the first line of 4.2: 'Heere once againe we sit: once again crown'd' (1718); John has been recognized as king a second time, much to the consternation of his nobles. In 5.1 John's kingship is recognized a third time as

Pandulph replaces the crown upon his head. Against this repetitious, hollow pageantry is set the stony reality of the citizens of Angiers – who cannot and will not recognize John as their rightful king, or Philip of France either.

The Bastard is also the focus of three acts of recognition. In 1.1 Eleanor recognizes Faulconbridge as the son of Richard *Cordelion*. In 5.1, the despairing John recognizes the Bastard as the leader of the English armies, saying, 'Have thou the ordering of this present time' (2246). There is a final act of recognition in the play – when the Bastard kneels before the boy-king Henry, saying, 'with all submission on my knee, / I do bequeath my faithfull services / And true subjection everlasting' (2714–16). Shakespeare found all these acts of recognition in some form in *The Troublesome Reign*.

But Shakespeare added another act of recognition in *King John*. It occurs in a scene which pre-echoes the opening scene of *Hamlet*. Both scenes take place in perfect darkness; the characters on stage cannot see one another's faces. *King John* 5.6 begins,

Hub	Whose there? Speak hoa, speak quickely, or I shoote.
Bast	A Friend. What art thou?
Hub	Of the part of England.
Bast	Whither doest thou go?
Hub	What's that to thee?
Hub	[*Bas.*] Why may not I demand of thine affaires,
	As well as thou of mine?
Bast	Hubert, I think.
Hub	Thou hast a perfect thought … (2550–60)

The moment is eerily reminiscent of the opening of *Hamlet* Q2:

Bar	Whose there?
Fran	Nay answere me. Stand and unfolde your selfe.
Bar	Long live the King.
Fran	Barnardo.
Bar	Hee.
Fran	You come most carefully upon your houre.
Bar	'Tis now stroke twelfe, get thee to bed *Francisco*.

(1.1.1–6)[123]

In *Hamlet* as in *King John*, a watchful soldier issues a challenge only to find himself challenged. In *Hamlet* the speakers recognize one another by voice. But in *King John* the challenger must ask, 'Who are thou?' to which the Bastard pregnantly replies, 'Who thou wilt; and if thou please / Thou mayst befriend me so much as to think / I come one way of the Plantagenets' (2564–6). Whereas *The Troublesome Reign*'s acts of recognition were all matters of *political* recognition, Shakespeare's 5.6 has an elusive, almost existential quality. 'Who's there?' is the question of *identity* which haunts both the bastards of *King John* and *Hamlet*.[124] Shakespeare, commencing work on an encomium for George Carey in *Hamlet* Q2 may have looked back at his memorial for Henry Carey in the *King John* of 1596. The common thread tying the two plays is the bastardy of the protagonist – which links both Faulconbridge and Hamlet with the Careys. We might say *The Tragedie of Hamlet Prince of Denmarke* begins at *King John* 5.6.1.

In addition to time-shifting the onstage action from the thirteenth to the sixteenth century and creating a new and suggestive act of recognition, Shakespeare sketched into *King John* minute details which link his Bastard with Henry Carey. These instances are particularly inscrutable; overt references to the newly deceased Carey in late 1596 would certainly have run afoul of the censor and new Lord Chamberlain, William Brooke. But as inscrutable as Shakespeare's Carey-Faulconbridge links may be, they are also unmistakable. The first appears moments after Eleanor recognizes Richard *Cordelion* in Philip Faulconbridge:

> *Eleanor*   He hath a trick of *Cordelions* face,
> The accent of his tongue affecteth him:
> Do you not read some tokens of my sonne
> In the large composition of this man?
>
> (93–6)

Henry Carey, of course, was said to strongly resemble Henry VIII both in his face and burly physique. But this might have been said of any number of men. Now comes one of Shakespeare's almost-invisible innovations which links Faulconbridge and Carey; this is the name of Lady Faulconbridge's attendant, who does not appear in *The Troublesome Reign* but with whom Shakespeare's Bastard seems to enjoy familiar relations. The name appears as 'Gurney' in the Folio stage direction 'Enter Lady Faulconbridge and James Gurney' (232.sd). But the stage direction may have been a book-keeper's interpolation; Shakespeare spells the name *Gournie* in the Bastard's speech, 'James Gournie, wilt thou give us leave a while?' (241). As to the particularity Shakespeare lends to *Gournie* – who appears here and never again – Braunmuller notes that 'Shakespeare rarely names plebian characters so precisely unless there is an ulterior motive.'[125] As in the case of Lamord, Shakespeare's invented name *Gournie* – with its final -*ie* – points to France and, particularly, to Normandy, the ancestral home of the Careys. The names 'Gournie' and 'Gurney' derive from the town of Gournay in Haute-Normandie not far from Lisieux.[126] Ascelin and Hugh de Gournay fought beside William the Conqueror at Hastings in 1066; perhaps some Carreys of Lisieux or Guernsey accompanied them.

Another of these barely detectable nods to the Careys can be found in Prince Henry's only memorable speech. When Pembroke says of the prince's dying father 'even now he sung' (2618), Henry seems as nonplussed as we are; he muses, ''Tis strange yt death shold sing' (2626). An Elizabethan audience would have found this moment not quite so strange as we do. Shakespeare's cue for a singing king was John's declaration in *The Troublesome Reign*, 'the spirit I cry unto my god, / As did the Kingly prophet David cry' (2.1079–80). King David, of course, was the author of the psalms. Shakespeare's John, who died on the night of 18/19 October 1216, was singing the psalms prescribed for that night of the month.[127] Henry continues,

> I am the Symet to this pale faint Swan
> Who chaunts a dolefull hymne to his owne death,
> And from the organ-pipe of frailety sings
> His soule and body to their lasting rest.

> (2527–30)

Scholars attribute this passage to folk-lore which held that the otherwise silent swan sang a dying 'swan-song' with its last breath.[128] But it is apparent that Shakespeare has gone a very long way around to tell us of a singing John and liken him to a swan. Swans figured prominently in the Carey coat of arms. Henry Carey's crest was a swan. Honigmann speculates that Folio's 'Symet' is a typesetter's misreading and that Shakespeare wrote 'Sycnet.'[129] I suspect this is correct; 'sycnet' meant both 'cygnet' and 'signet,' i.e. 'a small seal, usually one fixed on a finger-ring' (*OED*). If Shakespeare's cygnet is emblematic for George Carey mourning his late father, the playwright must have written *King John* after 23 June 1596, the day on which Henry Carey died leaving his swan-crest signet to his mourning son.

Above I offered to demonstrate that in *King John* Shakespeare alludes to *Magna Carta* in a way designed to escape the notice of the censors and all but the wiser sort among his auditors. Though long overlooked by scholars, Shakespeare's mischief is readily made clear. At the start of the Folio's *Actus Tertius* the kings John and Philip enter followed by Lewis, Eleanor, and others. Expansively, Philip opens the scene by addressing his newlywed daughter-in-law, Blanche: "'Tis true (faire daughter) and this blessed day, / Ever in *France* shall be kept festivall' (1000–1). It is the wedding day of Lewis and Blanche – the day of the uniting of the kingdoms – and the day which dashes Constance's hopes for Arthur's ascendancy. Shakespeare based these passages on Scene V of *The Troublesome Reign* which begins with an expansive King John declaring 'This is the day, the long desired day / wherein the Realmes of *England* and of *France* / Stand highly blessed in a lasting peace' (904–6). In both *The Troublesome Reign* and *King John* a king's speech provokes a bitter response from Constance (though in the former play her principal railing on her misfortune occurs in the prior Scene IV).

Aside from telling us it's a happy day, the author of *The Troublesome Reign* tells us nothing about the day upon which his scene takes place. By contrast, Shakespeare is particular about the day of Constance's lament; it is a Solstice, as we learn from Philip's 'the glorious sunne / Stayes in his course' (1002–3).

There are two Solstices, in June and in December. We know Philip is referring to the Summer Solstice because the siege of Angers occurred during the month of June 1200 – in proof of which the next scene opens with the Bastard's 'Now by my life, this day grows wondrous hot' (1285). From this information modern auditors or readers would infer that Shakespeare conceived his scene unfolding during the interval 20–23 June, the usual dates of the Summer Solstice. But this would not be correct.

The Summer Solstice came to fall in the interval 20–23 June only after the Gregorian calendar reform of 1582, long after the era of King John. In the 13th century the Julian calendar prevailing in Europe was 6.8 days in error; consequently, the Summer Solstice occurred each year in the interval 13–16 June. Constance's lament takes place on the Solstice. So did the signing of *Magna Carta*. The charter was signed on 15 June 1215. Elizabethan mathematicians and astronomers could easily divine that in 1215 the Summer Solstice occurred on 15 June at 9:19 a.m.

Shakespeare has set Constance's lament on the solar anniversary of the most historic event of King John's reign.[130] Viewed in this context, Shakespeare's version of Constance's rant – which bears little resemblance to her railing in *The Troublesome Reign* – takes on a new, illuminating coloration. When Philip declares that 'The yearely course that brings this day about, / Shall never see it, but a holy day' Constance replies

> A wicked day, and not a holy day.
> What hath this day deserv'd? what hath it done,
> That in golden letters should be set
> Among the high tides in the Kalendar?

> (1006–11)

For 'tides' some editors infer 'times'; this is not correct. Constance's line is further evidence this scene takes place on the Summer Solstice. On the Solstice the tidal ranges in the oceans are increased, and high tide during daytime is significantly higher than the high tide at night. Constance continues,

> Nay, rather turne this day out of the weeke,
> This day of shame, oppression, perjury.
> Or if it must stand still, let wives with childe
> Pray that their burthens may not fall this day,
> Lest that their hopes prodigiously be crost.
> But (on this day) let Sea-men feare no wracke,
> No bargaines breake that are not this day made;
> This day all things begun, come to ill end,
> Yea, faith it selfe to hollow falshood change.

Intriguingly, Constance's lament echoes John's lamentations after his nobles compelled his signature to *Magna Carta;* in Holinshed Shakespeare would have read how 'the king [John] having condescended to make such grants of liberties, farre contrarie to his mind, was [afterward] right sorrowfull in his heart, cursed his mother that bare him, the houre that he was borne, and the paps that gave him sucke, wishing that he had received death by violence of sword or knife, instead of naturall nourishment: he whetted his teeth, he did bite now on one staffe, and now on another as he walked, and oft brake the same in pieces when he had done, and with such disordered behavior and furious gestures he uttered his greef...' (2.186). Holinshed goes on to describe how John immediately took himself away to the Isle of Wight where he schemed how to break his *Magna Carta* bargain – and his faith – with the magnates.

To understand the (in)significance of *Magna Carta* and why Shakespeare treated the event in this manner one must know the real history of John's reign as well as did his lettered Elizabethan auditors. *Magna Carta* was signed between John and twenty-five 'surety' barons at Runnemede on 15 June 1215. The charter solemnly declared *inter alia* that no one – not even the king – was above the law. In this sense *Magna Carta* was a tremendous innovation which entailed an unprecedented grant by the crown to peers and population of what we now call 'civil rights.' However, though *Magna Carta* is cited as an antecedent of various constitutions in America and elsewhere, the glorious document was an utter failure. It remained in force barely a hundred days and its signing had bloody consequences. As lettered Elizabethans knew, in September 1215 Pope Innocent III abrogated *Magna Carta* and directed his handpicked Archbishop of Canterbury, Stephen Langston, to excommunicate the surety barons. The following May (1216), a French armada of 600 ships under Lewis landed at Stanhope. On learning of this adventure Innocent promptly excommunicated Lewis along with King Philip Augustus and the leading French barons. Notwithstanding these papal interdicts, on 2 June 1216 John's renegade English barons crowned Lewis King of England at London's St Paul's cathedral. Civil war ensued; it took a genuine popular uprising and much letting of blood to drive the French from England and restore boy-king Henry III to the throne. In 1217 Lewis and his defeated army finally were disarmed and packed off back to France. But only after they had signed an ignominious surrender at Runnemede. Considered in the light of historical fact, *Magna Carta* was a catastrophe. The charter sparked a conflagration which very nearly brought England, Scotland, and Ireland under French rule. The wiser sort would have remembered this when reminded of King John's era and a Summer Solstice. Little wonder Shakespeare put such a towering lament into the mouth of Constance.

In sum, what do Shakespeare's tributes to his three Lords Chamberlain tell us about the playwright and these, his plays? First, these instances must convince us that Shakespeare had a profound interest in chronometry and special knowledge of the subject. Recovering Shakespeare's tribute to William Brooke also restores the paradigm of Henry Chettle's man of civil demeanor; we can recognize that Shakespeare's supposed slights to Brooke are susceptible of other, kinder explanations. Far from being snide or petty toward this Lord Chamberlain, Shakespeare composed for Brooke a tender memorial, one which may have been cherished by his heirs.

To honor Henry Carey Shakespeare created one of his most dashing heroes – witty in speech, bold in action, royally magnanimous, loyal in life and to the death – and as humble and unselfish as Carey himself. Knowing that Henry Carey stands behind the flashing tongue and warlike arm of Philip Faulconbridge must deepen and excite anew our appreciation of the much underappreciated *King John*.

And recognizing Henry and son George behind the mask of Hamlet brings new and tremendous pathos to the bastard prince's lament for the ineradicable stain on his soul. The only way a bastard could erase this stain would be to undo his birth. And that paradox underlies the haunting question, 'To be or not to be ...'

Notes

1 To cite a few: G.P.V. Akrigg, *Shakespeare and the Earl of Southampton* (Cambridge: Harvard University Press, 1968); C.C. Stopes, *The Life of Henry [Wriothsley], the Third Earl of Southampton, Shakespeare's Patron* (Cambridge: Cambridge University Press, 1922); Gerald Massey, *The Secret Drama of Shakespeare's sonnets, etc.*, (London: K. Paul, 1888); and, of course, Oscar Wilde, 'The portrait of Mr. W.H.,' *Blackwood's Edinburgh magazine* (July 1889), pp. 1–21.

2 Unless otherwise noted, biographical data in this chapter relies on *The Oxford Dictionary of National Biography Online* (Oxford: Oxford University Press, 2004).

3 David McKeen, *A Memory of Honour: the Life of William Brooke, Lord Cobham* (Salzburg: Universitat Salzburg, 1986), p. 647. The office of Lord Chamberlain was prestigious, powerful and lucrative; it carried an annual stipend of some £160 plus numerous emoluments. In addition to arranging the Queen's progresses and entertainments the Chamberlain supervised her household, and controlled her calendar and access to the presence.

4 Brooke's death and the nasty politicking for his offices are recounted in C.L. Kingsford (ed.), *Report on the Manuscripts of Lord de l'Isle and Dudley Preserved at Penshurst place* (London: H.M. Stationery Office, 1925–66), II. 233ff.

5 The historical Oldcastle came by the Cobham addition via his marriage in 1409 to Joan, granddaughter of the third Lord. When Oldcastle went to the flames the Cobham title went up in smoke with him. Subsequently, his stepdaughter, Joan Braybrooke, married Sir Thomas Brooke, a socially ambitious sometime sheriff of Somerset. They saw to it that the Cobham title was revived in 1445 for their son,

Edward. See McKeen 1.15–18 and W.T. Waugh, 'Sir John Oldcastle,' *English Historical Review* 20 (1905), 434–56 and 637–68.

6 On this theory see *inter alia* Giorgio Melchiori, *The Second Part of King Henry IV* (Cambridge: Cambridge University Press, 1989), p. 10; John Dover Wilson, 'The origins and development of Shakespeare's Henry IV,' *The Library* (4th series, 24, 1945), 15–16; E.A.J. Honigmann, 'Sir John Oldcastle: Shakespeare's martyr,' in John W. Mahon and Thomas A. Pendleton (eds), *Fanned and Winnowed Opinions, etc.* (London: Methuen, 1987), pp. 118–31.

7 See Foxe or, more handily, Peter Corbin and Douglas Sedge, *The Oldcastle Controversy* (Manchester: Manchester University Press, 1991), pp. 2–6.

8 On the date of the play and the writing of the Epilogue see A.R. Humphreys (ed.), *King Henry IV Part 2* (London: Routledge, 1966), pp. xiv–xxi.

9 Text and lineation from Melchiori. For a detailed discussion see Gary Taylor, 'The Fortunes of Oldcastle,' *Shakespeare Survey* 38 (1985), 85–100. For other perspectives on these murky matters see: Samuel Burdett Hemingway, *The New Variorum Shakespeare: 1 Henry IV* (Philadelphia: Lippincott, 1936), p. 355, and Alice Lyle Scoufos, *Shakespeare's Topological Satire, etc.* (Athens: Ohio University Press, 1979), or her lesser-known but more accessible 'Nashe, Johnson, and the Oldcastle Problem,' *Modern Philology* 65:4 (May 1968), 307–24.

10 Nicholas Rowe (ed.), *The Works of Mr. William Shakespear* (London: 1709), I.ix. The summa on this topic is Rudolph Fiehler, 'How Oldcastle became Falstaff,' *Modern Language Quarterly* 16 (1955), 16–28.

11 For Cobham's turn as master of the plays see McKeen, pp. 648–51.

12 For example, Melchiori, p. 188n.

13 The relevant passage reads: 'One word more, I beseech you: if you be not too much cloyed with fat meat, our humble author will continue the story with Sir John in it, and make you merry with fair Katherine of France, where, for anything I know, Falstaff shall die of a sweat, unless already a be killed with your hard opinions; for Oldcastle died martyr, and this is not the man' (*2 Henry IV*, Epilogue 20–4).

14 T.W. Craik (ed.), *The Merry Wives of Windsor* (Oxford: Oxford University Press, 1989).

15 See Craik's concise epitome of the play's debut, pp. 1–13. It's no great leap to Ford a Brook(e). See Taylor, 'Fortunes.'

16 *The Merry Wives of Windsor* may contain another glance at Brooke; while cloaked in the alias 'Brooke' Ford tells Falstaff, 'they say if money go before, all ways do lie open' (2.2.164–5). Shakespeare may imply that Brooke bought the post of Lord Chamberlain; then as now such arrangements were not uncommon. McKeen (pp. 642–4) argues that this was not the case, and that the relations between Brooke and the Careys remained amicable.

17 See for examples Taylor and Scoufos.

18 Henry Chettle, *Kind-Harts Dreame* (London: 1592), c4v; Ben Jonson's 'To the memory of my beloved … Shakespeare, etc.,' Hinman, p. 10.

19 McKeen, p. 649.

20 First proposed by John Dennis in his preface to *The Comical Gallant* (1702) and recapitulated by Rowe (1709). David Wiles, among others, believes the play was

written 'at the behest of [George] Lord Hunsdon.' David Wiles, *Shakespeare's Clown: Actor and Text in the Elizabethan Playhouse* (Cambridge: Cambridge University Press, 1987), p. 117 and p. 203n.2.

21 Text and lineation from Gary Taylor (ed.), *Henry V* (Oxford: Oxford University Press, 1982).

22 The Cobham who emerges from McKeen's definitive biography is conscientious, competent, not unlearned, and scrupulously modest. He refused burial in Westminster Abbey, preferring the simpler church of St Mary Magdalene near his country estate. His will was a model of Christian charity. He handsomely endowed Cobham College, an institution which succored (and succors) the poor. McKeen, pp. 686–9.

23 Shakespeare's text contains no mention of Falstaff receiving the sacrament of extreme unction.

24 Oldcastle smuggled Wycliffite texts to the Continent where they inspired Jan Hus and perhaps Martin Luther.

25 Hostess recalls Falstaff 'babbled of green fields,' which scholars receive as an allusion to the 23rd Psalm. The Book of Common Prayer enjoined Elizabethan believers to read (or recite from memory) all 150 Psalms in the course of their morning and evening oblations during each calendar month. To regulate this practice the Book of Common Prayer provided a calendar which prescribed exactly those psalms to be read on each day of the month. As believing Elizabethans knew, the 23rd Psalm was calendared for the evening of the fourth day of the month. In an earlier comment on Falstaff's death in *Notes and Queries* (March 2003, 39) I erroneously connected Psalm 23 to the fifth day of the month. It's possible that Shakespeare mistook the date of Brooke's death as the night of 4/5 March rather than 5/6 March. Then again, 4 March was Henry Carey's birthday.

26 Surviving letters convey a sense of the venal politicking for Brooke's offices as he lay dying. On 18 February 1597 Whyte reports 'My Lord Chamberlain is sayd to be very ill ... My Lord of Hunsdon [George Carey] is thought shalbe Lord Chamberlain by his death, or by resignation if he live, for his body to to weake to brave the burden of the place ...' The politicking for the succession to Brooke's many powerful offices had already begun. On 21 February, Whyte writes to Sidney that Cecil 'went on Saturday to blackfriars [*sic*] to see my Lord Cobham' in his illness while Henry Cobham is reported to be daily pleading with the Queen for his father's offices. On 25 February, 'The physicians vary in their opinion of [the survival] of Lord Cobham.' On 28 February, My Lord Chamberlain grows weaker; his eldest son earnestly sues [the Queen] to be Lord Warden of the Cinque Ports.' On 1 March Whyte's letter begins, 'This day a speach was at Court that my Lord Chamberlain cannot live,' and the following day, 'It is now held certain Lord Cobham cannot live.' On 4 March, Essex writes to Sidney, 'I do believe now that my Lord Chamberlain will dy.' On that day Whyte reports that 'Mr. Hen. Brooke, Sir Ed. Wooton and the two Lords Buckhurst and Hunsdon do stand for [have declared their candidacy for warden of the] Cinque Ports.' On 6 March Whyte reports the death of Brooke and notes, 'The Court is full of who shall have this and that office; most say Mr. Harry Brooke shall have Eltham and the Cinque Ports ... Lord Hunsdon is named for Lord Chamberlain ...' Kingsford, II.233–46.

27 Recovered by the author using *Autotide 7.0*, Linden Software Ltd. (Liverpool) 2000. The date 16 March must be used to compensate for English Julian calendar which was then ten days behind the reformed Gregorian.

28 See Wiles' luminous assessment, pp. 116–35. Whether Falstaff's death was the cause or result of Kemp leaving the company is a matter of debate.

29 Holinshed. References from the online *Horace Howard Furness Memorial (Shakespeare) Library*. Folio DA130. H7 1587.

30 Kingsford, II.234.

31 Brooke had made his will some ten days before his decease, which gave his family and intimates time to assemble at his bedside.

32 Gabriel Harvey (1550?–1631), manuscript note in Spaeght's *Chaucer's Works* (London: 1598).

33 These would have included Henry Brooke, whose star was still in the ascendant when he was created Knight of the Garter around the time of the stage debut of Shakespeare's *Henry V*.

34 Harold Jenkins (ed.), *Hamlet* (London: Methuen, 1982), p. 20.

35 See for example: Jenkins, 11–13. Henslowe recorded a play entitled *Hamlet* performed at The Rose in 1594.

36 W.W. Greg, *Hamlet 1603* (Oxford: Clarendon Press, 1965), 3v.

37 W.W. Greg, *Hamlet, Second Quarto 1604–5* (London: Sidgwick and Jackson, 1940), 5v.

38 G.R. Hibbard (ed.), *Hamlet,* (Oxford: Oxford University Press, 1987), p. 3.

39 Hibbard, pp. 3–4.

40 Jenkins, p. 13. Andrew Gurr, '*Hamlet* and the *auto de fé*,' *Around the Globe* 13 (Spring 2000).

41 'Dead Shepheard, now I find thy saw of might, / Who euer lov'd, that lou'd not at first sight?' (*As You Like It* TLN 1853–4). See *2 Henry VI* 2.1.2 for Shakespeare's use of the phrase 'seven years' day.'

42 That Laertes, recently returned from Paris, knows the Frenchman's name and reputation lends solidity to his existence.

43 '*Scrimer* is properly a Gladiator, Fencer; from which we have deriv'd our Word, *Skirmish*.' L. Theobald, *The Works of Shakespeare* (London: 1733), 7.340.

44 One wonders whether Claudius' admiration for *Lamord's* horsemanship is a polite nod to the calling of Carey's nominal father, William, Master of the Horse for Henry VIII.

45 There is some question whether Mary was born in 1508 or in 1506, and whether she was younger or older than Anne, born 1507. My inference is that Mary was born in 1506 and was older than Anne, for two reasons: (1) Mary married first, as the elder daughter did traditionally; (2) fourteen was the age of consent under prevailing English and Canon law.

46 With manors, stewardships, and an annuity.

47 Reginald Pole reported that, in 1528, a member of parliament insulted the king's morals by accusing Henry of sleeping with Anne's mother as well as her sister. The flustered king replied, 'Never with her mother!' The anecdote is recounted in numerous sources.

48 As it was, in 1527 Henry was forced to seek a papal dispensation to vacate his

connection with Mary in order to marry Anne. The document reads, in part: 'In order to take away all occasion from evil doers, we do in the plenitude of our power hereby suspend ... all canons affecting impediments created by affinity rising *ex illicito coitu*, in any degree even in the first ... or of any affinity contracted in any degree even the first, *ex illicito coitu*, etc.'

49 Mary's subsequent marriage to commoner William Stafford (1534) estranged her from her ambitious family and royal in-laws; she descended into poverty and died (19 July 1543) dependent on the kindness of strangers.

50 His tutor was Nicholas Bourbon, the French poet and Latin doggerel writer; Hamlet, of course, fancies himself poetical.

51 About this time Hunsdon and Robert Dudley, the Queen's Master of the Horse, whipped all comers in a tournament at Greenwich honoring Elizabeth's Accession Day.

52 He is named among the list of the Earl of Leicester's players in a document of 7 May 1574.

53 The Carey family had close ties to other members of Shakespeare's circle. George Carey's wife and daughter, both named Elizabeth, were patrons of poets including Edmund Spenser and Shakespeare's chum, Thomas Nashe. George's daughter and heiress, Elizabeth, married Sir Thomas Berkeley, son and heir of Henry, Lord Berkeley.

54 They amassed land and influence, and are numerous today. In Normanville, La Courture, Guernsey, stands an imposing house which, according to the *Livre de Perchage*, was owned in 1573 by Jean de Vic, husband of Anne Careye [*sic*]. See www.careyroots.com.

55 By AD 1085 there were four branches of Careys in Somerset and Devonshire. See www.careyroots.com.

56 The original Carey arms had been 'Gules, a chevron between three swans proper, one thereof they still retain in their crest.' *Remarkable antiquities of the city of Exeter giving an account of the laws and customs of the place, the officers, courts of judicature, gates, walls, rivers, churches, and privileges; together with a catalogue of all the bishops, mayors, sheriffs, from the year 1049 to 1677*, collected by Richard Izacke (London, 1681), p. 71.

57 Carey named a younger son Robert.

58 Izacke, 72. At www.careyroots.com Paul Dobree-Carey records that 'The arms were first noted in Guernsey in documents borne by Nicolas Careye as Lieutenant of Thomas Wygmore, Bailiff of Guernsey, dated 1582 ... the arms for the English branch having been registered by the Heralds College in 1531.'

59 Rowe, 5.245.

60 Alexander Pope, *The Works of Shakespear* (London: 1725), 6.446.

61 Citing 'the next speech but one: "he is the brooch, indeed, And gem of all the nation."' Edmond Malone, *The Plays and Poems of William Shakspeare* (London, 1821), 7.452.

62 By J.P. Collier (1858), Dyce (1877), Wright (1894), Verity (1911), and Brook's and Crawford's *Yale* (1917). Only Craig (1905) held out for *Lamord*.

63 'This name, so suggestive of *La Mort*, looks the right name for the centaur-like Norman conjured up out of nowhere [and] *Lamound* seems more like to be a misreading of it ...' Hibbard, p. 315n.80.

64 E. Dowden, *The Plays of Shakespeare* (London, 1899), 6.179. He did, however, perceive that his proposed emendation – *Lamords* – would be fractured French since 'the word *mords* is masculine.' He attributed this to printing-house error: 'the printer of Q may be responsible for *La,*' the feminine article instead of a masculine *Le*.

65 Jenkins, p. 369n.

66 Verity detected the tension in Shakespeare's introduction of a French form: 'Some think that the name [Lamord] covers (in a semi-French form) an allusion to a famous Italian cavalier and huntsman, Pietro Monte, instructor in horsemanship at the Court of Louis VII.' A.W. Verity (ed.) *Hamlet* (Cambridge: Cambridge University Press, 1911), p. 108. The Monte connection was and is irrelevant; but Verity, as Dowden, sensed something amiss in Shakespeare's French and that there was more to *Lamord* than met the ear: 'That some personal allusion is intended seems probable; for the whole passage (lines 83–94) has rather the air of being specially introduced.' In the 1930s the reading *Lamound* made a comeback, thanks to Harrison (1937) and Kitteredge (1939). In 1934 Dover Wilson produced this epitome of received opinion: '*Lamord*, (Q2) F1 '*Lamound*.' Most read '*Lamond*'; Malone conjectures '*Lamode*,' Grant White '*Lamont*.' Possibly '*Le Monté*' was intended. Dowden follows Q2, 'having noticed in Cotgrave "*Mords,* a bitt of a horse."' I agree with Verity that some personal allusion is prob[able], more esp. as the whole passage (80–93) does not arise naturally out of a context in which the accomplishment dwelt on is fencing, not horsemanship. Then Wilson added to the confusion: 'Sh.'s patron, the Earl of Southampton, was created Master of his Horse by Essex in 1599, while in Ireland'; and this may be the point of the allusion. 'The brooch indeed And gem of all the nation' would suit well with Southampton's reputation at this period.' J.D. Wilson, *Hamlet* (Cambridge: Cambridge University Press, 1934), pp. 228–9. A brilliant trope, but wrong.

67 *H5* 3.1.1–34.

68 *Le Manoir Carrey* still stands in the town, the present structure being a 16th-century half-timbered, three-storey dwelling.

69 Jenkins' note on 'to the manner born' is useful: 'Not merely familiar with the custom from birth, but committed to it by birth. It is part of his [Hamlet's] heritage.' Jenkins, p. 208n.15.

70 We know Hamlet is a 'particular man' from a prior exchange with Gertrude, i.e. He: 'I Maddam, it is common.' She: 'If it be / Why seems it so perticuler with thee?' (Q2 1.2.74–6). And just in case we missed the particular-man-Hamlet connection the Ghost threatens to make 'each particuler haire [on Hamlet's head] to stand an end, / Like quils upon the fearfull Porpentine.' (1.5.19–20). For a broader perspective on Hamlet's questionable birth see S. Sohmer, 'Certain Speculations on Hamlet, the Calendar, and Martin Luther,' *EMLS* 2.1 (April 1996).

71 Deuteronomy 25:5, the law of the Levirate which required a brother to marry his dead brother's wife, provided one basis for Pope Julius II's dispensation (26 December 1503) which allowed Prince Henry to become betrothed to Katherine of Aragon, recently widowed by his brother Arthur. Two decades later, Deuteronomy 24:1, which requires a husband to divorce a wife in whom he finds

'uncleanesse,' formed a pillar of Henry's appeal to Pope Clement VII to let him put Queen Katherine away. The king claimed to be haunted by Leviticus 20:21: 'And if a man shall take his brother's wife, it is an unclean thing: he hath uncovered his brother's nakedness; they shall be childless.'

72 There's an uncanny series of illuminating echoes in Posthumus' rant, 'We are bastards all, / And that most venerable man which I / Did call my father was I know not where / When I was stamped. Some coiner with his tools / Made me a counterfeit; yet my mother seemed / The Dian of that time: so doth my wife / The nonpareil of this. O vengeance, vengeance!' (*Cymbaline* 2.5.2–8). Likewise in *Titus Andronicus,* when the Nurse presents Tamora's illegitimate child to Aaron: 'The Empress, sends it thee, thy stamp, thy seal, / And bids thee christen it with thy dagger's point' (4.2.69–70). Elsewhere, Shakespeare uses 'fault' as a euphemism for the female genitalia (*King Lear* 1.1.15), and 'stamp' as a euphemism for the begetting of illegitimate children: 'Ha, fie, these filthy vices! It were as good / To pardon him that hath from nature stolen / A man already made, as to remit / Their saucy sweetness that do coin God's image In stamps that are forbid.' (*Measure for Measure* 2.4.42–6). Hamlet's phrase 'Carrying ... Natures livery, or Fortune's star' may employ 'star' in the sense of a white spot or patch of hair on the forehead of a horse or ox (*OED* star n.6.b). Did Olivier/Branagh find a cue here for their platinum-blond Hamlets?

73 The Geneva Bible, 90v.

74 *Nobody and Somebody* (London: 1592) E2b.

75 *Cymbeline,* 1.4.135; *Winter's Tale,* 2.1.138.

76 See M.M. Mahood's *Shakespeare's Wordplay* (London: Methuen, 1957) for other examples of Shakespeare's unspoken puns.

77 The quibble on alcoholic beverages has an after-echo at 1.4.40 when Hamlet speculates whether the ghost is a *'spirit* of health.'

78 There are numerous references to *bastarde* wines in medieval and Renaissance literature, e.g., 'The fellows of Merton ... purchase some bastard in 1399.' Rogers, *Agric. and Prices* (London: 1866), 1.xxv.619.

79 'Bastards ... seeme to me to be so called because they are oftentimes adulterated and falsified with honey.' Surflet and Markham, *Country Farm etc.* (London: 1616), p. 642.

80 In the vinification of Falstaff's favorite, sack (modern: sherry), there are two intrusions into the fermentation and aging process. The first is the introduction of *flor,* a mold peculiar to the Xeres region of Spain which gives the wine its nutlike flavor. Secondly, sherries are aged (and dated) by the *solera* method. In this process small quantities of older sherries are added to young wines. The introduction of a few drams of older wine alters the new wine's character by a remarkable degree. a phenomenon well-known to sherry vintners and drinkers in Shakespeare's time.

81 Hamlet's 'dram of eale' is a metaphor for 'semen,' a word which may have been considered too rude for Shakespeare's stage. His three detectable references are scrupulously oblique: (1) when Cleopatra refers to her eunuch, Mardian, as being 'unseminared' (*Antony and Cleopatra* 1.5.11); (2) when Emelia upbraids Iago (*Othello* 1.4.149–52) for allowing his wit to be turned 'the seamy side without'; (3) when Hamlet refers to the 'rank sweat of an enseamed bed' (3.4.92).

82 The name of the familiar elder tree, *Sambucus nigra,* derives from the Old English word 'ellfrn' (*OED*). Also related to the Danish 'hyld' or 'hyldetrf.' The elder is typically a low tree or shrub, and its young branches are remarkable for their abundance of pith. The qualities of elder wood were well known to Shakespeare, who refers to its soft, removable pith in *Henry V:* 'that's a perilous shot out of an elder-gun' (4.1.198). Elder pith could be hollowed out to leave a tube suitable for the making of a toy gun. In *Love's Labour's Lost,* Shakespeare remembers the tradition that 'Judas was hang'd on an elder' (5.2.606). We may detect a glance at this quality of the elder tree in Hamlet's 'indeede it takes / From our atchievements, though perform'd at height / The pith and marrow of our attribute' (1.4.20–2).

83 The English vernacular name for the elder tree is 'Danewort,' from the tradition that the plant sprang up in places where Danes slaughtered Englishmen or *vice versa;* Hamlet, of course, will be packed off to England for slaughter before the end of the play. *OED* cites: 1538 Turner *Libellus;* an annoymous *Herbal* of 1568, and 1578 Lyte *Dodoens,* iii.xlv.380: '*This herbe is called . . . in Englishe Walwort, Danewort, and Bloodwort.*' While suggested in part by the abundance of the plant at certain spots historically or traditionally associated with slaughter, there was also an element of fanciful etymology in explaining the Latin name *Ebulus* from *ebullire* to bubble forth, with reference to the flowing of blood.' The plant was noted also for its diuretic qualities. *OED* citation: 1398 Trevisa Barth. *De R.,* xvii. cxliv. (1495) 700, '*The Ellern tree hath vertue Duretica*'

84 Fortescue fought at the battle of Towton (1461) and was subsequently attainted by the victorious Edward IV. In the aftermath, Fortescue 'followed Queen Margaret to Flanders, and remained abroad, living in poverty, with her and the Prince of Wales ...' *DNB.* During their exile, Fortescue undertook the education of the Prince. His *De Laudibus* is a dialogue between the student prince and Fortescue who offers many illustrations of the superiority of English Common Law over the Roman civil law prevailing on the Continent. Elements of this argument appeared in S. Sohmer, *EMLS* 6.3 (January, 2001), 13:1–7.

85 A translation from Latin by Robert Mulcaster appeared in at least six editions between 1573 and 1672. These citations are from the London edition of 1599.

86 Under law, a bastard child has no father and is nameless. Fortescue quotes a doggerel: 'To whom the people father is, / to him is father none and all. / To whom the people father is, / well fatherless we may him call' (fol. 93v).

87 Another striking linguistic parallel between the two texts: toward the end of his discourse on the laws of bastardy, Fortescue paraphrases Luke 6:43–4: 'For an evil tree saye they can not brynge furthe good fruites, nor a good tree beare evyll fruites (99r).' A few pages later Fortescue amplifies this principle: 'And what then if he have graffed a slyppe of a swete nature in a stock of a sower tree: So that the tree be his owne, shall not the fruites, thoughe they ever savor of the stocke, be his owne fruites' (fol. 102v). When Hamlet chides Ophelia that 'vertue cannot so enoculat our old stock, / but we shall relish of it' (3.1.119–20) Fortescue's 'savor' has become Shakespeare's 'relish.' Indeed, one meaning of 'savor' is 'to relish' (*OED* savor v. 11). For Fortescue as a source of *Hamlet* see *EMLS* 6:3, 13.1–7.

88 See www.careyroots.com/crest.html.

89 Geneva Bible, 91r. The widow apparently had no say in the matter. 'The widow had no hereditary rights in her husband's property, but was considered a part of the estate, and the surviving brother of the deceased was considered the natural heir. The right to inherit the widow soon became a duty to marry her if the deceased had left no sons, and in case there was no brother-in-law, the duty of marriage devolved on the father-in-law or the agnate who inherited, whoever this might be. The first son of the Levirate marriage was regarded as the son of the deceased.' James Orr (ed.), *International Standard Bible Encyclopedia: Electronic Edition* (Parsons Technology 1998), search = Brother's Wife.

90 Robert became an intimate of James' son and was named Earl of Monmouth in 1626.

91 Or, for the same reasons, these changes were made by a bookkeeper or editor prior to 1623.

92 Consider Hamlet's cry in Q1, 'Then venom to thy union here' as he stabs Claudius.

93 [My emphasis].

94 Thanks to Lucy Cullen of the Department of Sculpture, Metalwork, Ceramics and Glass, Victoria and Albert Museum.

95 'The celebrated Hunsdon onyx cameo, set in an enameled gold pendant worn from a chain, represents the mythological hero Perseus rescuing Andromeda. It illustrates marvelously the virtuoso talents of one of the best – albeit anonymous – hardstone engravers of the Renaissance. From the complex panorama of town and sea with ships and sea creatures, men and women stare in amazement as the young warrior flies down from the sky holding up the Gorgon's head on his shield and brandishing his sword. This tour-de-force matches the best engraving of the great cameo-cutters of ancient Greece and Rome.' Diana Scarisbrick, *Ancestral Jewels* (New York: Vendome Press, 1989), p. 15.

96 Philip Edwards (ed.), *Hamlet* (Cambridge: Cambridge University Press, 1985), p. 209n.

97 Shakespeare's decision to rework *The Troublesome Reign* in 1596 may have also been occasioned by the death of George Peele, who was buried in St James' on 9 November 1596. Peele may have co-authored with Shakespeare *Titus Andronicus;* see R.F. Hill, 'The Composition of Titus Andronicus,' *Shakespeare Survey* 10 (1957), pp. 60–70. Brian Vickers attributes *The Troublesome Reign* to Peele in '*The Troublesome Reign,* George Peele, and the Date of *King John,*' *Words That Count. Early Modern Authorship: Essays in Honor of Macdonald P. Jackson,* (ed.) Brian Boyd (Newark: University of Delaware Press, 2004), pp. 78–116 (particularly 111).

98 *Calendar of State Papers Dom.,* addenda, 1566–79, pp. 245–6.

99 *Dictionary of National Bibliography.*

100 Of alabaster and marble, gilded, swarming with heraldry, and thirty-six feet tall.

101 Lettered Elizabethans would have recognized that the opening scene of King John is rife with bastards – indeed, far more of them than modern auditors perceive. John, though perhaps legitimately born, illegitimately possesses the crown; we have his mother's word for that. For her part, Eleanor had been divorced by her first husband, King Louis VII of France, in 1152 on the grounds of consanguinity (shades of Henry VIII). In fact, Eleanor was a notorious sexual adventuress,

reputed to have experimented with infidels while on crusade in the Holy Land and having almost certainly bedding Geoffrey of Anjou; awkwardly, the latter proved to be the father of Eleanor's second husband, Henry II of England – coupling incest to adultery. Shakespeare's awareness of Eleanor's peccadilloes are almost certainly behind the moment when she and Constance fall to hair-pulling over the bastardy of their respective children in 2.1. For her part, Constance – after being widowed by Geoffrey Plantagenet – deserted her second husband, the Earl of Chester, in 1199 and married Guy de Thouars without the niceties of divorce. To compound matters, the man at the John's right hand – Salisbury – was John's half-brother, being the bastard son of Henry II. And all of these are in place before the ahistorical Bastard Faulconbridge makes his entrance.

102 *DNB Online* cites R. Naunton, *Fragmenta regalia* (1649), 102. In the original 'mistress,' signifying Queen Elizabeth, stands in place of my 'monarch.'
103 McKeen, ii.645.
104 Thomas Fuller, *The History of the Worthies of England* (London: 1662).
105 A.R. Braunmuller, *King John* (Oxford: Oxford University Press, 1998), p. 92.
106 See for example: Julia C. Van de Water, 'The Bastard in *King John*,' *Shakespeare Quarterly* 11 (1960), 137–46, and Lily B. Campbell, *Shakespeare's 'Histories' etc.* (San Marino: The Huntington Library, 1947), pp. 126–67.
107 Sigurd Burckhardt, '*King John*: The Ordering of this Present Time,' *English Literary History* 33:2 (June 1966), p. 133.
108 Campbell, p. 166.
109 Eric Sams, 'The Troublesome Wrangle Over *King John*' *Notes and Queries* 35 (March 1988), 41–4.
110 Burckhardt, p. 140.
111 *Minutes of the Privy Council* 12 November 1589: 'whereas there hathe growne some inconvenience by comon playes and enterludes ... in that the players take upon themselves to handle in their plaies certen matters of Divinytie and of State unfitt to be suffred ...' Cited in E.K. Chambers, *Stage*, 4.306.
112 William H. Matchett, 'Richard's Divided Heritage in *King John*,' *Essays in Criticism* 12 (July 1962), p. 2.
113 Citations from *King John* and throughline numbers from Hinman, pp. 323–44. Modern act/scene numbers from E.A.J. Honigmann (ed.), *King John* (London: Methuen, 1954).
114 Another time-shift signal – one which is clear to scholars and could not have escaped the notice of Elizabethan auditors who had seen *The Troublesome Reign* – is the absence from Shakespeare's *King John* of the Earl of Essex. In *The Troublesome Reign* it is Essex who mediates between Robert Faulconbridge, the Bastard, and their mother. It is Essex who demands freedom for Arthur and – when he discovers the prince dead – urges the lords to rebellion. Essex leads the traitors to Bury St Edmunds where they take the sacrament to serve the French king after Essex delivers a lengthy speech which makes the case for deposing King John. In Shakespeare's play it is Salisbury – Henry II's bastard – who leads the lords in taking the treasonous oath to serve the French king. Both Pembroke and Salisbury appear in *King John*, but not Essex.
115 Shakespeare also contrives for his Bastard to free the captured Queen Eleanor in

3.2, a feat performed by John in *The Troublesome Reign.* This nods at Carey's body-guarding Queen Elizabeth during the Armada scare.

116 Burckhardt, p. 143.

117 Campbell, p. 154.

118 Thomas More (St), *Apology* xlv, *Works* 915/1.

119 Henry's acts can be found in Gerald Bray (ed.), *Documents of the English Reformation* (Cambridge: James Clarke, 1994).

120 Braunmuller, p. 178n.3.1.176–7

121 Dover Wilson identified anomalies in the Folio *King John* which led him to conclude the text had been typeset from the author's foul papers. John Dover Wilson (ed.), *King John* (Cambridge: Cambridge University Press, 1934), 92–4. This view still prevails among the majority of scholars, for example Honigmann, *King John*, xxxiii–xliii. We can say for certain that the Folio act/scene divisions of *King John* are pied, i.e. there are only four acts, which is curious since those plays in the Folio which have act divisions are otherwise divided into five acts, e.g., *The Tempest, Richard III, Coriolanus. King John's Actus Secundus* consists of a single scene (Hinman, p. 330) and there are two *Acti Quarti* (pp. 335 and 340). It is possible that the typesetters were baffled because Shakespeare uncharacteristically divided *King John,* each beginning with an act of recognition: Act One with the coronation of John; Act Two rather than *Actus Tertius* beginning with the recognition of the newlywed Dolphin and Blanch; Act Three rather than the first *Actus Quartus* beginning with Hubert's preparations for the blinding, Arthur's entrance, and Hubert ironically kneeling to him as rightful King of England; Act Four beginning (as the second *Actus Quartus*) with Pandulph crowning John.

122 For example L.A. Beaurline (ed.), *King John* (Cambridge: Cambridge, University Press 1990), p. 63n.

123 Moments later in *Hamlet* Q2, Horatio and Marcellus will enter and declare themselves 'Friend to this ground. And Leedgemen to the Dane' (1.1.12–13) echoing Hubert's 'Of the part of England.'

124 There are more pre-echoes of *Hamlet* in *King John.* In both plays the death (murder) of a rightful king is compared with the first murder; Constance's 'For since the birth of Cain, the first male child, / To him that did but yesterday suspire' (3.4.79–80) pre-echoes Claudius' 'From the first course [corpse, Abel], till he that died to day' (Q2 1.2.104–5). Young Prince Lewis' state of mind when he expresses his *ennui*, 'There's nothing in this world can make me joy. Life is as tedious as a twice-told tale, etc.' (3.4.107–11) is very like young Hamlet losing his mirth and taste for exercise (2.2.306–15).

125 Braunmuller (133n) speculates that the name might have been modeled after a Hugh [de] Gourney to whom Holinshed refers elsewhere, which tends to support my inference. Holinshed also mentions the village Gornay in John's Normandy campaign of 1202. He writes that while the English succeeded in raising the French siege of Radepont, 'Howbeit after this the French king wan [won] Gourney.' Bullough, p. 30. Radepont is some fifty miles from Lisieux.

126 W. Arthur, *An Etymological Dictionary of Family and Christian Names, etc.* (New York: Sheldon, Blakeman, 1857). But 'Gurnie' is also marvelously close to

'Gurnsie,' an old variant spelling of the Channel Island's name; this may link 'James Gurnie' to Guernsey where the Careys were (and are) prominent.

127 Holinshed noted that 'Henrie, the third of that name, the eldest sonne of K. John, a child of the age of nine yeres, began his reigne over the realme of England the nineteenth day of October, in the yeare of our Lord 1216' (3.197). In fact, Henry's first regnal year commenced on 28 October. The Book of Common Prayer prescribed Psalms 93 and 94 for evening prayer on the eighteenth day of the month. Ironically, John would have chanted, 'O God, to whom vengeance belongeth, show thyself … / Lord, how long shall the wicked, how long shall the wicked triumph? / … and all the workers of iniquity boast themselves? / They break in pieces thy people, O LORD, and afflict thine heritage. / They slay the widow … and murder the fatherless' (Ps. 94:1–6). Constance was a widow and Arthur fatherless.

128 Braunmuller, p. 165n.21.

129 Honigmann, *King John*, p. 142n.

130 As distinct from the calendrical anniversary, a very astute piece of reckoning. The Solstice in 1215 was 15 June. The Solstice in the year of the marriage of Louis and Blanche (1200) was at 6:20 p.m. on 14 June. Shakespeare links Constance's lament with the Solstice rather than with the date of the signing of *Magna Carta*. This illustrates Shakespeare's remarkably detailed knowledge of chronometry.

Appendix

What Cicero said[1]

In 1.2 of Shakespeare's *Julius Caesar*, Caska describes for the benefit of Cassius and Brutus the circumstances of Antony's off-stage offer of a crown to Caesar. As Caska completes his tale of Antony's three offers, Caesar's refusal, his swoon and the reaction of the multitude, Cassius inquires:

> *Cassius* Did *Cicero* say any thing?
> *Caska* I, he spoke Greeke.
> *Cassius* To what effect?
> *Caska* Nay, and I tell you that, Ile ne're looke you i'th'face againe. But those that understood him, smil'd at one another, and shooke their heads: but for mine owne part, it was Greeke to me.
>
> (382–8)[2]

Caska's circumspection is tantalizing. He implies that if he repeats Cicero's words he may not be able to face his friends again. Then he describes other *cognoscenti* who witnessed Caear's swoon and heard Cicero's words; these men shared stealthy grins and headshakes.

Clearly, the implication of Shakespeare's passage is that Caska understood what Cicero said but dared not repeat a remark so unflattering to Caesar. The mystery surrounding what Cicero is said is heightened by the likelihood that Shakespeare and some of his first auditors knew Caska spoke fluent Greek. Plutarch's dramatic report of Caesar's assassination begins:

> *Caska* behinde him [Caesar] strake him in the necke with his sword, howbeit the wounde was not great nor mortall, bicause it seemed, the feare of such a develishe attempt did amaze him [Caska], and take his strength from him, that he killed him not at the first blowe. But *Caesar* turning straight unto him, caught hold of his sword, and he held it hard: and they both cried

out, *Caesar* in Latin: O vile traitor *Caska,* what doest thou? And *Caska* in Greeke to his brother, brother, helpe me.[3]

Although it has long been thought what Cicero said was unrecoverable, it is possible some of Shakespeare's auditors would have detected in Caska's report certain clues to a passage in Euripides' *Phoenician Women.* This couplet was first associated with Caesar's ambition by Cicero, and later reiterated in that context by Suetonius. Though now largely forgotten, the epigram was apparently a Renaissance commonplace for grasping ambition, employed even by Queen Elizabeth in correspondence.

Of course, in Plutarch and Cicero's own letters there are many expressions of the old republican's contempt for Caesar's imperial ambitions. Elizabethans familiar with *De Officiis* could recall that Cicero wrote that Caesar

> used to have continually upon his lips the Greek verses from the *Phoenissae,* which I will reproduce as well as I can – awkwardly, it may be, but still so that the meaning can be understood: … *if wrong may e'er be right, for a throne's sake / We wrong most right: – be God in all else feared!*[4]

Cicero's jibe caught the notice of Suetonius, who reproduced it in his *Historie of Caius Julius Caesar Dictator:*

> … in his 3. book of duties [Cicero] writeth, that Caesar had alwaies in his mouth, these verses of Euripides … which Cicero himselfe translated thus. '*Nam si violandum est ius, impery^{um} gratia Violandum est, alijs rebus pietatem colas.*'

> > For if thou must do wrong by breach,
> > Of lawes, of right and equitie,
> > Tis best thereby a Crowne to reach,
> > In all things els keepe pietie.[5]

This is what Cicero said, mocking Caesar's feignéd swooning piety.

Holland's Elizabethan translation of Euripides highlights its relevance to the Caesar of Shakespeare's play. As the *Pontifex Maximus* Caesar enters with his entourage on the holy feast day of the Lupercal, he flaunts his piety–

> > … our Elders say
> > The Barren touched in this holy chace,
> > Shake off their sterrile curse.
> > …
> > Set on, and leave no Ceremony out.

> > > (95–100)

Moments later Caesar is the object of his sycophant Antony's three offers of a crown.

In the Renaissance, Euripides' verses were a commonplace for importunate royal ambition:

> 'But to continue our matter,' writes La Primaudaye, 'if right (say ambitious men) may be violated, it is to be violated for a kingdome.' The employment of the same caustic argument is also noted by Charron in his anatomy of the passion of ambition, *'Si violendum est jus, regandi [sic] causa violendum est, in caeteris pietatem colas.'* If a man may at any time violate Justice, it must be to gaine a kingdome; in the rest observe justice and piete.[6]

Queen Elizabeth herself was known to have played upon the trope: 'This Latin tag seems to have had a popular currency; Queen Elizabeth writes to Sir Henry Sidney, Governor of Ireland, *"Si violandum jus regnandi causa."*'[7]

If Shakespeare was alluding to Euripides' couplet via Cicero's *De Officiis*, this recovery may cast new light on another crux in *Julius Caesar*. Writing *"De Shakespeare nostrati"* in the posthumously published *Timber: or, Discoveries; Made upon Men and Matter,* Ben Jonson recalled:

> I *remember,* the Players have often mentioned it as an honour to *Shakespeare,* that in his writing, (whatsoever he penn'd) hee never blotted out line. My answer hath beene, would he had blotted a thousand … Many times hee fell into those things, could not escape laughter: As when hee said in the person of *Caesar,* one speaking to him; *Caesar thou dost me wrong.* Hee replyed: *Caesar did never wrong, but with just cause* and such like: which were ridiculous.[8]

Jonson's recollection deserves consideration; playwrights' ears are keenly tuned to one another's lines.[9] No doubt the speech, as Jonson recalls it, provoked ridicule. Doing wrong for just cause would appear an oxymoron to those (including Jonson) who underestimated Shakespeare's knowledge of the classics and, therefore, did not recognize the glance at Cicero's *De Officiis* and Euripides. If what Cicero said on Shakespeare's Lupercal has now been recovered, Caesar's 'does not wrong without just cause' ought to be restored, and–ironically–Jonson thanked for remembering it.

Were two kings the first auditors for Shakespeare's *Macbeth*?[10]

If William Shakespeare were sufficiently curious about the astronomical details of the night of Duncan's murder to have recovered the true time of moonset, might the playwright (or someone who commissioned the writing of *Macbeth*) have given equal attention to identifying an appropriate occasion for the performance of the play? And wouldn't this attention have been heightened if *Macbeth* were purpose-written (or substantially revised) for performance before two royal kings, one himself a descendant of Banquo?

Scholars have long pondered the possibility that Shakespeare wrote (or substantially revised) *Macbeth* for a royal performance during the interval 17 July–11 August 1606; King Christian IV of Denmark was then in England visiting his brother-in-law King James I and sister, Queen Anne. Indeed, the Revels records indicate that Shakespeare's company, The King's Men, performed before the two monarchs twice at Greenwich and once at Hampton Court during this interval. Unfortunately, neither the precise dates of these performances nor the identities of the plays have come down to us. Notwithstanding this bar to certainty, there is one concordance of dates which provides an attractive (if admittedly speculative) instance for the 'occasional' and 'Royal' performance of *Macbeth*.

Although historians ascribe the date of the murder of King Duncan I of Scotland to the night of 13/14 August 1040, Shakespeare (apparently following Holinshed) erroneously ascribed the event to the night of 13/14 1046. By this reckoning the 560th anniversary of the murder which eventually brought the Stuart line to the thrones of Scotland and England was 13/14 August 1606.[11] Certainly, the anniversary of Duncan's murder would have been an appropriate occasion for a performance of *Macbeth* before Kings James and Christian. But Christian parted from James and departed England on Monday 11 August, sailing from Gravesend.[12] Therefore, it would appear the two monarchs could not have been together on the anniversary of the fateful night.

However, thanks to the anomaly in the Julian calendar which prevailed in England until 1752 and in Denmark until 1700, the two monarchs were indeed together on the true anniversary of the events depicted in Act Two of *Macbeth*. Scotland's King James VI was a calendrical man, and 'the wiser sort' among his English subjects (including Shakespeare) must have recognized this bent of mind. In December 1599 James had decreed that 1 January would henceforth be observed as New Year's day in Scotland as it was 'in all well governed countries,' a plain enough slap at Elizabeth's antiquated Julian calendar.[13] Although king and council stopped short of adopting the Gregorian reform by advancing their calendar ten days, they must have closely examined the Gregorian formulation. Certainly, James would have understood that the length of the Julian year (365.25 days) was inaccurate. Observers since at least the time of the Venerable Bede had calculated that Julius Caesar's year was eleven minutes fourteen seconds too long. In Jacobean England in 1606 there were any number of astrologers, mathematicians, and common almanac readers who understood the Julian calendar slipped one day every 128.19 years. Anyone with this knowledge could calculate the number of days slipped since Duncan's putative murder on the night of 13/14 August 1046:

$$1606 \qquad annus\ praesens$$
$$\underline{(1046)} \qquad \text{erroneous year of the murder}$$
$$560 \qquad \text{intervening years}$$

$$560\ /\ 128.19 = 4.37\ \text{days}$$

By this calculation, the calendar had slipped four days plus eight hours fifty-three minutes since Holinshed's erroneous date of the murder of Duncan on the night of 13/14 August 1046.

In Shakespeare's play the murder of Duncan takes place in the time of total darkness after Midnight and before daybreak. Anyone who has traveled to Scotland – or any other location 56° North or closer to the pole – knows how short true night can be in mid-August. On the morning of 14 August 1046 the sun rose at Dunsinane at 4:48 a.m. But daybreak – the hour associated with the crowing of the second cock – was 1:48 a.m.[14] That Shakespeare imagined the murder of Duncan taking place during the brief interval of complete darkness is suggested by the Torchbearer who accompanies the entrance of Banquo and Fleance at the beginning of Act Two. It's a nice question whether the bell that rings at 2.1.62 signaled that the murder scene was prepared *and* that the hour was 1 a.m. By the time the garrulous Porter enters at the beginning of 2.3 Shakespeare signals his audience that dawn has broken; 'the second cock' has crowed (2.3.23) and neither the Porter nor Macduff or Lennox carries a torch.

If Shakespeare imagined that Duncan's murder occurred between Midnight and 1:48 a.m. on 14 August 1046, then the precise anniversary of the event date fell between the hours of 4 p.m. and 6 p.m. on the afternoon of 9 August 1606. On this date Kings James and Christian were together at Greenwich.[15] The afternoon of 9 August 1606 seems a provocatively appropriate date for a royal performance of *Macbeth*.

On Copernicus, stars, and fire

This note was supplied by Dr Peter Usher, Professor Emeritus of Astronomy and Astrophysics at The Pennsylvania State University, and a member of the Royal Astronomical Society and the Historical Astronomy Division of the American Astronomical Society.

The Aristotelian position on the nature of the four basic elements Fire, Air, Water, and Earth, is arguably inconsistent, as he endows these elements with properties suited to the sublunary region of corruption and decay yet makes use of them in the superlunary realm. In sublunary space, for example, their motion is by and large rectilinear, whereas circular motion is the natural property of celestial objects. He explains the brightness of the stars by supposing that their motion causes the elemental essence Fire to interact with Air, producing flame and rendering them visible.

As the Dark Ages descended, the encyclopedist Isidore stated belief in the four elements, and in the Fire of stars. I take this view to have survived at least to around the turn of the seventeenth century. I assume that 'stars' are of two kinds, 'fixed' and 'wandering.' Sixteenth-century poets who speak of 'stars' imply either or both kinds. The fixed stars are the stars that are fixed in position relative to one another, and the wandering stars move relative to the fixed stars. Each class has motion, and each shines.

The class of wandering star has seven members, known today as Ancient Planets, which divide into two sub-classes: five are unresolved to the naked eye and undergo retrograde motion, and two are resolved and do not retrogress. Of the two Ancient Planets that are resolved, one, the Sun, is manifestly fiery. Democritus, Plato, and later philosophers recognized that the other resolved object, the Moon, borrows its light from the Sun. The Moon is not inherently fiery, owing, they say, to its lesser distance.

The five unresolved objects divide into two further categories, viz. two so-called 'inferior' Ancient Planets, Mercury and Venus, and three so-called 'superior' Ancient Planets, Mars, Jupiter, and Saturn. The first two never stray more than about 22 and 45 degrees from the direction of the Sun, whereas the other three can lie at any angle to the Sun.

Superior Ancient Planets have the further property, best seen for Mars, that they are brightest at times of achronical risings (corresponding to Opposition with the Sun) than at heliacal risings (corresponding to Conjunction). In the standard geocentric planetary model, however, the situation is reversed. Copernicus uses this argument to support his theory of a heliocentric planetary system.

There is a corresponding supporting datum from the inferior Ancient Planets, in that their perpetual angular proximity to the Sun implies that they orbit it. But they lend no other support. Mercury is too difficult to observe, and although there are isolated reports that 'Ishtar' (Venus) has 'horns,' these are not substantiated by what we might term "scientific" studies. Even if these had been attempted, most of the time the observations would have been at or below the limit of the best visual acuity (30 arc seconds). As a result, there were no reports of systematic changes in the appearance of the planet. Thus the empirical data were insufficient to confirm what Copernicus and the earlier Capellan variation posited, viz. a heliocentric orbit for Venus.

Thus at the turn of the seventeenth century, available empirical evidence did not suffice to establish heliocentricism as the model of choice. Added to this is the fact that ephemeredes calculated on the basis of that model had recourse to the old idea of epicycles, and in any case its predictions were just as poor as those calculated from the old geocentric theory. In fact, failures of both

Ptolemaic and Copernican theory were partly responsible for the emergence of the hybrid Tychonic model. Despite the oftentimes Whiggish interpretation of the Copernican Revolution, it cannot be said that heliocentricism dominated at that time.

Heliocentricism was revolutionary in other ways. According to Copernicus, the Sun rests stationary at the center of the sphere of stars, which is also at rest. (Copernicus had left aside all talk of supernumerary spheres that were supposed to account for Precession of the Equinoxes, etc.) Thus the fixity of the Sun and the fixed stars extinguishes their Fire (or else the properties of Fire need redefining). Copernican theory disputes that Fire plays a role in the visibility both of the fixed stars and one of the Ancient Planets, the Sun. The Moon, being a borrower and not a lender of light, is already excepted, but there remain the other five Ancient Planets. According to Copernicus these belong to a new class of Modern Planets, of which the Earth is one. The Earth is a 'dark star,' and is not burning, so it is possible that all modern planets are 'dark stars.' Thus in theory, Copernicanism imperils the Fire of all celestial luminaries, but the arguments are mainly theoretical, of the sort that might appeal to the armchair philosophers of antiquity. In order to tip the scales in favor of Copernicus, empirical evidence is needed over and above that which Copernicus supplied.

In 1610, Galileo published *Sidereus Nuncius* in which he announces that Venus has phases like the Moon, and that these correlate with that planet's position in respect to the Sun. Venus has a heliocentric orbit and so is also a 'dark star.' For the first time, a celestial luminary in superlunary space had been shown by direct observation to shine without need of Fire. Thus direct evidence established one heliocentric orbit and one 'dark star' among the Modern Planets, so it became much easier to accept the intrinsic darkness of all Modern Planets, and with it the demise of Fire.

In effect, it was Galileo's telescope that tipped the scales in favor of heliocentricism, and that extinguished the Fire of the stars. Support for the conclusion comes from the writings of the 'Copernicus in Poetry,' John Donne. In *The First Anniversary, An Anatomy of the World* of 1611, he wrote that the fire of stars is quite put out by the New Philosophy. He wrote this the year after *Sidereus Nuncius* appeared. The timing could be coincidental, but the science suggests otherwise. The combination of Copernican theory and Galilean telescopy dowsed Fire, and Donne refers to these two facets together as the New Philosophy.

More than a decade earlier, Shakespeare said the same thing, and in a manner suitably disguised so as not to alarm the masses. In the first line of Hamlet's doggerel verse, he could justly write that Ophelia should doubt that the stars are fire by appealing to the same item of information that Donne used to extinguish Fire, viz. telescopic observations of the phases of Venus, to which he refers in the same play.

Notes

1 An early version of this note appeared in *Notes and Queries*, n.s. 44, no. 1 (March 1997), pp. 56–8.

2 Text and lineation from Hinman, *First Folio*.

3 North, p. 794.

4 W. Miller (tr.), *Cicero: De Officiis* (Cambridge: Cambridge UP, 1990), pp. 356–7.

5 P. Holland (tr.), *Suetonius: The Historie of the Twelve Caesars, etc.* (London: M. Lownes, 1606), p. 14.

6 W.A. Armstrong, 'The Elizabethan Conception of the Tyrant,' *Review of English Studies* 22: 87 (1946), p. 178.

7 F. Chamberlin (ed.), *The Sayings of Queen Elizabeth*, (London: John Lane, 1923), p. 152. The Queen modifies Cicero's language to suggest wrong is right only to defend a lawful crown.

8 Reprinted by E.K. Chambers, *William Shakespeare*, 2.210, and commented upon by W.J. Velz, 'Clemency, Will, and Just Cause in Julius Caesar,' *Shakespeare Survey* 27 (1969), pp.109–18. Jonson's phrase 'hee said … Hee replyed' might lend credence to the notion that Shakespeare played the part of Caesar.

9 J.D. Wilson makes the case for Jonson's recollection in 'Ben Jonson and *Julius Caesar*,' *Shakespeare Survey* 2 (1949), 39–42.

10 An early version of this note appeared in *Notes and Queries*, n.s. 49, no. 2 (June 2002), pp. 231–4.

11 To the throne of Scotland on 26 March 1371 and the throne of England on 24 March 1603

12 Letter of 'Mr. Pory to Sir Robert Cotton' in Thomas Birch (ed.), *The Court and Times of James the First*, (London: H. Colburn, 1849), 1.66.

13 Holyrood House, 17 December 1599. SRO *Registrum Secreti Concilii; Acta* (1598–1601) PC 1/17 fols. 205–6.

14 Shakespeare is, elsewhere, notably precise about the reckoning of daybreak. Amid the bustling preparations for the wedding feast in *Romeo and Juliet*, Old Capulet exclaims, 'Come, stir, stir, stir, the second cock hath crow'd! The curfew bell hath rung, 'tis three o'clock [in the morning]' (4.4.3–4). The setting of this scene is Verona and the season July, when sunrise could be expected *ca* 4:40 a.m. and daybreak began *ca* 2:30 a.m.

15 G.P.V. Akrigg, *Jacobean Pageant*, (London: H. Hamilton, 1962), p. 83.

Bibliography

The Bible and Holy Scriptures (Geneva: Rouland Hall) 1560.

The Book of Common Prayer (London: C. Barker) 1599.

Encyclopedia Britannica on CD-ROM (1999).

The Catholic Encyclopedia on CD-ROM (2003).

Anonymous, *A coppie of the letter sent from Ferrara the xxii of November 1570* (London: 1571?, STC 10830).

Adams, Henry Hitch, *English Domestic or, Homiletic Tragedy, 1575–1642* (New York: Columbia University Press, 1943).

Akrigg, G.P.V., *Shakespeare and the Earl of Southampton* (Cambridge: Harvard University Press, 1968).

—— *Jacobean Pageant* (London: H. Hamilton, 1962).

Alastos, Doros, *Cyprus in History* (London: Zeno, 1955).

Allen, Ned B., 'The Two Parts of *Othello*,' *Shakespeare Survey* 21 (1969), 16.

Apostle, Hippocrates G. [!] (tr.), *Aristotle's Metaphysics* (London: Indiana University Press, 1966).

Arkangel Complete Shakespeare, *Romeo and Juliet* (New York: Penguin Audio Books, 1989).

Armstrong, W.A., 'The Elizabethan Conception of the Tyrant,' *Review of English Studies* 22: 87 (1946).

Arthur, W., *An Etymological Dictionary of Family and Christian Names* (New York: Sheldon, Blakeman, 1857).

Asquith, Clare, *Shadowplay: The Hidden Beliefs and Coded Politics of William Shakespeare* (New York: Public Affairs, 2005)

Bandello, Matteo, *Novelle* (Lucca, 1554).

Beaurline, L. (ed.), *King John* (Cambridge: Cambridge University Press 1990).

Berry, Philippa, 'Double Dying and Other Tragic Inversions,' in *Shakespeare's Feminine Endings* (London: Routledge, 1999).

Birch, Thomas (ed.), *The Court and Times of James the First* (London: H. Colburn, 1849).

Birt, Henry Norbert, *The Elizabethan Religious Settlement: A Study of Contemporary Documents* (London: G. Bell, 1906).

Black, James, 'Henry IV's Pilgrimage,' *Shakespeare Quarterly* 34 (1983), 18–26.

Blatherwick, S. and A. Gurr (and J. Orrel), 'Shakespeare's Factory,' *Antiquity* 66:251 (1992), 315–33.

Boaistuau, Pierre, *Histoires Tragiques* (Paris: 1559).

Boccaccio, *Il Decamerone* (Firenze [really Venice]: 1527).

Bond, John J., *A Handy-Book of Rules and Tables* (London: 1869).

Bosquet, R. (ed.), *Albertus Magnus, Summa,* I, tr. xiii; Q. liv, vol. 31, p. 551 (Paris: 1895).

Bradshaw, Graham, 'Obeying the Time in *Othello:* a Myth and the Mess it Made,' *English Studies* 73:3 (1992), 211.

Braunmuller, A.R. (ed.), *King John* (Oxford: Oxford University Press, 1998).

Bray, Gerald (ed.), *Documents of the English Reformation* (Cambridge: James Clarke, 1994).

Brodrick, James, *Galileo and the Roman Inquisition* (London: Catholic Truth Society, 1963).

Brognoligo, Gioachino (ed.), *Matteo Bandello: Le Novelle* (Bari: Laterza & Figli, 1928).

Brooke, Arthur, *The Tragicall Historye of Romeus and Juliet* (London: Richard Tottel, 1562).

Brown, John Russell (ed.), *The Merchant of Venice* (London: Methuen, 1955).

Bryant, J. C., *Tudor drama and religious controversy* (Macon: Mercer 1984).

Bryson, Graeme, *Shakespeare in Lancaster* (Liverpool: Sunwards, 1997)

Buchman, Lorne M., 'Orson Welles's *Othello,' Shakespeare Survey* 39 (1987), 59.

Bullough, Geoffrey (ed.), *Narrative and Dramatic Sources of Shakespeare* (New York: Columbia University Press, 1957).

Burckhardt, Sigurd, *Shakespeare's Meaning*, (Princeton: Princeton University Press, 1968), p. 6.

—— '*King John:* The Ordering of this Present Time,' *English Literary History* 33:2 (June 1966).

Campbell, Lily B., *Shakespeare's 'Histories'* (San Marino: The Huntington Library, 1947).

Carr, Richard A. (ed.), *Histoires tragiques / Pierre Boaistuau* (Paris: Librarie Honoré Champion, 1977).

Carter, T. *Shakespeare and Holy Scripture* (London: Hodder and Stoughton, 1905).

Chambers, E.K., *William Shakespeare: a Study of Facts and Problems* (Oxford: Oxford University Press, 1930).

—— *The Elizabethan Stage* (Oxford: Clarendon Press, 1923).

Chang, Joseph S.M.J., '*Julius Caesar* in the Light of Renaissance Historiography,' *Journal of English and Germanic Philology* 69 (1970).

Chapman, Raymond, 'Double Time in *Romeo and Juliet*,' *MLR* XLVI (1949).

Chaucer, Geoffrey, *The assemble of foules* [*Parliament of Fowls*] (London: de Worde, 1530). Bodleian Facs. e112.

Cheney, C. R., *Handbook of Dates for Students of English History* (London: Royal Historical Society, 1991).

Chettle, Henry, *Kind-Harts Dreame* (London: 1592).

Churchill, Awnsham (ed.), *A Collection of Voyages and Travels* (London: 1704).

Cobham, Claude Delaval (ed.), *Excerpta Cypria* (Cambridge: Cambridge University Press, 1908).

Coghill, Nevil, *Shakespeare's Professional Skills* (Cambridge: Cambridge University Press, 1964).

Collier, J.P., *Notes and Emendations to the Text of Shakespeare's Plays* (London: Whittaker and Co., 1853).

Collison, Patrick, *Archbishop Grindal and The Struggle for a Reformed Church* (London: Jonathan Cape, 1979).

Cook, Ann Jennalie, *The Privileged Playgoers of Shakespeare's London* (Princeton: Princeton University Press, 1981).

Corbin, Peter and Douglas Sedge, *The Oldcastle Controversy* (Manchester: Manchester University Press, 1991).

Coyne, S.T., M.A. Hoskin, and O. Pedersen (eds), *The Gregorian Reform of the Calender* (Città del Vaticano: Specola Vaticana, 1983).

Craig, J.W., *The Oxford Shakespeare* (Oxford: Oxford and Company, 1905).

Craik, T.W. (ed.), *The Merry Wives of Windsor* (Oxford: Oxford University Press, 1989).

Crawford, J.R. (ed.), *Hamlet* (New Haven: Yale University Press, 1917).

Cross, F.L. and E.A. Livingston (eds), *The Oxford Dictionary of the Christian Church* (Oxford: Oxford University Press, 1997).

Dampier, William C., *A History of Science and its Relation with Philosophy and Religion* (Cambridge: Cambridge University Press, 1961)

Daniel, P.A. (ed.), *Parallel Texts of Romeo and Juliet* (London: Trubner, 1874)

—— 'Time Analysis of the Plots of Shakespeare, etc.,' *The New Shakspere Society's Transactions 1877–9*, series 1, Vols. 5–7 (London 1879), 6.191–4.

Daniell, David, *William Tyndale* (New Haven: Yale University Press, 1994)

—— *Julius Caesar* (London: Thomas Nelson, 1998).

Davidson, Clifford, *History, Religion, and Violence: Cultural Contexts for Medieval and Renaissance English Drama* (Aldershot: Ashgate, 2002).

Dickinson, Hugh, 'The Reformation of Prince Hal,' *Shakespeare Quarterly* 12 (1966), 33–46.

Digges, Leonard [Thomas], *A prognostication everlastinge, etc.* (London: Thomas Marsh, 1576).

—— *An arithmeticall militare treatise, named Stratioticos, etc.* (London: Henrie Brynneman, 1579).

Dobson, Michael and Stanley Wells (eds), *The Oxford Companion to Shakespeare* (Oxford: Oxford University Press, 2001).

Dodson, Sarah, 'Notes on the Earthquake,' *Modern Language Notes* (February 1950), 144.

Dollimore, Jonathan, *Radical Tragedy: Religion, Ideology and Power in the Drama of Shakespeare and his Contemporaries* (Basingstoke: Palgrave/Macmillan, 2003).

Donno, Elizabeth S. (ed.), *Twelfth Night* (Cambridge: Cambridge University Press, 1992).

Dowden, E., *The Complete Works of William Shakespeare* (London: London and Company, 1910).

Duff, E. Gordon (ed.), *Information for Pilgrims unto the Holy Land by William Wey* (London: Lawrence and Bullen, 1893).

Duffy, Eamon, *The Stripping of the Altars* (New Haven: Yale University Press, 1992).

Dutton, R., *Mastering the Revels* (Iowa City: University of Iowa Press, 1991).

Dyce, Alexander, *The Works of William Shakespeare* (London: Chapman and Hall, 1956–7).

Edelman, Charles, *Shakespeare's Military Language* (London: Athlone P, 2000).

Edwards, Philip (ed.), *Hamlet* (Cambridge: Cambridge University Press, 1985).

Ellis, F.S. (ed.), *The Golden Legend ... as Englished by William Caxton* (London: J.M. Dent, 1900).

Engler, Balz, 'How Shakespeare Revised *Othello*,' *ES* 57:6 (1976), 515–21.

Evans, G. B. (ed.), *Romeo and Juliet* (Cambridge: Cambridge University Press, 1984).

Evans, Jessie Benton, *Giulietta and Romeo* (Portland: Mosher, 1934).

Everett, Barbara, 'The Nurse's Story,' *Critical Quarterly* 14 (1972), 132–3.

—— 'A Spanish Othello,' *Shakespeare Survey* 35 (1982), 103.

Evett, David, 'Types of King David in Shakespeare's Lancastrian Tetralogy,' *Shakespeare Survey* 14 (1981), 139–61.

Fiehler, Rudolph, 'How Oldcastle became Falstaff,' *Modern Language Quarterly* 16 (1955), 16–28.

Finocchiaro, Maurice A., *Retrying Galileo, 1633–1992* (Berkeley: University of California Press, 2005)

Fleissner, Robert F., 'The Three Base Indians in *Othello*,' *Shakespeare Quarterly* 22:1 (1971), 80–2.

Farmer, David Hugh (ed.), *The Oxford Dictionary of Saints* (Oxford: Oxford University Press, 1978).

Farmer, William, *The common Almanacke or Kalender* (London: Watkins and Robertes, 1586).

Fortescue, John, *De Laudibus Legem Angliae* (London: 1599).

Fowler, W. Warde, *The Roman Festivals of the Period of the Republic* (London: Macmillan, 1899).

Frazer, James (Sir) (tr.), *Ovid, The Fasti* (Cambridge: Cambridge University Press, 1989).

Freeman, Arthur, '*Othello's* 'Base Indian': v.ii.347,' *Shakespeare Quarterly* 13:2 (1962), 256–7.

Fuller, Thomas, *The History of the Worthies of England* (London: Grismond, Leybourne and Godbid, 1662). Wing CD-ROM 1996, F2440.

Furness, Horace Howard (ed.), *The Variorum Romeo and Juliet* (Philadelphia: Lippincott, 1874).

—— (ed.), *The Variorum Othello* (Philadelphia: Lippincott, 1886).

Gallyon, Margaret, *Margery Kempe* (Norwich: Canterbury Press, 1995).

Gatti, Hilary, *Giordano Bruno and Renaissance Science* (Ithaca: Cornell University Press, 1999).

Gibbons, Brian, *Romeo and Juliet* (London: Routledge, 1980).

Goldman, Lawrence (ed.), *The Oxford Dictionary of National Biography Online*, (Oxford: Oxford University Press, 2004).

Granville-Barker, Harley, *Prefaces to Shakespeare* (Princeton: Princeton University Press, 1947).

Greenblatt, Stephen, *Will in the World: How Shakespeare Became Shakespeare* (New York: Norton, 2004)

Greg, W.W. (ed.), *Hamlet, Second Quarto 1604–5* (London: Sidgwick and Jackson, 1940).

—— (ed.), *The Editorial Problem in Shakespeare* (Oxford: Oxford University Press, 1942).

—— (ed.), *Richard the Third: Shakespeare Quarto Facsimilies No. 12* (Oxford: Clarendon Press, 1959).

—— (ed.), *Hamlet 1603* (Oxford: Clarendon Press, 1965).

Gresham, Edward, *An Almanack and Progostication* (London: James Robertes, 1602).

Gurr, Andrew, '*Hamlet* and the *auto de fé,*' *Around the Globe* 13 (Spring 2000).

—— *Playgoing in Shakespeare's London* (Cambridge: Cambridge University Press, 2004).

Hacket, J., *A History of the Orthodox Church of Cyprus* (New York: 1901).

Hakluyt, Richard, *The Principal Navigations* (London, 1599).

Halio, Jay, *Shakespeare's Romeo and Juliet: Texts, Contexts, and Interpretation* (London: Associated University Press, 1995), p. 150.

Hall, Edward, *Chronicle; Containing the History of England* (London: 1548).

Harbage, Alfred, *Shakespeare's Audience* (New York: Columbia University Press, 1964).

Harrison, G.B. (ed.), *Shakespeare: Works* (New York: 1952).

Harvey, J. *Leape Yeares. A compendious Prognostication* (London: Watkins and Robertes, 1582).

Hassel, R. Chris, Jr., *Renaissance Drama and the English Church Year* (Lincoln: University of Nebraska Press, 1979).

Heath, Sidney, *Pilgrim Life in the Middle Ages* (London: T. F. Unwin, 1911).

Heath (Sir), Thomas, *A History of Greek Mathematics* (Oxford: Oxford University Press, 1921).

Hemingway, Samuel Burdett (ed.), The New Variorum Shakespeare: *1 Henry IV* (Philadelphia: Lippincott, 1936).

Hibbard, G.R. (ed.), *Hamlet* (Oxford: Oxford University Press, 1987).

Hill (Sir), George, *A History of Cyprus* (Cambridge: Cambridge University Press, 1949).

Hill, Janet, *Stages and Playgoers: From Guild Plays to Shakespeare* (Montreal: McGill-Queen's University Press, 2002).

Hill, R.F., 'The Composition of Titus Andronicus,' *Shakespeare Survey* 10 (1957), 68–9.

Hinman, Charles C., *The First Folio of Shakespeare* (New York: Norton, 1968).

Holinshed, Raphael, *The Chronicles of England, Scotland, and Ireland* (London: Henry Denham, 1587).

Holland, Philemon (tr.), *Suetonius: The Historie of the Twelve Caesars, etc.,* (London: M. Lownes, 1606).

Honigmann, E.A.J. (ed.), *King John* (London: Methuen, 1954).

—— 'Shakespeare's Plutarch,' *Shakespeare Quarterly* 10 (1959), 29.

—— *Shakespeare: The Lost Years* (Manchester: Manchester University Press, 1975).

—— 'Sir John Oldcastle: Shakespeare's martyr,' in John W. Mahon and Thomas A. Pendleton (eds), *Fanned and Winnowed Opinions* (London: Methuen, 1987).

—— (ed.), *Othello* (London: Methuen, 1997).

Hornblower, Simon and Anthony Spawforth (eds), *The Oxford Classical Dictionary* (Oxford: Oxford University Press, 1999)

Hotson, Leslie, *I, William Shakespeare* (London: J. Cape, 1937).

Hoyle, Fred, *Nicolaus Copernicus: an Essay on his Life and Work* (London: Heinemann, 1973).

Hughes, Philip, *The Reformation in England* (London: Hollis&Carter, 1952).

Humphreys, A. R. (ed.), *King Henry IV Part 2* (London: Routledge, 1966).

Humphries, Rolfe (tr.), *The Satires of Juvenal* (Bloomington: Indiana University Press, 1958).

Hunt, Maurice, 'Predestination and the Heresy of Merit in *Othello*,' *Comparative Drama* 30:3 (Fall 1996), 346–76.

Hunter, G.K., 'Shakespeare's Politics and the Rejection of Falstaff,' *Critical Quarterly* 1 (Autumn 1959), 229–36

Hunter, Joseph, *New Illustrations of the Life, Studies, and Writings of Shakespeare* (London: Nichols, 1845).

Izacke, Richard, *Remarkable Antiquities of the City of Exeter* (London: 1681).

Jeffrey, D.L., *A Dictionary of Biblical Traditions* (Ann Arbor: University of Michigan Press, 1992).

Jenkins, Harold (ed.), *Hamlet* (London: Methuen, 1982).

Johnson, Samuel (ed.), *The Plays of William Shakespeare* (London: 1765).

Johnson, Samuel and George Steevens (eds), *The dramatick writings of Will. Shakspere* (London: 1788).

Jones, Emrys, 'Othello, "Lepanto" and the Cyprus Wars,' *Shakespeare Survey* 21 (1968), 47–52

—— *Scenic Form in Shakespeare* (Oxford: Oxford University Press, 1971).

Jones-Davies, Margaret, '*Cymbeline* and the Sleep of Faith,' in *Theater and Religion: Lancastrian Shakespeare*, Richard Dutton, Alison Findlay, and Richard Wilson (eds), (Manchester: Manchester University Press, 2003).

Joseph, Sister Miriam, *Shakespeare's Use of the Arts of Language* (New York: Columbia University Press, 1947).

Kaula, David, 'Let Us Be Sacrificers': Religious Motifs in Julius Caesar,' *Shakespeare Survey* 14 (1981), 198–9.

Kelly, Henry Ansgar, *Chaucer and the Cult of Saint Valentine* (Leiden: Brill, 1986).

Kernan, Alvin, *Shakespeare: the King's Playwright* (New Haven: Yale University Press, 1995).

King, Pamela, 'Calendar and Text: Christ's Ministry in the York Plays' *Medium Aevum* 67 (1998), 30–59

Kingsford, C.L. (ed.), *Report on the Manuscripts of Lord de l'Isle and Dudley preserved at Penshurst* (London: H.M. Stationery Office, 1925–66).

Knapp, Jeffrey, *Preachers and players in Shakespeare's England* (Berkeley: Center for Hermeneutical Studies, 1995).

—— *Shakespeare's Tribe: Church, Nation, and Theater in Renaissance England* (Chicago: University of Chicago Press, 2002).

Kuhn, Thomas S., *The Copernican Revolution* (Cambridge: Harvard University Press, 1957).

Laroque, Francois, 'An Archaeology of the Dramatic Text: *Othello* and Popular Traditions' *Cahiers élisabéthains* 32 (1987), 13–35

—— Shakespeare's Festive World, (Cambridge: Cambridge University Press, 1993).

Leduc, D.C. and D. Baudot, *The Liturgy of the Roman Missal* (London: Burns Oates and Washbourne, n.d.)

Lemon, R. (ed.), *Calendar of State Papers, Domestic Series ... 1581–90* (London: Longman, 1865).

Levenson, Jill L. (ed.), *Romeo and Juliet* (Oxford: Oxford University Press, 2000).

Littleton (Sir), Thomas, *Littleton's Tenures in French and English* (London: Streater, 1671).

Machamer, Peter (ed.), *The Cambridge Companion to Galileo* (Cambridge: Cambridge University Press, 1998).

Mack, Maynard, 'Rescuing Shakespeare,' *International Shakespeare Association Occasional Paper* (no. 1, 1979).

McKeen, David, *A Memory of Honour: the Life of William Brooke, Lord Cobham* (Salzburg: Universitat Salzburg, 1986).

Mahood's, M.M., *Shakespeare's Wordplay* (London: Methuen, 1957).

Manning, Roger B., *Religion and Society in Elizabethan Sussex* (Leicester: Leicester University Press, 1969).

Mansfield, Harvey C. (tr.), *Niccolò Machiavelli: The Prince* (Chicago: University of Chicago Press, 1985).

Marlowe, Christopher, *The Famous Tragedy of the Rich Jew of Malta* (London: John Beale, 1633).

Massey, G., *The Secret Drama of Shakespeare's Sonnets* (London: Kegan Paul, 1888).

Matchett, William H., 'Richard's Divided Heritage in *King John*,' *Essays in Criticism* 12 (July 1962), 231–53

Melchiori, Giorgio, *The Second Part of King Henry IV* (Cambridge: Cambridge University Press, 1989).

Michie, James (tr.), *The Odes of Horace* (London: Hart-Davis, 1963).

Miller, W. (tr.), *Cicero: De Officiis*, (Cambridge: Cambridge University Press, 1990).

Mitchell, R.J., *The Spring Voyage* (New York: Murray, 1964).

Moore, Olin H., *The Legend of Romeo and Juliet* (Columbus: Ohio State University Press, 1950).

More (St.), Thomas, *The Complete Works* (New Haven: Yale University Press, 1963–97).

Muir, Kenneth, 'The Text of *Othello*,' *Shakespeare Studies* 1 (1965), 227–39.

Munro, John (ed.), *The London Shakespeare* (London: Eyre and Spottiswoode, 1957).

Nelson, T.G.A. and Charles Haines, 'Othello's Unconsummated Marriage,' *Essays in Criticism* 33 (January 1983), 1–18.

North, Christopher (John Wilson), *Blackwood's Magazine* (November 1849, April 1850, May 1850).

North (Sir), Thomas (tr.), *Plutarch, The Lives of the Noble Grecians and Romanes* (London, 1579).

Nosworthy, J.M. (ed.), *Cymbeline,* The Arden Shakespeare (London: Routledge, 1988).

Orr, James (ed.), *International Standard Bible Encyclopedia: Electronic Edition* (Parsons Technology, 1998).

Orrell, John, *The Quest for Shakespeare's Globe* (Cambridge: Cambridge University Press, 1983).

Painter, William, *The Palace of Pleasure* (London: Tottell and Jones, 1566).

Paster, Gail Kern, *The Body Embarrassed* (Ithaca: Cornell University Press, 1993).

Payne, John (tr.), *The Novels of Matteo Bandello* (London: 1890).

Pedersen, Olaf, *Galileo and the Council of Trent* (Città del Vaticano: Specola Vaticana, 1991).

Pendergast, John S., '*Cymbeline* and the Question of Genre,' *Journal of the Wooden O Symposium* 2 (2002).

Pickering, David, *Cassell Dictionary of Superstitions* (London: Cassell, 1995).

Pinciss, G.M., *Forbidden Matter: Religion in the Drama of Shakespeare and his Contemporaries* (Newark: University of Delaware Press, 2000).

Pont, Robert, *A New Treatise of the Right Reckoning Yeares* (Edinburgh: Robert Walde-Grave, 1599).

Pope, Alexander, *The Works of Shakespear* (London: Tonson, 1735).

Porto, Luigi da, *Istoria novellamente ritrovata di due Nobili Amanti* (*ca* 1530).

—— *Giulietta e Romeo, Novella Storica* (Pisa, 1831).

Pye, Thomas, *The Houreglasse* (London: 1597).

Rayso, Thomas M., 'The Aesthetic Significance of Shakespeare's Handling of Time,' *Studies in Philology* 32 (1935), 197–209.

Ridley, M.R. (ed.), *Othello* (London: Methuen, 1958).

Rodgers, Edith Cooperrider, *Discussion of Holidays in the Later Middle Ages* (New York: Columbia University Press, 1940).

Rogers, L.W., *Occultism in the Shakespeare Plays* (1909, rpt. Kila, Montana: Kessinger, 1996)

Rose, Martial (ed.), *The Wakefield Mystery Plays* (New York: Doubleday. 1962).

Ross, Lawrence J., 'The Meaning of Strawberries in Shakespeare,' *Studies in the Renaissance* 7 (1960), 255–40.

Rowe, Nicholas (ed.), *The Works of Mr. William Shakespear* (London: 1709).

Rozett, Martha Tuck, *The Doctrine of Election and the Emergence of Elizabethan Tragedy* (Princeton: Princeton University Press, 1984).

Ryan, W. G., *The Golden Legend* (Princeton: Princeton University Press, 1993).

—— with Helmut Ripperger (trs.), *The Golden Legend of Jacobus de Voragine* (New York: Arno Press, 1941).

Rymer, Thomas, *A Short View of Tragedy* (London: 1693).

Sams, Eric, 'The Troublesome Wrangle Over *King John*' *Notes and Queries* 35 (March 1988).

Sanders, Norman (ed.), *Merchant of Venice* (Cambridge: Cambridge University Press, 1984).

—— (ed.) *Othello* (Cambridge: Cambridge University Press, 1984).

Scarisbrick, Diana, *Ancestral Jewels* (New York: Vendome Press, 1989).

Schanzer, Ernest, 'Thomas Platter's Observations on the Elizabethan Stage,' *Notes & Queries* (November 1956), 466–7.

Schoenbaum, Samuel, *Shakespeare: a Documentary Life* (Oxford: Oxford University Press, 1975).

—— *Shakespeare: A Compact Documentary Life* (Oxford: Oxford University Press, 1977).

Scoufos, Alice Lyle, 'Nashe, Johnson, and the Oldcastle Problem,' *Modern Philology* 65:4 (May 1968), 307–24

—— *Shakespeare's Topological Satire* (Athens: Ohio University Press, 1979).

Seng, Peter J., 'Songs, Time, and the Rejection of Falstaff,' *Shakespeare Survey* 15 (1962), 31–40.

Shaheen, Naseeb, 'Like the Base Judean,' *Shakespeare Quarterly* 31:1 (1980), 93–5.

—— *Biblical References in Shakespeare's History Plays* (Newark, NJ: University of Delaware Press, 1989).

Simmons, J.R., *Shakespeare's Pagan World* (London: Harvester 1973).

Simpson, John (ed.) *The Oxford English Dictionary on CD-ROM Version 3.0* (Oxford: Oxford University Press, 2002).

Singer, Dorothea Waley, *Giordano Bruno: His Life and Thought, etc.* (New York: Henry Schuman, *ca* 1950).

Sohmer, Steve, 'Certain Speculations on Hamlet, etc.,' *Early Modern Literary Studies* 2.1 (April 1996).

—— 'What Cicero Said,' *Notes and Queries* (vol. 44, no. 1, March 1997), 56–8.

—— 'The Lunar Calendar in Shakespeare's *King Lear*,' *Early Modern Literary Studies* 5:2 (September, 1999) 2.1–17.

—— *Shakespeare's Mystery Play and the opening of the Globe Theater 1599* (Manchester: Manchester University Press, 1999).

—— 'Another Time: The Venetian Calendar in Shakespeare's Plays' in Holger Klein and Michele Marrapodi (eds), *Shakespeare in Italy* (New York: Lewiston, 1999).

—— 'A Note on Hamlet's Illegitimacy Identifying a Source of the '*Dram of Eale*' Speech (Q2 1.4.17–38), *Early Modern Literary Studies* 6:3 (January 2001).

—— 'The 'Double Time' Crux in *Othello* Solved,' *English Literary Renaissance* (Spring 2002), 214–38.

—— 'Shakespeare's Time-Riddles in *Romeo and Juliet* Solved,' *English Literary Renaissance* (Autumn 2005), 407–28.

Speght, T., *The workes of our antient … Geffrey Chaucer* (London: Impensis George Bishop, 1598).

Spurgeon, Caroline, *Shakespeare's Imagery* (Cambridge: Cambridge University Press, 1935).

Stopes, C.C., *The Life of Henry [Wriothsley], the Third Earl of Southampton, Shakespeare's patron* (Cambridge: Cambridge University Press, 1922).

Strype, John, *The Life and Acts of Matthew Parker* (London: John Wyat, 1711).

Tanselle, G. Thomas, 'Time in *Romeo and Juliet*,' *Shakespeare Quarterly* 15 (1964), 349–61.

Taylor, Gary, 'The Fortunes of Oldcastle,' *Shakespeare Survey* 38 (1985), 85–100.

—— (ed.), *Henry V* (Oxford: Oxford University Press, 1982).

Theobald, Lewis, *The Works of Shakespeare* (London: Bettesworth and Hitch, 1733).

Thoren, Victor E., *The Lord of Uraniborg* (Cambridge: Cambridge University Press, 1990).

Tittler, Robert, *Nicholas Bacon: The Making of a Tudor Statesman* (Athens: Ohio University Press, *ca* 1976).

Tyrwhitt, Thomas, *Observations and Conjectures upon some Passages of Shakespeare* (London: Rivington and Payne, 1766).

Van de Water, Julia C., 'The Bastard in *King John*,' *Shakespeare Quarterly* 11 (1960), 137–46.

Velz, W.J., 'Clemency, Will, and Just Cause in Julius Caesar,' *Shakespeare Survey* 27 (1969).

Verity, A.W. (ed.) *Hamlet* (Cambridge: Cambridge University Press, 1911).

Vickers, Brian, 'The Troublesome Reign, George Peele, and the Date of King John,' in *Words That Count* (ed.) Brian Boyd (Newark: University of Delaware Press, 2004).

Wallis, Charles Glenn (tr.), *Copernicus' On the Revolutions of the Heavenly Spheres* (New York: Prometheus, 1995).

Walter, J.H. (ed.), *King Henry V* (London: Methuen, 1954).

Waugh, W.T., 'Sir John Oldcastle,' *English Historical Review* 20 (1905), 637–58.

Wells, Stanley and Gary Taylor, *William Shakespeare: a Textual Companion* (Oxford: Clarendon Press, 1987).

Wentersdorf, Karl P., 'The Time Problem in Othello: a Reconsideration' (Bochum: *Jahrbuch der Deutschen Shakespeare-Gesellschaft West*, 1985), 63–77.

Wheatly, Charles, *The Church of England Man's Companion* (Oxford: The Theater, 1710).

Wickham, G., *Early English Stages* (London: Routledge and Kegan Paul, 1981).

Wilde, Oscar, 'The Portrait of Mr. W.H.,' *Blackwood's Edinburgh magazine*, (July 1889), 1–21.

Wiles, David, *Shakespeare's Clown: Actor and Text in the Elizabethan Playhouse* (Cambridge: Cambridge University Press, 1987).

—— *Shakespeare's Almanac* (Cambridge: Cambridge University Press, 1993).

Wilson, John Dover (ed.), *King John* (Cambridge: Cambridge University Press, 1934).

—— *Hamlet* (Cambridge: Cambridge University Press, 1934).

—— 'The Origins and Development of Shakespeare's Henry IV,' *The Library* (4th series, 24, 1945), 15–16

—— 'Ben Jonson and *Julius Caesar*,' *Shakespeare Survey* 2 (1949).

Wilson, Richard, *Secret Shakespeare: Studies in Theater, Religion, and Resistence* (Manchester: Manchester University Press, 2004)

Wordsworth, Christopher (ed.), *The Ancient Kalendar of the University of Oxford* (Oxford: Clarendon Press, 1904).

Wright, William Aldus, *The Works of William Shakespeare* (London: Macmillan, 1893–4).

Yates, Frances, *The Occult Philosophy in the Elizabethan Age* (London: Routledge, 1979).

Index

CABRINI COLLEGE LIBRARY
610 KING OF PRUSSIA ROAD
RADNOR, PA 19087-3699

DEMCO